Praise for *Creating Visual Experiences with Flex 3.0*

"Adobe Flex is changing the face of the Web by enabling developers to create rich Internet applications quickly. This book provides developers a way to get a jump on the competition by enabling them to quickly learn how easily they can set their application apart from the rest."

—Gary Mangum, Principal Engineer, The Generations Network

"Juan and Andy do a great job breaking ground on a vast and exciting topic. This book moves beyond learning the syntax of the language and gets to the heart of what Flex was really made for—building immersive user experiences."

—R.J. Owen, Senior Developer, EffectiveUI

"This is a fantastic source to get you started on your way to prettying up your Flex Applications."

—Jeffry Houser, Producer of The Flex Show

"*Creating Visual Experiences with Flex 3.0* takes a thorough look into the design side of Flex application development and is a must-have book for any Flex developer."

—Sean Moore, Flex and AIR Developer, Kannopy, Inc.

"*Creating Visual Experiences with Flex 3.0* is an outstanding book written by two of the most well-known industry experts. The book is highly accessible, concise, and understandable even for non-designer types such as myself. It is a much needed breath of fresh air in a market chock full of developer-centric Flex books. "

—Jun Heider, Sr. Developer and Technical Trainer, RealEyes Media

"I first saw Juan and Andy give a visual effects presentation at 360/Flex Conference. It was clear they were experts on the subject, so I was excited when I heard they were writing a book. And they delivered; I wish I had this book in my hands a long time ago."

—Leonard Souza, Interactive Creative Director

Creating Visual Experiences with Flex 3.0

Creating Visual Experiences with Flex 3.0

Juan Sanchez
Andy McIntosh

✦✦Addison-Wesley

Upper Saddle River, NJ • Boston • Indianapolis • San Francisco
New York • Toronto • Montreal • London • Munich • Paris • Madrid
Capetown • Sydney • Tokyo • Singapore • Mexico City

Many of the designations used by manufacturers and sellers to distinguish their products are claimed as trademarks. Where those designations appear in this book, and the publisher was aware of a trademark claim, the designations have been printed with initial capital letters or in all capitals.

The authors and publisher have taken care in the preparation of this book, but make no expressed or implied warranty of any kind and assume no responsibility for errors or omissions. No liability is assumed for incidental or consequential damages in connection with or arising out of the use of the information or programs contained herein.

The publisher offers excellent discounts on this book when ordered in quantity for bulk purchases or special sales, which may include electronic versions and/or custom covers and content particular to your business, training goals, marketing focus, and branding interests. For more information, please contact

U.S. Corporate and Government Sales
1-800-382-3419
corpsales@pearsontechgroup.com

For sales outside the United States, please contact

International Sales
international@pearsoned.com

Visit us on the Web: informit.com/aw

Library of Congress Cataloging-in-Publication Data

Sanchez, Juan, 1980-
  Creating visual experiences with Flex 3.0 / Juan Sanchez, Andy McIntosh. – 1st ed.
    p. cm.
  Includes bibliographical references and index.
  ISBN 0-321-54537-0 (paper back : alk. paper)
1. Flex (Computer file) 2. Internet programming. 3. Application software—Development.
4. Web site development—Computer programs. I. McIntosh, Andy, 1982- II. Title.

  QA76.625.S23 2008
  006.7'6—dc22

                                                  2008033095

ISBN-13: 978-0-321-54537-4
ISBN-10:   0-321-54537-0

Text printed in the United States on recycled paper at R.R. Donnelley in Crawfordsville, Indiana.
First printing, November 2008

Editor-in-Chief
Karen Gettman

Senior Acquisitions Editor
Chuck Toporek

Development Editor
Sheri Cain

Managing Editor
John Fuller

Project Editor
Sally Gregg

Copy Editor
Kelli M. Brooks

Indexer
Jack Lewis

Proofreader
Diane Freed

Technical Reviewers
Gary Mangum
R.J. Owen

Interior Designer
Gary Adair

Cover Designer
Gary Adair

Composition
Kim Arney

Contents at a Glance

Table of Contents

Foreword

Over the past few years, the boundaries of what designers and developers can create on the Web have expanded enormously. Web sites increasingly integrate pixel-perfect visual design, video, animation, and advanced user interaction to create rich experiences that are both fun and useful. Many of these sites are built using the Adobe Flash platform. And more and more Flash sites are being built using Adobe Flex.

One of the most common misconceptions about Flex is that it's different from Flash. It's not: Flex is Flash. Flex applications run in the Flash Player; Flex is built on top of the Flash file format, language, and API. Through Flex, you have access to all the richness of the Flash Player, with the added benefit of being able to work more seamlessly with traditional development tools.

If you looked at Flex applications a couple of years ago, you might not have believed this seamless story. Flex applications looked like, well, Flex applications. They looked pretty nice right out of the box, but once you'd seen a few, you could instantly spot others.

Why was this? The focus of the first version of Flex was to make the Flash platform accessible to traditional software developers, and to make it easy for them to produce applications that looked good right out of the box. And it worked: People who would never have even conceived of using Flash began building enterprise-quality applications using our technology. Flex removed their barrier for entry to developing rich applications.

But you can only do so much in a release, especially a 1.0 release, and we didn't have time to also reinvent the world of *designing* rich applications. We did a lot to make the built-in component skins flexible—providing a large set of style parameters to allow people to tweak the visual appearance of components—but we knew that in order to really bring designers into Flex, we would need to do a lot more.

So, in Flex 2 and 3, we've been making it easier to build great visual and motion design into Flex applications. In Flex 2, we created view states and transitions to help designers and developers organize the appearance and behavior of complex dynamic applications. We also added a constraint-based layout mechanism that makes it easy to go from a pixel-perfect static design to a resizable application. In Flex 3, following the acquisition of Macromedia by Adobe, we built a streamlined skinning workflow between the Adobe Creative Suite tools and Flex Builder, and added a CSS design view to Flex Builder that lets you visually tweak the built-in appearance of components.

Andy McIntosh and Juan Sanchez are the perfect guides for your exploration into the visual design features of Flex. As designers who have crossed over into the world of development, and with their years of experience at EffectiveUI and other rich application design and development studios, they have been deeply engrossed in the world of Flex. In this book, they start with the basics of what designers and developers need to know about getting Flex applications to look good, then dive into more advanced topics and realistic examples showing how to create the look and feel of a complex application.

If you're a designer who's willing to leap into writing code once in awhile, or a developer with an eye for design, this book will help you build great Flex interfaces yourself. If you're a designer who never touches code, but wants to understand what your Flex developers will be able to deliver, or if you're a pure developer who needs to learn how to implement the beautiful mockup a designer gave you, this book can help you work more effectively with your design/development partner.

Of course, Adobe isn't stopping here. We've got a lot of great stuff coming in Flex 4 and beyond to make it even easier for designers and developers to work together to build even richer experiences. But with this book in hand, you can get started today designing and building engaging applications. Go forth and create!

Narciso (nj) Jaramillo
Product designer, Adobe Flex Team

Preface

The Web is always evolving as new technologies and greater user demands bubble to the surface. With the introduction of Flash in 1996, Web pages started to change from a static point-click-reload experience to a dynamic experience void of page refreshes and back button reactions. Since then, many technologies have risen to meet the ever-growing needs of the user, each proposing new conventions for reaching a final goal. As Flash matured, it became more frequently used for replicating interactions a user might expect from a robust desktop application. Flash was a usable solution for creating browser-based applications, but not necessarily the most approachable.

Now with Adobe Flex, the Flash player has matured to the point that it can be considered a target for enterprise-level applications. Along with Flex, there have been lots of competing technologies breaking onto the scene, underscoring the importance of rich user experience. New focus has been placed on the processes surrounding innovation, collaboration between designer and developer, usability, and deployment. These advancing facets pose new challenges for both designers and developers to overcome in order to create compelling visual experiences in Flex 3.

Creating Visual Experiences with Flex 3.0 is a compilation of knowledge gathered from a myriad of real-world scenarios involving customization of Flex applications and creating rich user experiences.

Scope of This Book

Rarely is there a case when no visual customization is required while creating a Flex application. It can be hard to find all the necessary information that covers the many approaches that can be taken to customize the visual experience of a Flex application. Interpreting that information to an actual use-case within an application can also be a daunting task. Our focus is to expose the knowledge we wished we had when we first started working with Flex. It is by no means meant to be an end-all be-all, but a starting point for your journey into working with the visual aspects of Flex 3. The goal is to give enough information to answer immediate questions and directions to find additional answers.

Everything discussed in this book can be used in some way, shape, or form, from robust enterprise-level applications to a simple RSS reader. The walkthroughs in this book are meant to be to-the-point and clearly communicate the approaches discussed. Since we learned Flex by pulling bits and pieces from a number of different examples to meet the needs of our applications, there is an *a la carte* presentation of walkthroughs. This will make it easy for you to grab what you need without foraging through massive lines of code to find the one bit you're interested in.

Most of the topics discussed in this book surround features immediately available in Flex. Creating custom components, advanced data visualization, and nonvisual components will not be covered. Although those things are also essential to enhancing the user experience, it extends beyond the scope of this book.

This book is not meant to be a rule-book of standards or a rigid set of guidelines. Each project is different and has its own requirements. There is always a judgment call to be made between deadlines, budget, client needs, and user feedback that will dictate what approach you may take to implementing your own version of a unique visual experience. In the end though, you want to be happy with what you release, from the back-end architecture to the customer facing offering.

Audience for This Book

The primary audience is designers and developers interested in translating design visions to Flex while maintaining the highest fidelity. Topics discussed revolve around some light design theory of rich user experiences and the visual presentation of user interface components. Designers and developers can use the information in this book to gain an understanding of the advanced level of customization that can be implemented in Flex. Also, those who may not be fully immersed in Flex development may find this book helpful in understanding what can be achieved visually with Flex.

The level of knowledge required for this book ranges from beginner to somewhat advanced, but the approach is always to make sure there is a guided sense of understanding. In the process of writing this book, we found ourselves referring to our own draft versions of chapters to find answers to a variety of questions that arose while working on a client project in Flex. We can only hope that this book may also serve as a solid reference that can help guide you in your own projects.

Background

As Flex developers who are pretty involved with the Flex community, we get questions all the time through email and blog comments about the nuances of customizing Flex applications. It is a rare occurrence to *not* get approached at least once at a conference by someone with a laptop eager to find an answer or to gain some insight. In fact, this whole project was started based on a co-presentation that was given at a Flex-focused conference, called 360|Flex. The thought was to bottle our collective knowledge in a way that was more approachable than reading documentation and span the concepts we valued as we worked to implement our designs in Flex.

How This Book Is Organized

The beginning of this book sets the stage for the rest of the chapters by introducing the capabilities of Flex and discussing some of the design foundation behind creating a visual experience. The remaining chapters go into more technical detail about visual customization and implementation in Flex. Because each chapter discusses techniques that may complement others, chapters have been ordered to take advantage of material presented in previous chapters. This is not to say that you can't jump into any given chapter at any point throughout your reading.

> **Chapter 1: Rich Internet Applications.** Design plays a large role in the final appearance of your Flex application. This chapter gives a general overview of design fundamentals and thinking points that can transfer to your application's final design.

Chapter 2: Adobe Flex and AIR. An overview of Adobe Flex 3 and the Adobe Integrated Runtime (AIR) sets the stage for some of the technical aspects in the remainder of the book.

Chapter 3: Dynamic Layout. Layout defines the visual structure of your application. Learn about the various components and techniques you can use to create the visual skeleton of your application.

Chapter 4: Styling. Using styling properties, you can customize components rapidly and easily. Styling lays the groundwork for other methods when customizing a user interface.

Chapter 5: Graphical Skinning. When styling a component isn't enough, skinning can step in and take customization to the next level. You can leverage existing graphics applications like Adobe Illustrator, Flash, Fireworks, and Photoshop to customize the look of your Flex application.

Chapter 6: Programmatic Skinning. Drawing graphics programmatically to be used for the appearance of components is very powerful, but also more complex than graphical skinning. Learn how you can leverage the power of programmatic skinning to create customizable interfaces.

Chapter 7: Lists and Navigation Components. The additional challenges for customization posed by List and Navigation controls, including item renderers and a data-driven display, are addressed. Lists and navigation components present different challenges for customization because they are primarily data driven and comprise many pieces.

Chapter 8: Indicators and Cursors. Guiding a user through an application is instrumental to a user achieving a goal. Steer your customers in the right direction by adding another level of customization.

Chapter 9: Fonts and Text. The way you display text and how it looks can play an emotional role as well as an informational one. Establishing structured and well-placed text is well within reach when working with Flex.

Chapter 10: Filters and Blends. Adding a sense of layering and depth can add a level of richness to an application. Flex provides a number of filters and blends that can be applied to components for a variety of purposes.

Chapter 11: Effects and Transitions. By deploying in the Flash player, Flex applications can capitalize on the advantages of using motion to create a fluid and immersive experience. Learn how you can leverage motion-based features of Flex in a variety of ways.

Chapter 12: Flex and Flash Integration. Flash and Flex share a common ground: ActionScript 3 and the Flash player. Flash CS3 and plugins can be used to create custom components, skins, containers, and motions.

Chapter 13: Customizing AIR Applications. AIR allows you deploy desktop applications using the same code-base as Flex applications. However, AIR applications have additional parameters that can be customized and are specific to the desktop environment.

Conventions Used in This Book

As you read this book there are a number of conventions used to guide you through varying types of information. You will find the code hosted at http://www.cveflex.com. At any given point you may encounter the following:

Tables. Used to group items and descriptions in a structured format for quick and easy reference.

Figures. Range from screenshots to diagrams to graphical instructions.

Listings. Code that supports discussed concepts and can include MXML, CSS, ActionScript, and comments.

Exercises. Longer walkthroughs that may involve code, graphic creation, traversing multiple applications, and running sample applications.

Tips. Used as pointers for clarifications and suggestions.

Notes. Used to provide further information.

In every case, these items are noted by their type, chapter number, and a sequential number (e.g., Table 5-3, Figure 7-13, etc.). For Exercises, a number for the exercise is introduced (e.g., Figure 5.1-4, Listing 4.3-7). This convention is used to refer to these items in the text and to allow you to cross-reference things as you move through the book.

Styling and Skinning Diagrams

You will frequently be referred to Appendix A's, "Skinning and Styling Diagrams," throughout the book. This reference is a series of diagrams that point out the customizable parts of visual Flex components, including containers and controls. It is meant to be a complementary reference during the process of customizing components in your Flex application.

Additional Resources

Other references you will find include Appendix B, "Filters Cheat Sheet," and Appendix C, "Resources and Cool Stuff." These cheat sheets are meant to act as quick references that expose the properties for these Flex 3 features along with a brief description of the property.

Acknowledgments

Writing a book was one of those ideas that was frequently talked about but hardly entertained. However, when the opportunity presented itself, we jumped in with both feet. During the process, jobs changed, relocation occurred, other enticing projects popped up, and jobs remained demanding. Needless to say, we never would have moved forward with this project if it wasn't for the support and guidance from a number of individuals, both in our professional and personal lives.

Beyond the technical aspects of working with Flex and wanting to increase our own knowledge of creating better experiences, the most enticing part of working with Flex is the community. A lot of the knowledge we've gained has been a result of engaging with other members of the Flex community, some of whom have become good friends. Our hopes are that this book can expand on that dialogue.

Thank you to everyone at EffectiveUI; our contacts from the Flex team: Narciso "nj" Jaramillo, Heidi Williams, Rob Adams, George Comninos, Deepa Subramaniam, and Peter Flynn; Tom Ortega and John Wilker of 360 Conferences; Chuck Toporek of Addison-Wesley; and everyone who took time out of their busy lives to help and teach us along the way.

A special thanks to Patrick Hansen, who read and reviewed the book pro bono, and to RJ Owen for the wonderful candid feedback and comma assassination.

Andy McIntosh—For their endless patience, support, and inspiration, I'd like to thank my mom, dad, and the rest of my family; Angela Schuman and her family; Juan Sanchez; and Anthony Franco and Robb Wilson.

Juan Sanchez—I'd like to say thanks to: my mom, dad, sisters Monica, Maria, and Alicia, and brother Fernando for their constant encouragement and support in whatever I do. Grace, you were there for every second of it; your caring, love, and support is beyond words; you rock! Andy, for agreeing to write this book with me. Everyone at Atomic Curve, where my journey with Flex first began. Finally, to every friend and family member that has been there for me along the way.

About the Authors

Andy McIntosh is one of the first members of EffectiveUI, a Denver-based rich Internet application agency. As an Experience Architect, he specializes in interaction design, custom component development, and programmatic skinning. His recent focus has been on migrating enterprise applications to Flex/AIR-based solutions.

Andy attended The Art Institute of Colorado in Denver where he earned a BA in Interactive Media Design. While in school, he discovered that merely designing applications wasn't enough and that he wanted to make them come to life. A lifelong fan of Lego and gadgetry, he learned development by taking applications apart and putting them back together. His attention to detail, in both development and design, add a mark of quality to his work that is second to none. In his own words, "Development is design, but with different tools."

Blending his technical expertise with his formal training in visual design, Andy has played a major role in successful projects for clients such as Adobe, Workday, Scion, United Airlines, and others. Additionally, Andy is an advisor for Degrafa, an open-source declarative graphics framework for Flex.

He currently resides in downtown Denver, and frequently travels to both coasts for business and pleasure. His interests include books, cars, music, industrial design, and remodeling his loft. He blogs useful findings and random thoughts at andymcintosh.com.

Juan Sanchez is an Experience Architect for EffectiveUI, a leading provider of rich Internet applications, based in Denver, Colorado. He graduated from California State University, Chico, with a BA in communication design. Juan's background is primarily in print design, branding, and advertising; however, his skills quickly expanded into Web technologies like HTML, CSS, Flash, and eventually Flex.

Equipped with a creative eye and logical mind, Juan walks the line between designer and developer. Juan's interests lie in user experience, usability, designer/developer collaboration, and open-source projects. As an active Flex community member, Juan manages ScaleNine.com, a Web site dedicated to compiling skins and themes for Flex. He is a regular speaker at user groups, corporate workshops, and conferences, including 360|Flex and WebManiacs. Juan is also a founding member of Degrafa, a declarative graphics framework for Flex.

Juan currently lives in downtown Denver with his girlfriend, Grace, and a little Chihuahua named Maddie. Now that he is done with "The Book," Juan hopes to get back to restoring his '66 Ford Mustang, running, enjoying Denver, and maybe taking up drums again.

Introduction

Rich Internet Applications

A rich Internet application (RIA) engages users, allows them to accomplish tasks, and can be downright enjoyable. It allows colleagues to collaborate simply and seamlessly, and customers to interact with products in compelling and exciting ways. RIAs go beyond the static views of the traditional Web and put dynamic, tailored content right into the user's hands. They often transcend the perceived limitations of the Web browser and deliver experiences users have come to expect from their desktop applications. The bottom line: Rich Internet applications don't just look great; they improve user satisfaction and productivity.

User expectations and market competition are constantly increasing the demands for awesome Web applications that provide a great experience from start to finish. A successful rich Internet application must deliver quality content; it must perform well and seem immediately responsive to user input; and it must be easy to use and understand with very little instruction. Failure to execute in any of these areas can result in an unsuccessful application, even if it excels in all other areas.

When creating rich Internet applications, designers and developers are presented with new opportunities and unique challenges. There is no secret recipe for creating successful RIAs; however, there are several design principles and best practices you can follow. It's tempting to concentrate on just aesthetics or just usability, but a great RIA combines both. Careful consideration in the following areas can set you on the right path to an engaging Web application.

The Audience

Before building any rich Internet application, you need to think about the people who will be using it. You'll want to know as much as you can about your users. Age, interests, income, and physical location are just some of the demographics you might be interested in. You may also be interested in their work environment, profession, and specialty. Knowing these things about your users can help you understand their goals and tasks so you can deliver an application that they'll find intuitive and useful.

If possible, study the way your users work with their existing tools, or similar applications. Sometimes leveraging existing metaphors in your RIA can lead to wider adoption and understanding. For example, if users rely on a system of sticky notes to keep organized, that familiar paradigm could be effective in your application. Understand their mission-critical workflows and think of ways to improve them if possible, but be cautious of innovating for the sake of innovation.

Defining user personas to capture the findings of your research can provide guidelines when determining the feature set of your application. Beware that trying to address too many workflows at once may dilute the usability for any particular user persona. A one-size-fits-all solution is often not the right one.

You may find it useful to describe the way a particular persona will utilize the features of your application by writing it out as a story. The following "user story" describes how one persona might interact with an online banking application.

> Mark is a 19-year-old college student who needs a quick and easy way to manage his finances. When Mark logs into the application, he sees an overview of where his finances stand as well as an idea of his spending habits. He needs to pay some bills, so he accesses the Bill Pay area of the application where he specifies the bills he would like to pay as well as the amount of each. With a single click, Mark pays all his bills and he's on his way.

The Content

People use Web applications to browse videos, edit photos, check their latest bank statements, or watch an item they're bidding on. As the cliché goes, "content is king." No matter how snazzy your interface is, if there's no interesting content, users will find little value in the application. A user's goals are often based around viewing or manipulating some piece of content.

An effective rich Internet application presents users with the content they care about and provides intuitive ways for them to interact with it. For example, take an application like Adobe Media Player. Immediately, the user has access to several videos, right on the first screen. After he clicks to view a video, he is presented with additional videos and information about the current video. If the user's goal is to spend an evening watching video content, he can do so without much effort.

A nonintrusive interface is also key to delivering the content users desire. Many applications, like Adobe Photoshop Express, utilize a high-contrast visual theme so that the content stands out against the interface, as shown in Figure 1-1. When absolute focus and maximum screen real estate is required, an application can be designed to employ a full-screen mode, like that of Adobe Media Player (see Figure 1-2).

As with many other facets of rich Internet application design, working with content is a matter of striking a balance. Too much content at once can overwhelm your users, and not enough content can frustrate them, especially if they have to click a hundred times to get to what they want. If you understand your users' goals and tasks, you can

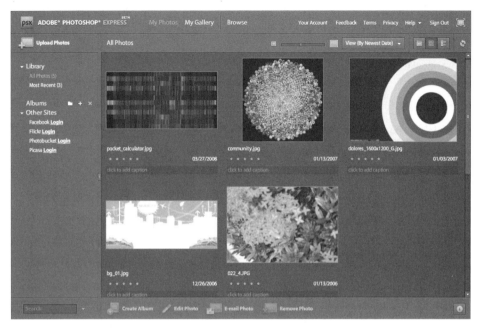

Figure 1-1   The dark visual theme of Photoshop Express
makes the images stand out vividly from the interface

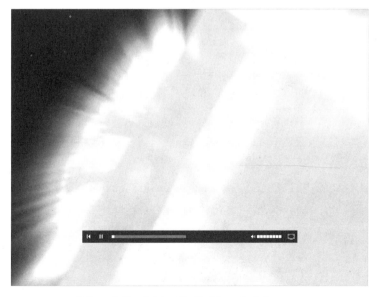

Figure 1-2   Adobe Media Player in full-screen
mode with a controller overlaying the video

anticipate what content they're interested in and progressively disclose it to them as it becomes relevant. If you must display large amounts of content—as is often the case with media-centric sites—your users will expect a natural way to filter and browse the content to locate what they're interested in.

User Interaction

An effective application enables users to access content, perform tasks, and accomplish their goals through obvious interactions and meaningful feedback. A good interaction model should give users the freedom to explore various paths with comfort, knowing they can always return to familiar territory or correct mistakes. It should establish context for the users as they perform tasks and help them make informed decisions throughout their experience.

User interaction determines the structure of an application. There are three high-level structure types that are based on the activity that the application facilitates. Some applications are intended to present information, others allow users to carry out a process, and some are used to create things. The structure influences how users will navigate from section to section and/or switch between an application's modes, and dictates the layout of the elements within a section and how those elements behave and work together.

User interaction describes how users will achieve their goals. One goal of a Photoshop Express user is to choose an image from her library and enter a mode in which she can edit it (see Figure 1-3). To accomplish this, Photoshop Express allows a user to either double-click an image, or select an image and then click the Edit Photo button. The application responds by expanding the image and offering a set of options for manipulating and interacting with the photo. Providing alternative methods to complete a task is common in good interaction design as it enables users to operate in the way that is most comfortable or familiar to them, and it promotes discoverability of features.

Performance is an important aspect of user interaction. Users rely on quick responses to their input to help inform their next move. A slow response may result in your users feeling disconnected or deter them from exploring the features of your application. Imagine an application used for searching a database of movie titles. If the search results

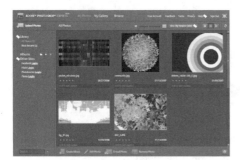 

Figure 1-3   Adobe Photoshop Express browse and edit modes

come back very slowly, the user may be compelled to spend more time when defining the search criteria because executing a search feels like an investment of time. A better solution is something that gives the user the freedom to rapid-fire several queries to hone in on the information he desires.

The Presentation

The presentation layer of a rich Internet application comprises look and feel through the use of color, motion, typography, and iconography, and the implementation of visual metaphors such as layering and depth. The presentation elements of an application should support the user interaction and may be influenced by branding or other external elements. The presentation of an application is often the first thing that draws a user to an application, so a little extra pizzazz for aesthetics' sake isn't necessarily bad, but should be implemented strategically to balance form and function.

Color

Color is a powerful mechanism that can be used to evoke emotion and reinforce meaning and/or context. It can guide a user by signifying an error, calling attention to an important area within a view or creating associations between elements. Also, color is one of the most important elements of a corporate brand. Utilizing it appropriately can help the application integrate with related marketing materials.

Using color "incorrectly" or nontraditionally can rapidly degrade the user experience.

Figure 1-4 illustrates a mixed message being sent to the user by displaying the message "Upload Successful" in red. This could evoke a negative reaction to a positive message since red is usually associated with errors. When considering color, it is important to understand your target audience because colors may have different meaning in different cultures.

Figure 1-4   Be careful how you use color. In this case,
red projects a negative relation to a positive message.

Motion

Motion can be used to draw attention, help users visually understand what's changing during a transition, smooth out interactions, and add aesthetic value. Consider the *genie effect* that OS X uses when minimizing windows (see Figure 1-5): although somewhat

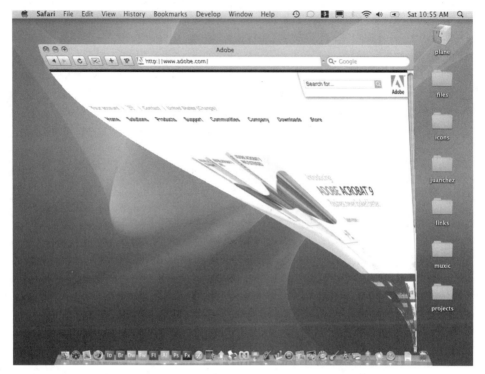

Figure 1-5   Macintosh OS X's genie effect, used when minimizing
a window to the dock is an effective use of motion

superfluous, there's no question about where the window is going. Using motion in Web applications is very powerful, but can be challenging to use effectively. A particular transition might seem fun at first, but your users may quickly tire of it if they have to wait for it to complete. Simply put, motion for motion's sake is a one-way ticket to fractured user experience.

Typography

Good use of typography transcends designing a rich Internet application; it can also be a fundamental aspect of the experience you're trying to create (see Figure 1-6). Using type, you can reinforce structure within your application without having to rely heavily on visual containers. If you've ever looked at the text on a newspaper, you'll see that text is not thrown together in a haphazard manner; there is hierarchy and flow. Using similar tactics of hierarchy within your application, you can present text in a clear and concise manner that effectively guides the user's eye. For example, you may choose to set a call to action in a slightly larger font and a different color than other surrounding text.

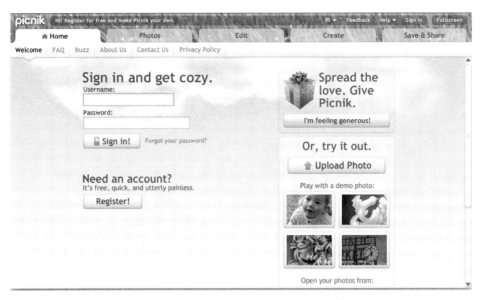

Figure 1-6   Picnik uses typography to group messages and
establish a sense of hierarchy according to areas of importance.
The choice of font supports the clean look of the application.

Fonts, which are a part of typography, can say a lot about the text it represents. For
example, you may be familiar with Comic Sans, which probably wouldn't be the best
choice for a font to use in a commercial application, unless you're working with content
that it can support, like a comic strip, storyboard, or child-focused application. Be considerate of the font you use and the way it is arranged within your application views to
be sure there is a clear message that reinforces good usability.

Iconography

There are a number of universally recognized symbols and icons that, when seen, can
speak more than words. Road signs, logos, packaging, and other visual displays rely on
these recognized symbols to strengthen the level of understanding or recognition of the
message that is being sent. This can also be applied in your applications to display recognizable symbols to the user, whether through icons, instructional graphics, buttons, or
other components.

Consider a button that, when clicked, deletes a photo from the user's photo gallery.
You could just use a generic Button with a label that reads "Delete Photo from Gallery"
or you could describe the action using a descriptive icon shown in Figure 1-7. Not only
does the icon speak volumes about its prescribed function, it is very noticeable, which
helps distinguish it from other controls that may be occupying the same space.

Figure 1-7   Iconography can strengthen the perceived functionality
of controls. In this case, an icon can be used to clearly
communicate its function of deleting a photo gallery.

Layering and Depth

Many of the characteristics of objects in the physical world are influenced by the
environment they sit in and the other objects they interact with. Light cascades across
their surfaces, their forms are reflected on other surfaces, and they cast shadows on
the ground around them. Additionally, each object occupies a different area of space
along common planes. All of these same characteristics can be used to model surfaces
within your applications.

Realistic styling of panels, buttons, combo-boxes, and other interface controls can
help users know how to work with your application and promote understanding of how
the elements work together (see Figure 1-8). Using gradients, highlights, and shadows on
buttons and other components can invite a user to click on them and can simulate the
button being indented while the mouse is down. It gives your users a small bit of instant
gratification as your application responds to their input in a way they've come to expect
from real physical objects. Attention to details like these can make your application feel
more "realistic."

Figure 1-8   A glossy, raised button design using gradients, highlights, and shadows

Simulating depth by layering visual elements can emphasize or deemphasize portions
of your application. The interface on the left in Figure 1-9 is an example of a "flat"
design that makes it hard to distinguish the content from ancillary controls. Notice that
by applying depth cues to the interface on the right in Figure 1-9 the distinction
between content and controls is more clear and defined.

Layering elements can also provide a way to achieve progressive content disclosure
while keeping a user in context. For example, you can use a drawer metaphor to reveal
additional content and expose additional controls without taking a user to a completely
new screen.

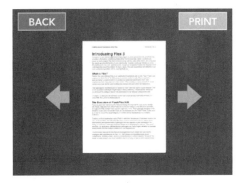 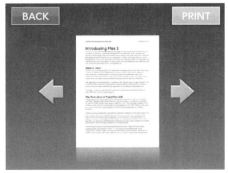

Figure 1-9   The interface on the left has a very "flat" design, which diluties the separation between content and controls, whereas the interface on the right uses depth to clearly define those aspects

External Elements

Rich internet applications often share screen real estate with other elements of a Web page, such as advertisements, text, or even other Web applications. Consider an interactive product configurator embedded in a page on a car manufacturer's Web page: It's likely to coexist with promotional offers and site navigation.

External elements can have implications on the user experience of an RIA and should be taken into consideration when designing the application. If you do not have the option to alter the external elements, choose colors, fonts, and form to help your application integrate seamlessly with the surrounding content.

Summary

There are several aspects of successful rich Internet applications, each very important and connected. Rich internet applications are user-centered, so perhaps the most important aspect to consider is the target audience. Who's going to be using the application, what do they want to do, and what do they expect? The goals of users are based around interacting with some sort of content: watching videos, customizing products, or learning information. This means an application lacking content offers very little value to users.

When you understand your users, the content they want, and what they hope to accomplish, you must design the interactions that will satisfy them and make them productive. The type of interactions should dictate the overall structure of your RIA. When the functionality and interactions of the application have been established, you must figure out how to present it through color, motion, typography, iconography, and simulated layering and depth. The presentation aspect offers the most room for creativity, but should support the user's goals while adding aesthetic value.

The next chapter introduces Adobe Flex and AIR, and why it is the perfect medium for creating rich Internet applications.

2

Adobe Flex and AIR

Adobe Flex is a development framework designed specifically for creating rich Internet applications (RIAs). At its core is the Adobe Flash Player, which has long been used for delivering expressive and immersive content consistently across major browsers on several operating systems. The Flash Player enables Flex to break free of the link-and-page metaphor and leverage more fluid and granular interactions. This experience allows users to accomplish more tasks in one "view," avoid potentially slow page refreshes, and progressively load content.

The Flex framework offers an extensible set of visual and nonvisual components similar to those offered in many desktop development suites, including things like data grids, layout containers, and a variety of interactive controls. These components, combined with immersive content and motion, can be used to implement elements of a rich user experience.

The Adobe Integrated Runtime (AIR) allows developers to deploy HTML, AJAX, and Flash-based applications to the desktop. When combined with Flex, AIR makes it easy to build desktop applications with the same ease of design and development as rich Web applications. These features, along with the ability to be launched from the Windows start menu or Mac OS dock, enable AIR applications to run along side first-class applications such as Microsoft Office, Adobe Photoshop, and the like.

The community surrounding Flex has rapidly grown to bring additional component libraries, application frameworks, and a wide variety of other useful resources. These community offerings can act as a means to further extend Flex or create a starting point to take Flex applications in new directions. All these factors combined make Flex an enticing solution for creating intriguing experiences in the RIA ecosystem.

Flex 3.0 Framework

The core portions of the Flex framework include a variety of visual components that allow for rapid development and deployment of rich Internet applications. The user sees and interacts with these components as he navigates through your application. As such, it is important to have a good understanding of their capabilities as well as where they may fall short. In any case, there are ways to fully customize the experience to fully cater to your users.

Dynamic Layout

One of the most powerful features of the Flex framework is the ability to create dynamic layouts. The visual structure of a Flex application can adjust to support the content and immediate tasks of the user. Components can dynamically alter their properties in fluid ways to help guide users, free up space, or progressively reveal pertinent content.

Extensible Visual Components

Flex comes with a number of visual components that can be used to create a fully functioning application. Visual components within Flex are comprised of containers, which handle layout, and controls, which implement interaction. With the provided components that come "out-of-the-box" with Flex, it's relatively easy to rapidly prototype a concept or spend an extended period of time finessing a release-worthy product.

Flex components can be altered, or extended, to create your own custom components. With a little development time and effort, these components can become completely modular and distributed across applications. The ability to do this has enabled the Flex community to create a variety of custom visual components and distribute them to anyone one who may be interested. For example, FlexLib, an open source library of user interface components, has a component that extends the Flex Tab Navigator to include additional functionality (see Figure 2-1). You can view the FlexLib components at http://code.google.com/p/flexlib/.

Figure 2-1   FlexLib provides a Tab Navigator (left) that extends the default
Flex Tab Navigator (right) to include functionality for moving tabs, closing
tabs, and the ability to navigate to tabs that extend beyond the visible area

Custom Appearance

Beyond functionality, the visual components within the Flex framework can be customized to take on any look dictated by a design vision down to the finest detail. Cursors can be customized, color palettes defined, and much, much more. This may involve altering visual properties, creating custom graphics, embedding fonts, or programmatically drawing visual assets.

You can also take advantage of the integration between Adobe Creative Suite applications like Flash, Fireworks, Photoshop, and Illustrator to bring functionality to even the most complex designs. Ultimately, these visual modifications support the other aspects of a well-planned application to create a memorable experience. By taking the time to add a bit of polish, you can create an application that stands out against the competition (see Figure 2-2).

Flex has a variety of bitmap effects called filters and blends that allow you to add Photoshop-like graphic treatments to your Flex application. Effects like drop shadows, glows, color effects, and more can be used strategically to visually enhance and entice your users.

Figure 2-2   Customize the appearance of Flex components—in this case, a button is shown

The Power of Motion

Animation is at the core of the Flash Player, and Flex has many ways to leverage this feature. There are a wide variety of motion-based effects that can influence components to glow, move, resize, or play a sound at any given point during a user interaction. Using motion you can add a whole new dimension to a Flex application and make it even more dynamic.

With Flex, you trade in page refreshes and static content loads for dynamic and engaging transitions between views. Layouts can fluidly change, visual properties can elegantly respond to user interaction, and entire views can take on whole new meanings to bring a user even closer to the content she seeks.

Developing Flex Applications

Flex offers an XML-based markup language called MXML to define the various aspects of a rich Internet application. From UI controls to data-structures and visual effects, everything created in MXML translates to ActionScript when compiled, and the mapping is fairly straightforward. A button described in an MXML will end up as an instance of an ActionScript Button class, initialized with parameters specified in the markup tag. Likewise, any class you create with ActionScript is available for use in MXML.

Using MXML to build a Flex application simplifies layout and abstracts much of the tedious work necessary to wire the elements of an application together. For these reasons, MXML is suitable for creating both rapid prototypes and production-quality applications.

Flex 3 SDK and MXML Compiler

Developing Flex applications is completely free using a text editor and the Flex Software Development Kit, which includes the Flex framework and the MXML Compiler (MXMLC). Using this compiler, you can package your code and assets into a working Flex application. However, this is not a very practical method for rapidly developing Flex applications.

Adobe provides a standalone application called Flex Builder that is built on the Eclipse platform. However, if your development environment already includes Eclipse, Adobe also provides a Flex Builder plugin. Both of these solutions provide essentially the same functionality and are available for Windows, Mac OS X, and Linux. Visit http://www.adobe.com/products/flex/ to learn more about Flex Builder.

> **Note**
>
> Students have access to Flex Builder for free, and Adobe offers a 30-day trial version. Check www.adobe.com for more details.

With Flex Builder, you get a robust feature set to help you rapidly develop not only Flex applications, but AIR applications as well. For editing MXML, ActionScript, and CSS, you get syntax coloring, code hinting, statement completion, and more. You also have the options to switch between Source View and Design View to get a visual representation of your application. There are plenty of features that can ease the development process and set you on track to rapid development.

Adobe Creative Suite

At some point, you'll want to explore giving your application a custom user interface and overall appearance. Having a custom-looking application helps it stand apart from the competition, reinforce branding, and presents the user with a visual design that supports the experience. It is completely possible to create the supporting graphics for your application using a variety of different graphics programs; however, the Adobe Creative Suite of applications provides a number of features that are directly integrated with Flex (see Figure 2-3). Throughout this book, you will be exposed to these features, and if you'd like to try these applications, you can download free trials at http://www.adobe.com/downloads/.

Distributing a Flex Application

Flex applications are distributed as SWF files that run in the browser through the Flash Player. A Flex application may take up an entire Web page or intermingle with other HTML content. For breaking beyond the browser and onto the desktop, you can use your same code base within the Adobe Integrated Runtime. AIR applications run on Mac OS X, Windows, and Linux, so you can develop once and deploy everywhere (see Figure 2-4).

Figure 2-3   The Adobe Creative Suite of applications that integrate with
Flex: Adobe Illustrator, Flash, Fireworks, and Photoshop. (Adobe product
screenshot reprinted with permission from Adobe Systems Incorporated.)

Figure 2-4   Flex applications can be deployed in the browser or as an
AIR application using the same code base. (Adobe product screenshot
reprinted with permission from Adobe Systems Incorporated.)

Summary

The Flex framework provides a powerful development environment that enables you to
rapidly deploy very rich and immersive experiences. There are various features that can
be leveraged using a number of development and design tools to create Flex applications.
When you're ready to deploy your Flex application, you can keep it in the browser or
break out onto the desktop using AIR and the same code base.

In the next chapter, you will begin your journey into the specific visual components Flex has to offer, beginning with layout. When designing your application, layout is the first thing you want to start thinking about. Layout determines how the rest of your application's components relate to each other, and in many cases, it is a direct reflection of any wireframes or interaction diagrams that have already been determined.

The Flex 3 Framework

3

Dynamic Layout

Layout deals with the size and position of the components that comprise a rich Internet application. With Flex 3, you can size and position these components based on other components and available space, which gives you a way to create dynamic layouts. Dynamic layouts can adapt to your users' screen resolution and allow you to hide, show, or resize content as necessary.

The type of application and your target audience can have a strong influence on the way you lay it out. Complex enterprise applications may utilize a rigid grid-based layout, whereas a children's educational application may benefit from a more free-form layout. An application like Scrapblog, a Flex-based scrapbooking tool, uses dynamic layout to maximize the space available for viewing and interacting with scrapbook pages (see Figure 3-1). This sort of functionality would have been challenging without dynamic layout.

This chapter offers an in-depth look at the elements of the Flex 3 layout mechanism, and discusses various techniques for positioning and sizing components and working with scrolling. After reading this chapter, you should have a general understanding of the layout options at your disposal and how to apply them.

Understanding Flex Layout

Flex 3 utilizes a system of containers and controls to provide a foundation for dynamic layout. Containers are components such as HBox, VBox, and Canvas that allow components to be nested inside of them to dictate the size and position of these components. In contrast, controls, such as Button and ComboBox, are components that cannot have other components added to them and are concerned with processing some type of user interaction. That is not to say that controls are not composed of other components, but that there is no external mechanism to add child components to a control. Virtually every visual component in the Flex universe is either a container or a control (see Figure 3-2).

Figure 3-1   Scrapblog uses Flex's dynamic layout to allow for areas to expand when needed or stay at a fixed size.

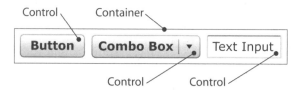

Figure 3-2   Several controls positioned within a container

Flex utilizes a variety of containers to achieve dynamic layout, each with different rules for sizing and positioning the components it contains. Complex layouts can be achieved by nesting containers within other containers, although too many nested containers can compromise performance. Generally speaking, having fewer containers is better, which should be considered when evaluating where to use automatic positioning and absolute positioning.

Automatic Positioning

Many containers in the Flex framework support automatic positioning and arrange their children based on specific rules such as layout direction, padding, and horizontal/vertical gap. Automatic positioning is sometimes referred to as *automatic layout*. Automatic layout frees you from having to constantly ensure that components are laid out correctly when your interface changes or resizes.

Linear Layout

Many of the containers that support automatic layout do so in a linear pattern. That is, they arrange their children in either a single row or single column (see Figure 3-3 and Figure 3-4). The most common linear-layout containers are HBox and VBox, which are simply Box components with their `direction` property predefined. However, other components, such as Panel and Application, also support linear layout when their `layout` property is set to `vertical` or `horizontal`.

Figure 3-3   Vertical linear layout

Figure 3-4   Horizontal linear layout

Multidimensional Layout

The Tile and Grid containers support a multidimensional layout pattern in which their children are arranged in rows and columns (see Figure 3-5). Tile lays out its children in equal-sized cells and determines the number of rows and columns automatically. Grid requires that you specify rows and columns, and explicitly define the child that goes in each

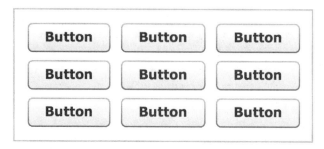

Figure 3-5   Multidimensional layout

cell. As of Flex 3, the Grid container has been deprecated in favor of the new Constraint-Row and ConstraintColumn features, described later in this chapter.

Understanding Padding and Gap

Padding is an attribute of a container that specifies the amount of space between its edges and its child components. The available padding attributes are `paddingLeft`, `paddingRight`, `paddingTop`, and `paddingBottom`.

Gap is the amount of space between the child components within a container. For containers with multidimensional layout pattern, both `horizontalGap` and `verticalGap` can be specified. Containers with a linear-layout pattern only reflect the value of one gap attribute, depending on the container's layout direction. (See Figure 3-6 for examples of padding and gap.)

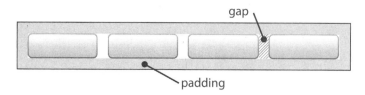

Figure 3-6   Padding and gap

> **Note**
> Style properties relating to padding and gap are only available to containers that support automatic layout.

Excluding Components from Automatic Layout

Even hidden (nonvisible) components occupy layout space and affect the position of other components in a container. To override this behavior, you must explicitly instruct the component to be excluded from layout by setting `includeInLayout` to `false`.

> **Tip**
> To make a component excluded from layout whenever it is hidden, you can bind its
> `includeInLayout` property to its `visible` property, as shown in Listing 3-1.

Listing 3-1   **Binding visible and includeInLayout properties**

```
<mx:Button id="btn" includeInLayout="{btn.visible}" visible="false" />
```

Using a Spacer Control

A Spacer control is a special nonvisual component designed to influence automatic layout.
It does not display anything, but it occupies whatever layout space you specify, which
affects the positioning of other children in the container (see Listing 3-2 and Figure 3-7).

Listing 3-2   **Using a Spacer control in an HBox container**

```
<mx:HBox>
    <mx:Label text="left" />
    <mx:Spacer width="100%" />
    <mx:Button label="right" />
</mx:HBox>
```

Figure 3-7   A Spacer control in an HBox container

Absolute Positioning

Some containers in the Flex framework support absolute positioning, meaning you can
explicitly define the location of the components within. Components in these containers
can overlap, and none of the children components are affected by the positioning of the
others. Absolute positioning may seem restrictive and nonconducive to dynamic layout;
however, properly leveraging the constraint properties of these containers can help you
control the size and position of your components. Additionally, absolute positioning can
help reduce the number of nested components, which can increase overall performance.

The containers that support absolute positioning are Panel, TitleWindow, Application
(when `layout` is set to `absolute`), and Canvas. The location of components within these
containers can be specified by setting their **x** and **y** positions, or by setting one or more of their

constraint properties, such as top, bottom, left, right, baseline, horizontalCenter, or verticalCenter. The available absolute positioning properties are described in Table 3-1.

Table 3-1   **Available Properties for Absolute Positioning**

Name	Description
x	The explicit x position of the component within its parent container, in pixels.
y	The explicit y position of the component within its parent container, in pixels.
left	The distance of the component's left edge from its parent container's left edge, in pixels.
right	The distance of the component's right edge from its parent container's right edge, in pixels.
top	The distance of the component's top edge from its parent container's top edge, in pixels.
bottom	The distance of the component's bottom edge from its parent container's bottom edge, in pixels.
baseline	The distance of the component's baseline from its parent container's top edge, in pixels. The baseline is usually a component's bottom edge or the bottom of the text in the control.
horizontalCenter	The distance of the component's horizontal center from its parent container's horizontal center, in pixels.
verticalCenter	The distance of the component's vertical center from its parent container's vertical center, in pixels.

Specifying Component Position as Cartesian Coordinates

Every visual component in Flex 3 has an x and y property. Setting these properties explicitly positions the component within its parent container's coordinate system (see Figure 3-8). The upper-left corner of a container is the (0,0) coordinate, and as you might expect, moving to the right along the x-axis increases the x value. However, unlike some coordinate systems, moving downward on the y-axis actually increases the y value. That is, a component positioned at (10,10) will be 10 pixels over from the left edge of the container and 10 pixels *down* from the top edge (see Figure 3-9).

> **Note**
>
> Setting the x and y properties on a component that is in an automatic positioning container will have no effect.

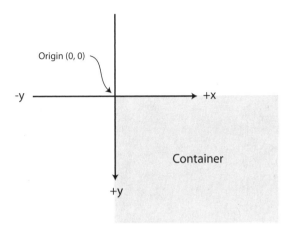

Figure 3-8   The coordinate system within a Flex container exists in the lower-right quadrant and has an inverted y-axis

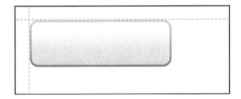

Figure 3-9   A button explicitly positioned at x:10, y:10 in a Canvas container

Specifying Component Position with Constraint-Based Layout

It is possible to specify a component's position in relation to the edges, center, or other points of its parent container. This anchors the component within the container and gives you a way to control its location, even when the container resizes.

> **Tip**
>
> Constraint-based layout properties are actually style properties and can be specified in CSS, which opens up some interesting possibilities. If your application is built using only constraints, it is possible to change the entire layout just by changing the style sheet.

Positioning Relative to Edges

A component can be positioned relative to the edges of its parent container by specifying its `left`, `right`, `top`, and/or `bottom` properties. This keeps the component's coordinating edges at the distance you specify. For example, if you place a button inside of a Canvas component and set the `right` property to 10, the right edge of the button will remain 10 pixels from the right edge of the container, even if the container changes size (see Figure 3-10).

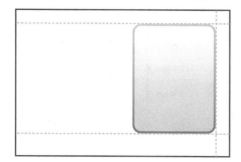

Figure 3-10   A button positioned at top:10, right:10, and
bottom:10 in a Canvas container

Positioning Relative to Centers

Similar to positioning a component relative to a container's edge, components can be positioned in relation to the horizontal and/or vertical center of their parent containers. This is accomplished by setting the component's `verticalCenter` and `horizontalCenter` properties, which are defined as numbers representing the positive or negative offset from its parent container's center point (see Figure 3-11).

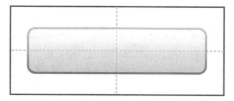

Figure 3-11   A button positioned at verticalCenter:0,
horizontalCenter:0 in a Canvas container

Using Constraint Rows and Columns

New to Flex 3, the space within an absolute positioning container can be divided up to create additional constraint areas. This is achieved by defining one or more ConstraintRow and/or ConstraintColumn classes (see Figure 3-12 and Figure 3-13). The size of these rows and columns can be specified as absolute values, as a percentage of the Canvas's size, or their size can be dynamically determined based on the components positioned within them. This is an incredibly powerful mechanism for creating dynamic layouts.

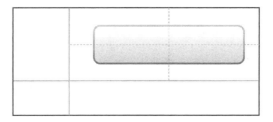

Figure 3-12   Centering a component within a constraint row and column

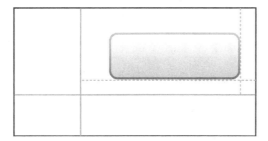

Figure 3-13   Positioning a component in the
bottom-right of a constraint row and column

Once defined, components can be positioned with their edges or centers relative to a ConstraintRow or ConstraintColumn. Additionally, you can specify the baseline position of a component in relation to a ConstraintRow or ConstraintColumn.

> **Note**
>
> Constraint rows and columns cannot be defined with CSS, and the values for constraint-based layouts are not inherited.

Sizing Components

There are several ways to size components in a Flex 3 application. The dimensions of a component can be specified in pixels or percentages, determined based on its contents and internal layout rules, or implied from its constraints. Table 3-2 describes the various size-related properties available to all visual components in Flex.

Specifying Size in Pixels

A component's size can be explicitly defined by setting its `width` and `height` properties. Setting these properties overrides any default sizing that the component might normally do (see Listing 3-3).

Table 3-2   **Size-Related Attributes**

Name	Description
width	The explicit width of the component, in pixels.
height	The explicit height of the component, in pixels.
percentWidth	The width of the component in relation to its parent container, as a percentage.
percentHeight	The height of the component in relation to its parent container, as a percentage.
actualWidth	The current width of the component, in pixels (read-only).
actualHeight	The current height of the component, in pixels (read-only).

Listing 3-3   **Explicitly defining the size of a Button component**

```
<mx:Button width="200" height="40" />
```

Specifying Size as a Percentage

It is possible to set a component's size to a percentage of its parent container's available size. To do this, set the `percentWidth` and/or `percentHeight` properties of a component. In MXML, if you set the `width` or `height` attribute to a percentage value, it automatically sets the `percentWidth` or `percentHeight` property for you (see Listing 3-4).

Listing 3-4   **Defining the size of a Button component using percentages**

```
<mx:Button width="30%" height="10%" />
```

If the parent container supports automatic layout, the padding of the container will be taken into consideration when calculating available space. Absolute layout containers do not support padding; however, the position of the component affects available space. Suppose a button is explicitly positioned at 30 pixels on the x-axis in a 100 pixel–wide container. Setting the button's `percentWidth` to 100% results in an `actualWidth` of 70 pixels (see Figure 3-14).

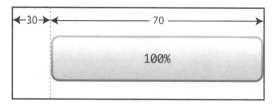

Figure 3-14   The x position of a button affects
its width when defined as a percentage

Letting Components Determine Their Own Size

If no size is specified, most components will invoke a measurement routine for calculating their ideal size based on their contents and layout rules. This is sometimes referred to as the component's *default size*. For example, if no `width` is specified for a Button component, it displays at a calculated width based on the length of its label, the size of its icon, the gap between the icon and the label, and any padding.

If the default size of a component is larger than the available space of its parent container, it is up to the parent component to decide how to display the component. Typically, the component is clipped and the container sprouts scroll bars to allow the user to see the entire component.

If the component's parent component does not have a size specified, the default size of the component is used in calculating the size of the parent container.

Understanding How Constraints Affect Size

Positioning components in relation to the edges of their parent containers can affect the size of the component, but only when two opposing sides are anchored. For example, if you set both the `left` and `right` attributes to 10 on a component inside a container that is 100 pixels wide, the `actualWidth` of the component will be 80 pixels (see Figure 3-15). Setting both `top` and `bottom` attributes would have a similar effect.

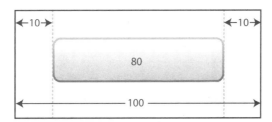

Figure 3-15   A button anchored to opposing
sides stretches as the container resizes

Managing Scrolling

When a component is larger than its container's boundaries, scroll bars often appear to allow the user to view the entire component. This behavior can be controlled using the `verticalScrollPolicy` or `horizontalScrollPolicy` properties available on most containers. However, getting scrolling to work as desired presents some unforeseen challenges. The following example encapsulates a very common pitfall when implementing layout.

Listing 3-5 creates Panel, which is nested within a dark grey Canvas component. The panel is absolutely positioned within the container by setting the `left`, `right`, `top`, and `bottom` properties to 10, effectively creating a 10-pixel gap around the panel on all sides and constraining it to a width of 180 pixels and a height of 280 pixels. By default, a Panel component has 10-pixel borders on the left, right, and bottom, and we've explicitly set the header height to 20 pixels. This leaves 250 pixels of height in the body of the panel for content, as shown in Figure 3-16.

Listing 3-5   **Constraining the size of a Panel component within a Canvas container**

```
<mx:Canvas
      width="200"
      height="300"
      backgroundColor="0x333333"
      >
      <mx:Panel
          left="10"
          right="10"
          top="10"
          bottom="10"
          headerHeight="20"
          >
      </mx:Panel>
</mx:Canvas>
```

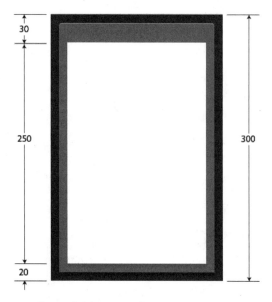

Figure 3-16   Constraints and borders leave
250 pixels in the body of the panel for content

If you add content to the panel that is taller than 250 pixels—in this case, a red canvas with a height of 400 pixels (see Listing 3-6)—you'd expect something similar to Figure 3-17.

However, what you actually get is shown in Figure 3-18. The height of the inner canvas is actually affecting the height of the panel, breaking the constraint, and causing the outer grey canvas to become scrollable.

Listing 3-6   **Adding content to the panel that extends beyond its constrained bounds**

```
<mx:Canvas
     width="200"
     height="300"
     backgroundColor="0x333333"
     >
     <mx:Panel
          left="10"
          right="10"
          top="10"
          bottom="10"
          headerHeight="20"
          >
          <mx:Canvas
               width="100%"
               height="400"
               backgroundColor="0xFF0000"
            />
     </mx:Panel>
</mx:Canvas>
```

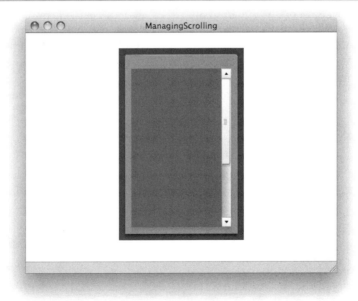

Figure 3-17   The expected behavior of adding content
that extends beyond the bounds of the Panel component

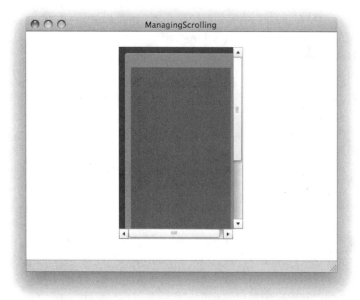

Figure 3-18   The actual behavior of adding content
that extends beyond the bounds of the Panel component

Rather than relying on the panel being constrained by its parent container, you could explicitly set a height on the panel, but this would mean that the panel would not respond to the outer canvas changing height. The actual solution is a somewhat counterintuitive one: You must explicitly specify a minimum height for the panel. During the measurement routine, when Flex noticed that the panel had no explicit sizing, it attempted to come up with a natural default size while taking many things into consideration, including content size and constraints. If no minimum height is set, the panel defines a default minimum size that is large enough to display all of its content. Since measurement occurs from the inside out, attempting to constrain the panel to the 280-pixel height described earlier is canceled out by the minimum height. Setting a minimum height prevents this default behavior, and the panel behaves as desired. Listing 3-7 shows the code that produces the expected results as pictured in Figure 3-16. This behavior is not unique to using constraints as demonstrated here. It can potentially occur anytime a container's dimensions are inferred, rather than set explicitly.

Listing 3-7   **Specifying a minHeight property on the panel produces the desired effect**

```
<mx:Canvas
     width="200"
     height="300"
     backgroundColor="0x333333"
     >
```

Listing 3-7   **Continued**

```
<mx:Panel
        left="10"
        right="10"
        top="10"
        bottom="10"
        headerHeight="20"
        minHeight="0"
        >
        <mx:Canvas
                width="100%"
                height="400"
                backgroundColor="0xFF0000"
                />
    </mx:Panel>
</mx:Canvas>
```

Summary

Dynamic layout is a key element of rich Internet applications. It makes optimum use of the user's screen and allows you to progressively display content. Flex 3 achieves dynamic positioning and sizing through a variety of containers that support different types of layout. Some containers support automatic positioning and others support absolute positioning. The size of components in a Flex application can be explicitly specified, defined as a percentage of available space, inferred from their position, or determined based on the contents of the components. The key to creating dynamic layout is understanding how the various positioning and sizing techniques work together, and applying them in the correct combinations.

4

Styling

Every visual component in the Flex framework has a default appearance, including colors, shape, font, and more. Although this default look, called the Halo theme, looks nice as a default, a custom look can help your application stand out among other Flex applications. The Flex framework allows you to customize the look of components using special properties called styles. Styles can define things like colors, fonts, and other visual characteristics, which makes styling one of the most powerful mechanisms in Flex, but also one of the most complex mechanisms. Mastering styling is key to creating expressive Flex and AIR applications.

Using styling you can easily change the appearance of your application. Each Flex component has its own set of style properties that allow you to alter different parts of it to create a custom look. If you're looking for the quickest way to divert from the default Halo Flex theme without too much effort, styling is the way to get there. Figure 4-1 shows variations of a button made to look different using just style properties, starting with the default look.

Figure 4-1   Visual variations of a button changed using styling

Understanding Style Properties

Not all properties of visual components can be specified as styles. Typically, style properties are those that modify only the appearance of a visual component such as color-related properties, font and font size, padding, and so on. Table 4-1 shows the types of properties that can be classified as styles and those that cannot. Style properties are used to specify skins and other visual elements (see Chapter 5, "Graphical Skinning," for more about skinning).

Table 4-1   Flex Properties That Can Be Applied as Styles and Those That Cannot

With styling you can specify:

Fonts	Text formatting	Colors
Icons, indicators and cursors	Skins	Alignment
Relative positioning	Padding	

With styling you cannot specify:

Absolute positioning	Size	Event handlers
Effects and transitions	States	Filters
Component properties		

Inheritance

Components may inherit styles from their parent containers. Consider a Button component within a Canvas container where the Canvas has the `color` style set to `0xFF0000` (red) as shown in Listing 4-1. Even though `color` has not been set directly on the Button component, it will still have a red label, just by virtue of being a child of the Canvas (see Figure 4-2).

Listing 4-1   The value of the color style that is set on the Canvas component will cascade to the Button component within

```
<mx:Canvas
      width="400"
      height="100"
      backgroundColor="0xFFFFFF"
      color="0xFF0000"
      >
      <mx:Button
            label="Button"
            verticalCenter="0"
            horizontalCenter="0"
            />
</mx:Canvas>
```

Figure 4-2   Button inheriting the color property from a canvas

Inheritance is a very powerful function of the styling mechanism, as it allows top-level style changes to propagate throughout the application. This behavior, coupled with the various CSS selectors discussed in the upcoming "Applying Styles with CSS" section, make it possible to change the visuals of an entire application rather easily.

> **Note**
>
> Not all style properties are inheritable. Refer to the Adobe Flex 3 Language Reference for more information.

Data Types and Formats

With the exception of class references and embedded assets, styles can only be of type String, Number, or an Array of Strings and Numbers. To validate values, styles have a format associated with them. For example, the `backgroundColor` style of a Canvas is associated with the "color" format, which means it can be specified as either hexadecimal, RGB, or qualified color name.

Table 4-2 describes the relationship between various data types, formats, and the units/syntax available when specifying styles.

> **Note**
>
> Embedding assets and using class references are discussed at length in Chapter 5 and Chapter 9.

Table 4-2   **Property Formats**

Name	Sample styles	Units / Syntax
Length (Number) style-name: length [unit]	fontSize borderThickness horizontalGap paddingTop paddingBottom paddingLeft paddingRight	pixels (px) inches (in) centimeters (cm) millimeters (mm) points (pt) picas (pc) keywords, for fontSize only: • xx-small • x-small • small • medium • large • x-large • xx-large
Time (Number) style-name: time	openDuration closeDuration selectionDuration	milliseconds

Table 4-2   **Continued**

Name	Sample styles	Units / Syntax
Color (String or Number) style-name: color	`backgroundColor` `borderColor` `color` `textSelectedColor`	hexadecimal (#000000 - #FFFFF) RGB (r%, g%, b%) VGA color names: • Aqua • Black • Blue • Fuschia • Gray • Green • Lime • Maroon • Navy • Olive • Purple • Red • Silver • Teal • White • Yellow

Applying Styles Inline

The simplest way to apply a style is to set a style directly on an instance of a visual component. Using MXML, the syntax is the exact same as setting a property (see Listing 4-2).

Listing 4-2   **Specifying the color style on a Button component inline with MXML**

```
<mx:Button color="0xFF0000" label="Red" />
```

Note

Note that syntax for setting the `color` style is the same used for setting the `label` property, which is not a style.

Style properties can be bound to variables, making it possible to create interactive or dynamic interfaces. For example, the `fontSize` property of a TextArea component could be bound to the value property of a NumericStepper. Interacting with the NumericStepper would affect the size of the text in the TextArea.

Applying Styles Using CSS

Although applying styles inline is easy, the real power of the styling framework is that you can define sets of styles, called selectors, and apply them to many component instances. Selectors are defined using CSS (cascading style sheets) syntax written in either external style sheets or in between `<mx:Style>` tags within a component.

The CSS syntax used in Flex is similar to that used in HTML; however, there are some important differences you should be aware of. This section discusses local and external styles, the various available selectors, and compares Flex CSS to HTML CSS.

> **Note**
>
> When working with styles using CSS, you have the option to reference styles using either inter-cap notation (someStyle) or hyphenated notation (some-style). Flex Builder's code hinting for styles automatically completes style names using hyphen notation.

Understanding Local and External Styles

Styles can be defined using CSS in either an external style sheet or within MXML `<mx:Style>` tags. Styles defined in the latter mode are available only to the components and their children that are created within that particular MXML file. Using an external style sheet is recommended because it keeps all the styles centralized, which can increase legibility and simplify maintenance. Also, external style sheets can be packaged into themes and then dynamically loaded to change the look of an application without needing to recompile the application, as described later in this chapter.

Unless otherwise specified, a Flex application loads the standard Halo theme. The style sheet associated with this theme is located at [Adobe Flex Builder 3]/sdks/3.0.0/frameworks/projects/framework/defaults.css. Although this style sheet doesn't define every property for all components, it does define a lot of them. If you replace this file or load a different style sheet, your application may look pretty plain unless you redefine a lot of styles.

> **Tip**
>
> Studying the defaults.css style sheet is a great way to become familiar with the elements of Flex applications that can be stylized.

Understanding CSS Selectors

Style definitions, whether created externally or locally, comprise a set of styles, called selectors. Based on how they're named, they are applied to components in one of several ways: per instance (class selector), per class (type selector), or globally (global selector). Listing 4-3 provides the general syntax of how styles are defined in CSS.

Listing 4-3   **Typical CSS selector syntax**

```
style_name
{
     style_property: value;
     [...]
}
```

Class Selectors

Class selectors define a set of properties that can be applied to specific instances of components. For example, a class selector named `bigRed` may specify `fontSize` of 24 and color
value of `0xFF0000` (see Listing 4-4). These properties can then be applied to any instance
of a component by setting the `styleName` property to `bigRed` (see Listing 4-5).

Listing 4-4   **The bigRed class selector definition**

```
.bigRed
{
     fontSize: 24;
     color: #FF0000;
}
```

Listing 4-5   **The bigRed class selector being applied to an instance of**
              button and an instance of ComboBox

```
<mx:Button styleName="bigRed" />
<mx:ComboBox styleName="bigRed" />
```

> **Note**
> The name of class selectors must start with a period (.) when they are defined, but the period
> is omitted when applying the styles. Class selector names typically use inter-caps, with a low-
> ercase first letter.

Type Selectors

Type selectors define a set of properties that are automatically applied to all instances of a
certain component. For example, a Button type selector that specifies a color value of
`0xFF0000` causes all instances of button to have red text (see Listing 4-6).

Listing 4-6   **A Button type selector specifying red text**

```
Button
{
     color: #FFFFFF;
}
```

The name of type selectors must exactly match the name of the MXML file or ActionScript class that defines the component; therefore, they typically begin with an uppercase letter, use inter-caps, and are not preceded by a period (.).

The Global Selector

The global selector is a special type selector that can impact nearly every component of a Flex or AIR application. Basically, if no other styles have been defined for a component, a value from the global selector will be applied, if available.

Because Application (or WindowedApplication in AIR) is typically the topmost container, defining a type selector for Application seems to behave very similarly to using the global selector. However, the key difference is that setting a style property in the global selector can affect even noninheriting properties. For example, setting `cornerRadius` to 8 in the global selector affects all components that have a `cornerRadius` style property, even though `cornerRadius` is not an inheritable style (see Listing 4-7). Setting `cornerRadius` to 8 in only the Application selector will not impact any components.

Also, the global selector impacts components that are not actually children of the main Application container, such as popup alerts or windows.

Listing 4-7   **The special global selector specifying a `cornerRadius` of 8 pixels**

```
global
{
    cornerRadius: 8px;
}
```

Note

The global selector does not need to be prefaced with a period (.) because it is a type selector, but it must be all lowercase.

HTML versus Flex CSS

If you've used CSS in HTML, the syntax for CSS in Flex will be familiar, but you'll find that the capabilities differ. Flex does not actually allow you to "cascade" styles in CSS as you can with HTML. For example, the CSS code snippet in Listing 4-8 will *not* apply styling to a button inside a component called SearchInput. CSS in Flex also does *not* support pseudo selectors, like `img:hover`. This means the code in Listing 4-9 would not affect the over state of a button in Flex, as it might in HTML. Furthermore, you cannot specify dimensions (such as `width` and `height`) and positioning (such as `x` and `y`), as you can in HTML.

Listing 4-8   **Cascading styles, as depicted here, will not work in the Flex CSS implementation**

```
SearchInput Button
{
    color: #FFFFFF;
    fillColors: #72CFFF, #165D81;
}
```

Listing 4-9   **Pseudo selectors, as shown here, will not work in the Flex CSS implementation**

```
Button:over
{
    color: #222222;
    fillColors: #72CFFF, #165D81;
}
```

Style Precedence

Depending on where and how they are defined, some styles may override others. Leveraging this gives you a lot of control over how styles are applied in your application, while still allowing you to make broad-stroke changes at a high level.

Redefining a selector does not completely replace the selector, but rather appends additional properties and overrides any existing ones. This means you can simply override the properties you wish, and keep everything else as it's been defined previously. For example, you like the way the Halo buttons look, but you want to shrink the corner radius to 0 pixels. All you have to do is create a Button type selector and set the `cornerRadius` property to 0 (see Listing 4-10). All instances of Button maintain the properties defined in the default style sheet, but will not have rounded corners (see Figure 4-3).

Listing 4-10   **Overriding the cornerRadius value for all Button components**

```
<mx:Style>

    Button
    {
        cornerRadius: 0px;
    }

</mx:Style>

<mx:Button label="Button 1"/>
<mx:Button label="Button 2"/>
```

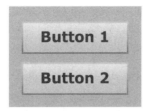

Figure 4-3   Halo buttons without rounded corners

Likewise, assigning a class selector to a component for which a type selector is also defined results in a combination of the style properties being applied. Listing 4-11 extends the previous example by creating a type selector and applying it to the second button. Both buttons still have square corners, but the second one also has a red label as specified by the type selector (see Figure 4-4).

Listing 4-11   **Overriding the cornerRadius value for all Button components and applying a class selector to a specific button**

```
<mx:Style>

    Button
    {
        cornerRadius: 0px;
    }

    .redText
    {
        color: #FF0000;
    }

</mx:Style>

<mx:Button label="Button 1"/>
<mx:Button label="Button 2" styleName="redText"/>
```

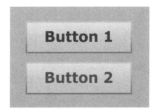

Figure 4-4   Halo buttons without rounded corners. Button 2 has a red label.

Generally speaking, styles applied inline override styles defined locally, which override styles defined in external style sheets. Moreover, inline styles override class selectors, which override type selectors, which override the global selector. Whew. Let's consider some examples.

Let's say you've defined that all buttons in your application should have a dark gray label by specifying the color style property in an external style sheet named myStyles.css (see Listing 4-12). However, in a particular view, like a high-contrast heads-up display panel (HUDPanel.mxml), you want all the buttons to have white labels. One way to accomplish this is to redefine the `color` property for all buttons in an `<mx:Style>` block in the MXML file that defines the panel (see Listing 4-13).

Listing 4-12   Button label color specified in an external style sheet

```
/* myStyles.css */


Button
{
      color: #333333 /* dark gray */
}
```

Listing 4-13   Overriding the Button type selector within a specific view

```
<!- HUDPanel.mxml ->

<?xml version="1.0" encoding="utf-8"?>
<mx:Panel xmlns:mx="http://www.adobe.com/2006/mxml" layout="">

      <mx:Style>

            Button
            {
                  color: #FFFFFF; /* white */
            }

      </mx:Style>

</mx:Panel>
```

You could also approach the challenge described previously by creatively using the different types of selectors. A Button type selector could still define the dark grey label, but you could create a class selector called hudButton (see Listing 4-14) and apply that to each button within the heads-up display panel (see Listing 4-15).

Listing 4-14   **Defining a type selector and a class selector**

```
/* myStyles.css */

Button
{
    color: #333333 /* dark gray */
}

.hudButton
{
    color: #FFFFFF /* white */
}
```

Listing 4-15   **Overriding the Button label color by applying the class selector**

```
<!- HUDPanel.mxml ->

<?xml version="1.0" encoding="utf-8"?>
<mx:Panel xmlns:mx="http://www.adobe.com/2006/mxml" >

    <mx:Button styleName="hudButton" label="click me" />

</mx:Panel>
```

Yet another way to approach this challenge is to utilize inheritance. Remember that the color style property propagates from a parent container to the children within. So, perhaps the easiest way to solve this problem is to set the `color` property for the entire HUDPanel container with a type selector and let the buttons inherit the value (see Listing 4-16). Keep in mind that this will change the `color` property of all eligible children components such as Labels and ComboBoxes, but this is probably desirable.

Listing 4-16   **Specifying the color for all components in the HUDPanel container with a type selector**

```
/* myStyles.css */

Button
{
    color: #333333 /* dark grey */
}

HUDPanel
{
    color: #FFFFFF /* white */
}
```

> **Tip**
>
> If you have similar styling for various style selectors, you can combine them using comma delimitation to cut down on the amount of code you have to write as well as maintain consistency. The CSS code in Listing 4-17 shows similar style properties for .downloadButton and .saveButton being grouped together, but redefined separately for their differences, in this case, icons.

Listing 4-17   Combining styles using comma delimitation

```
.downloadButton, .saveButton
{
      fillColors: #FFFFFF, #CCCCCC;
      borderColor: #666666;
      cornerRadius: 8;
      color: #222222;
}

.downloadButton
{
      icon: Embed(source="downloadIcon.png");
}

.saveButton
{
      icon: Embed(source="saveIcon.png");
}
```

Working with Styles Using ActionScript

So far, we've mostly discussed working with styles using MXML. If necessary, you can accomplish the same tasks, and more, using ActionScript. Perhaps your application requires a particular button to be red or green depending on the values of certain variables. You could execute a function that checks those variables and conditionally sets the **backgroundColor** style of your button. As with many things in application development, there are several ways to accomplish this, but let's have a look at how you might do it with ActionScript (see Listing 4-18).

To set a style on an instance of a component, you call the **setStyle** method available to any style-enabled component, passing it the name of the style property and the value you wish to set it to. This is basically the equivalent of specifying a style property inline in MXML. Because calling this method not only impacts the component on which it was called, but also any components contained within, it should be used judiciously. To get the current value of a style property using ActionScript, you use the **getStyle** method, which is a much lighter operation than **setStyle**.

Listing 4-18   **Conditionally setting style properties using ActionScript**

```
<mx:Script>
<![CDATA[
      public var valid:Boolean = true;
      public function changeButtonColor () : void
      {
            if ( valid == true )
            {
                  // make the background green
                  myButton.setStyle('backgroundColor',0x00CC00);
            }
            else
            {
                  // make the background red
                  myButton.setStyle('backgroundColor',0xCC0000);
            }
      }
]]>
</mx:Script>

<mx:Button id="myButton" click="changeButtonColor()" />
```

Warning

Because the `setStyle` method accepts the style name as a string, there is no validation as to whether that property actually exists. That means you could misspell the property name, and it would fail, and fail silently. You won't even get an exception when you try to set it.

Creating Stylable Widgets

It is common to composite two or more components to create a reusable widget for your application. For example, you might extend an HBox and stuff it with a TextInput and Button to create a SearchInputWidget to use throughout your application. Listing 4-19 demonstrates exactly that to create a component that looks like Figure 4-5.

Listing 4-19   **Applying style to an element of a widget with an explicit class selector**

```
<!- SearchInput.mxml ->

<?xml version="1.0" encoding="utf-8"?>
<mx:HBox xmlns:mx="http://www.adobe.com/2006/mxml" >
      <mx:TextInput
            width="100%"
            height="100%"
            />
```

Listing 4-19   **Continued**

```
    <mx:Button
        label="Search"
        height="100%"
        styleName="searchInputButton"
        />
</mx:HBox>
```

Figure 4-5   A stylable SearchInput widget that
combines a TextInput with a SearchButton

Notice in Listing 4-19 that the `styleName` of the button is set to `searchInputButton`. This approach exposes the style of the button so that it can be defined outside of the widget, but all instances of SearchInputWidget will have the exact same style. Although this is better than applying a bunch of inline styles to the button, there is still a better way. Changing the button definition as shown in Listing 4-20 allows you to customize each instance of the SearchInput widget differently (see Listing 4-21).

Listing 4-20   **Applying style to an element of a widget using a dynamic class selector**

```
...
<mx:Button
        label="Search"
        height="100%"
        styleName="{getStyle('buttonStyleName')}"
        />
...
```

Listing 4-21   **Applying two different styles to two instances of the same widget**

```
<local:SearchInputWidget buttonStyleName='redButton' />
<local:SearchInputWidget buttonStyleName='blueButton' />
```

For this trick to work, you must expose `buttonStyleName` as a style using metadata as shown in Listing 4-22. Style metadata tells the compiler which style can be used with a particular component, its format and data type, and whether children of this component should inherit this style.

Listing 4-22   **Style metadata used to define a buttonStyleName style**

```
[Style(name="buttonStyleName", type="String", inherit="no")]
```

Introducing the Style Manager

Behind all styling operations in Flex is the StyleManager. It is possible to access, modify, and define CSS selectors using ActionScript and the StyleManager. This opens a world of possibilities for creating dynamic styles or performing other tricks.

You can use ActionScript to directly access the selectors from the StyleManager to take an inside-out approach to styling. For example, you might define a selector that embeds several icons (see Listing 4-23). Next, from within your application, use ActionScript to access the values of that selector (see Listing 4-24). It's a pretty handy trick because it keeps all of your icons in one place.

Without this trick, you have to embed your assets within the component in which it will be used, which can get ugly if that component is buried deep in the application package structure. Imagine a SearchInput widget located in a com.cve.view.controls package. A reference to an icon located in an images folder at the root of the project might look something like Listing 4-25.

The StyleManager also enables you to load and unload entire style sheets at runtime, which enables you to create dynamic, on-the-fly customizations of your Flex application. For this to work, your style sheets must be compiled as SWF. Runtime styling is described at length in Exercise 4.1.

Listing 4-23   **Several assets embedded in a single selector**

```
.icons
{
    wrenchIcon: Embed('images/wrench.png');
    searchIcon: Embed('images/magnifier.png');
    loginIcon: Embed('images/lock.png');
}
```

Listing 4-24   **Accessing embed assets using the StyleManager**

```
<Button
    icon="{StyleManager.getStyleDeclaration('.icons').getStyle('wrenchIcon')}"
    label="Customize"
/>
```

Listing 4-25   **An ugly Embed statement within a component**

```
[Embed(source="../../../../images/magnifyer.png")]
public var searchIcon:Class;
```

Styling in Design View

You don't always have to assign styling properties to components directly in the Source View of Flex Builder. In Design View, you can access all the style properties for any component in the Flex Properties panel (Window > Flex Properties). With the Flex Properties panel visible, you can select any component to access visual selectors for the styles of that component. Figure 4-6 shows what the Flex Properties panel looks like when selecting a Button in Design View. You can also access other style properties in this same panel, as shown in Figure 4-7.

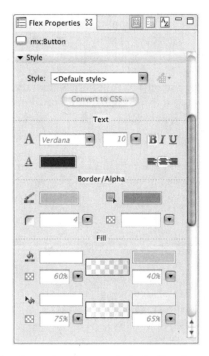

Figure 4-6   Styles for a button within the Flex Properties panel

Note

Not every style property is represented in the Style panel. To access more styles, click on the category list and scroll to the Styles category, or find a style via the alphabetized list of properties as shown in Figure 4-7.

Whenever you make changes to the styling of a component using the Flex Properties panel, the styles will be created inline of the component's MXML. However, you can easily convert your inline styling to CSS to use throughout your application. In Flex Builder, this is really easy to do by following these steps:

1. Once you have created styling for a particular component, select that component and, in the Flex Properties panel, click the Convert to CSS button as shown in Figure 4-8.

Figure 4-7   Accessing other style properties via the Flex Properties panel

Figure 4-8   The Convert to CSS button

2. When you click the Convert to CSS button, the New Style Rule window appears (see Figure 4-9). If you don't have a CSS file already created, you can click the New button to create one to hold your new style.

3. With your CSS file specified, you can select to apply the styling globally, as a type selector, to a specific component, or to a component using a style name. You can refer to the "Understanding CSS Selectors" section in this chapter for more information on the differences between these options. After selecting your desired option, click OK.

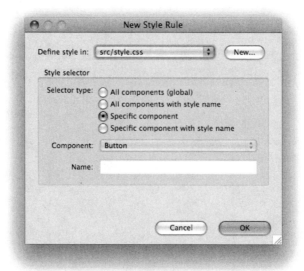

Figure 4-9   The New Style Rule window

4. When you click OK, the appropriate CSS is written to the specified CSS file and you are taken into CSS Design View where you have additional options to customize your components using a more visual tool set.

Tip
You can access CSS Design View any time you have a CSS file open in Source View mode.

CSS Design View

One of the new features of Flex Builder 3 is CSS Design View, which allows you to visually edit styles within a CSS file. In this view, you are presented with the various component parts that can be styled, as well as any available states. You can also do things like zoom in and out for pixel perfect accuracy, pan around using the Hand tool, or add and remove styles. Figure 4-10 is a snapshot of CSS Design View for the CSS of the styling of a button.

In CSS Design View, you can also easily assign other visual parameters like icons, fonts, and skins for your components. Refer to Chapters 5 or 9 for more information on using those features of CSS Design View.

In CSS Design View, you can also easily navigate between different styles. You can do this by selecting a style from the Style Combo Box. You can also move throughout the CSS code structure of your CSS file using the Outline panel (see Figure 4-11) when in CSS Source View, which you can access by selecting Window > Outline. Clicking on any of the properties in the Outline structure jumps you to the corresponding CSS code.

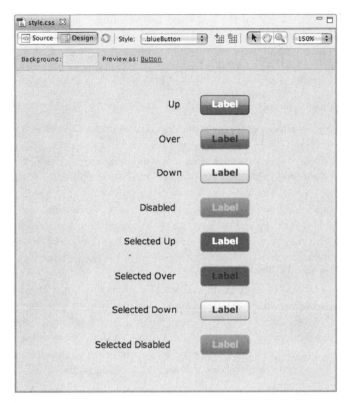

Figure 4-10   CSS Design View of a styled button

Figure 4-11   CSS Outline View with button styling and embedded font

Working in CSS Design View is a quick and easy way to get instant feedback on the look of a styled component. It's great for quick prototyping and rapid development. However, you may find it helpful to become familiar with working in the CSS Source View for code formatting and taking advantage of some of the tips discussed in this chapter.

Themes

A theme is essentially a look, generally a visually consistent one, for a Flex application that has been created using CSS and/or supporting assets. A theme can vary in complexity from simple color changes to graphic-rich styling. After spending the time and effort to create a theme for your Flex application, you can package it to be repurposed or distributed by creating a theme.

At a minimum, a theme can be used by passing its assets to others interested in implementing it into their Flex application. You can also package those assets as a single theme within a Flash Component file (SWC) to be easily distributed or compile that theme SWC to be used as a theme loaded at runtime. However, once you create a theme SWC, it will no longer be editable.

A theme SWC is basically a package of any CSS files, graphic assets, or programmatic skin classes that comprise your Flex application's appearance. Each of the supporting graphical assets or classes must be either embedded or use a ClassReference in order to ensure their inclusion into the theme SWC. You can learn more about embedding graphic assets in the Skinning chapter. You can use the Flex compiler to apply a theme SWC and the compc utility to create one. To learn more about working with theme SWCs, refer to the Flex 3 documentation.

Note

As a reference for creating your own theme SWCs, you may want to duplicate the defaults.css file that comes with the Flex 3 SDK and build upon it to make your own custom theme.

Summary

Styles are different from properties and exhibit several special behaviors, such as inheritance. The most powerful aspect of styling is that styles can be defined in sets and applied to components in a variety of ways.

Styling plays a major role in the way you define the look of your application. The more you work with it, the more you will see just how powerful it can be. Whether you just need to change the look of a single button or an entire application, styling is the root mechanism for complete customization.

The following chapters build on the concepts discussed here and introduce further customization techniques such as skinning and working with indicators, cursors, and text.

5

Graphical Skinning

How many times have you seen a Flex application that looks like Figure 5-1? After seeing the same user interface time and again, it gets old, which is not the best way to present a professional Flex application. The most successful Flex applications out there don't look or "feel" like Flex applications. For example, a Flex preloader is a dead give-away of a Flex application, whereas customizing it helps the application look unique. Attention to these types of details helps give an application the polished feel required for a truly engaging user experience. This detailed effect can be accomplished with skinning.

Figure 5-1   A Flex application with that default "Flex look."

Skinning is a Flex term that refers to the act of changing the way a component looks by replacing the assets that make up its visual appearance. It also allows you customize the appearance of your components beyond what can be achieved with styling. This chapter will focus on graphical skinning, which involves the use of bitmap or vector graphics to change the visual appearance of components versus using graphics that are drawn programmatically via ActionScript.

Each component within the Flex framework has its own "skinnable" parts. Some components, like a Container, are "invisible" by default and contain a single view or "state." Other components, like a Button, have several states that change depending on how the user interacts with the component. Assets can be created for each state of a component to create unique user interfaces and interactive graphics.

The process of graphically skinning a component involves embedding external assets, such as bitmap or vector graphics, for each state of a component. Creating graphical skins is typically easier than programmatic skinning because you can use visual tools such as Photoshop, Illustrator, Fireworks, or Flash to create your skin artwork. Each of these graphics tools has different capabilities and uses different methods to skin a Flex application. However, there are some general concepts, plugins, and conventions that apply to each of these tools that will help you skin a Flex component graphically.

As you may have noticed, the default look of Flex components is nice, but it doesn't have the visual appeal or in-depth branding that custom skinning provides. You can use graphical skinning to create an engaging experience your users will remember and want to return to. This is important because a unique and approachable user interface is one asset that can put your application ahead of competitors. As a small example of what you can do with graphical skinning, take a look at the varieties of buttons in Figure 5-2. Each is a Flex Button component underneath, but all have a different look to them.

Figure 5-2   A variety of skinned Flex buttons that demonstrate how bitmap and vector graphics can be used for custom skinning

As you become more familiar with skinning, you'll be able to discern how others skinned their Flex applications to create a truly custom look. An eye trained to see how custom-looking components were skinned can be helpful as you piece together your own application and formalize a plan to "get it skinned." Figures 5-3 and 5-4 are some examples of what you can do with graphical skinning. You can also go to the Flex application showcase at http://www.flex.org/showcase to see a wide range of custom-looking applications. If you know how to use any bitmap- or vector-based graphics editing applications, you can skin a Flex application.

In this chapter, you will learn about the differences between bitmap and vector graphics, bringing graphics into Flex, preventing your skins from distorting, naming conventions to smooth out the skinning process, and the skinning features Flex Builder has to offer. The information in this chapter will give you a good base of understanding what is involved with creating graphical skins and implementing them in Flex. To further your knowledge, you can read Exercises 5.1–5.4 or start using the skin templates discussed in each of those exercises.

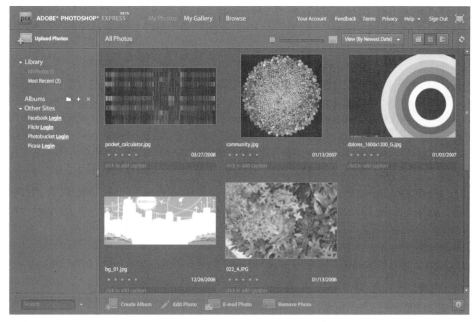

Figure 5-3   Photoshop Express uses extreme skinning to create a
custom user interface. (Adobe product screenshot(s) reprinted
with permission from Adobe Systems Incorporated.)

Figure 5-4   Discovery Earth Live creates a custom branded experience with
visually rich controls. (Compliments of Discovery Channel and Discovery.com.)

Difference Between Bitmap and Vector

Graphical skins can be bitmap or vector in nature. There are differences between these graphics that you should consider when deciding which type you will use to create your skins. In some cases, you may let the tool you're most familiar with dictate the approach you take when creating graphical skins.

Bitmap artwork is made up of rasterized graphics pixels, each with its own color. When scaling, bitmaps are subject to pixilation, also called rasterization, and become blurred when scaled above 100% of their original size as in Figure 5-5. Many graphical user interfaces (GUIs), like a computer's operating system and a majority of the images used on the Web, are made up of bitmap graphics.

Flex supports JPG, PNG, and GIF bitmap file formats to be used as assets for creating graphical skins. They do not support the rich animations that you can achieve when using Flash SWFs. Bitmap assets are exported from graphics applications like Photoshop and Fireworks. These applications fit into some of the workflows we'll be discussing for creating your own graphical skins. There are also some techniques that will discussed later that you can use to make sure your bitmap assets do not distort and scale cleanly.

Vector artwork is made up of shapes created using points, lines, and curves that are drawn using mathematical equations to form simple to complex graphics as in Figure 5-1. Vector artwork is ideal for creating scaleable graphics because, unlike Bitmap artwork, it does not pixelate when scaled. For example, something as simple as a Button scaling to accommodate the length of the label could result in pixelation. This is important to keep in mind when deciding which method to use when creating graphics for your application. These differences are described in Table 5-1. If any of your graphics are going to scale in your application, you will probably want to go the vector route by using graphics applications like Flash or Illustrator.

For vector-based formats, Flex supports the use of Flash SWF and SWC files, which are commonly exported from Flash or Illustrator. Scaleable Vector Graphics files (SVG), which may come from Illustrator, are also supported by Flex 3, but are not commonly used for graphical skinning. To get these bitmap or vector graphics in a Flex application, they must be embedded.

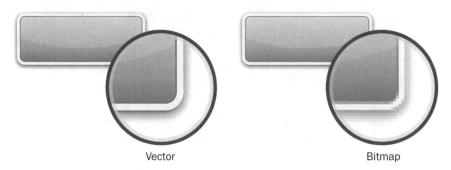

Vector   Bitmap

Figure 5-5   Vector and Bitmap graphic comparison

Table 5-1   Bitmap Versus Vector

	Bitmap	Vector
Pixelation	Subject to pixelation	Stays crisp and does not pixelate
Usage	Multiple files	Can contain many skins in one file
File size	Larger file size	Smaller file size

Embedding Graphics in Flex 3

To use a bitmap or vector graphic as a skin, it must be embedded. Graphics may be embedded using external CSS files, `<mx:Style>` tags in an MXML class, or inline. You can embed a bitmap graphic, a SWF (pronounced "swif"), or a symbol inside of a SWF. As an example, here's what the CSS looks like for a button style that uses embedded bitmap graphics (see Listing 5-1) and one that uses a symbol from a SWF (see Listing 5-2).

Listing 5-1   Embedding bitmaps

```
Button
{
    upSkin: Embed(source='images/Button_upSkin.png');
    overSkin: Embed(source='images/Button_overSkin.png');
    downSkin: Embed(source='images/Button_downSkin.png');
    disabledSkin: Embed(source='images/Button_disabledSkin.png');
}
```

Listing 5-2   Embedding symbols from a SWF

```
Button
{
    upSkin: Embed(source='skin.swf',symbol='Button_upSkin');
    overSkin: Embed(source='skin.swf',symbol='Button_overSkin');
    downSkin: Embed(source='skin.swf',symbol='Button_downSkin');
    disabledSkin: Embed(source='skin.swf',symbol='Button_disabledSkin');
}
```

If you use the Flex Component Kit, which is discussed in Chapter 12, "Flex and Flash Integration," you reference a `skinClass`, as in Listing 5-3. A skin class references a custom component created in Flash.

Listing 5-3   Referencing a skin class

```
Button
{
    upSkin:      Embed(skinClass='Button_upSkin');
    overSkin:    Embed(skinClass='Button_overSkin');
```

Listing 5-3   **Continued**

```
downSkin:     Embed(skinClass='Button_downSkin');
disabledSkin: Embed(skinClass='Button_disabledSkin');
}
```

Just bringing graphics into Flex and using them as a skin isn't always enough. Additional preparation of graphics for skinning is often required to make sure the graphic adheres to the dimensions of the component it is being used with. Luckily, you can use 9-slice grids to make sure your skinned components look pixel-perfect.

Using 9-Slice Grids

When you apply an embedded graphic as a skin, it must have the capability to change in size as the component it is applied to changes in size. Fortunately, there is a feature in Flex you can take advantage of to ensure that your graphics scale accordingly without getting distorted. This feature is called 9-slice scaling, or scale-9. This works by slicing up a graphic into nine different parts based on values for a top, left, right, and bottom slice to establish the scaleable areas of a graphic (see Figure 5-6). These four slices split your skin into nine sections that scale independently, hence the name 9-slice. In visual editors, these slices appear as dashed lines.

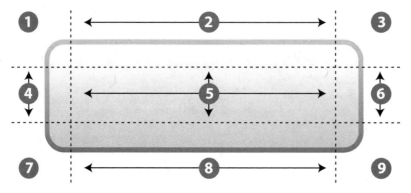

Figure 5-6   9-slice guides

The nine pieces each react differently when your skin is scaled. When a skin is scaled horizontally, pieces 2, 5, and 8 are the only pieces that stretch in that direction. When a skin is scaled vertically, pieces 4, 5, and 6 are the only pieces that stretch in that direction. In every case, pieces 1, 3, 7, and 9 do not stretch at all. This allows for skins to grow in size without being distorted as shown in Figure 5-7.

Figure 5-7   With and without 9-slice scaling. Notice that using
scale-9 prevents the image from distorting when horizontally stretched.

Setting 9-Slice Grids

There are different methods of applying these 9-slice guides to bitmap and vector graphics. Bitmap graphics require coordinates values specified in the `Embed` statement of a graphic. A vector graphic can either use coordinate values set in the CSS `Embed` statement (see Listing 5-4) or the 9-slice grid can be assigned visually in Flash or Illustrator (see Figure 5-8). Each method does the same thing; it's really up to what you prefer and how either method fits into your workflow.

If setting coordinate values sounds complex, don't worry. Flex Builder 3 offers a visual toolset to assign the coordinate values necessary for setting the 9-slice grid (see Figure 5-8). When the 9-slice grid properties are specified using that tool, the necessary values for `scaleGridLeft`, `scaleGridTop`, `scaleGridRight`, and `scaleGridBottom` are automatically assigned to the skin. You can also edit the 9-slice grid by clicking on the Edit Scale Grid button in the CSS Design View in Flex Builder 3.

Listing 5-4   **Setting scale grids in an Embed statement**

```
Button
{
    upSkin:    Embed(source="skins/assets/Button_upSkin.png",
                    scaleGridLeft="6",
                    scaleGridTop="6",
                    scaleGridRight="94",
                    scaleGridBottom="18");
}
```

You can use this same method for a symbol within a SWF; however, it requires that you reference a symbol as shown in Listing 5-5. You cannot apply 9-slice grids to the SWF itself.

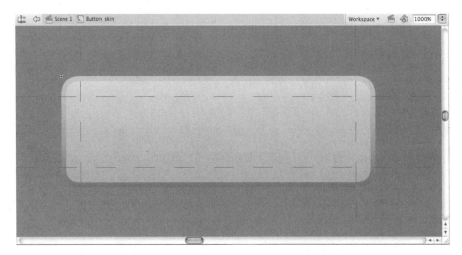

Figure 5-8   Visually setting scale grids in Flash CS3

Listing 5-5   **Setting scale grids in an Embed statement for a symbol within a SWF**

```
Button
{
    upSkin:   Embed(source="skins.swf", symbol="Button_upSkin"
                    scaleGridLeft="6",
                    scaleGridTop="6",
                    scaleGridRight="94",
                    scaleGridBottom="18");
}
```

At the bare minimum, you can create graphics, embed them, and apply 9-slice grids to skin your whole application. Doing that over and over can be a tedious process. You can leverage some of integration features the Adobe Creative Suite and Flex Builder share as well as use some strategies to further optimize your workflow.

Naming Conventions for Skin Importing

Creating your graphical skin assets is only half the battle. Bringing those assets into Flex is the other half. The second half is less difficult thanks to the Skin Import feature in Flex. Some of the examples that support this chapter will use this Skin Import Wizard, which is accessible by selecting File > Import > Skin Artwork. To smooth out the process of importing your skin assets and assigning skins to components, there are naming conventions you should be aware of before you start importing your skins.

These naming conventions do not have to be followed to use the wizard, but they help make the skinning process much quicker. If you don't use the naming conventions, you may find that specifying the `Embed` statements for all your components is a tedious process. For example, by using these naming conventions, the Skin Import Wizard (which we'll discuss later) automatically recognizes the skin parts specified by the naming convention and you don't have to sort through a long list of choices of how you want your skin applied to a component.

> **Note**
>
> If you're wondering where these naming conventions came from, they are used by Adobe for skin templates (which you'll learn about later) and discussed in a tutorial by Adobe's Narciso Jaramillo on designing skins for Flex 3. You can read his article at http://www.adobe.com/devnet/flex/articles/skins_styles.html.

When creating artwork for your component skins, you'll be asked to assign names to symbols if you're using Flash or Illustrator (when creating a SWF or SWC), names to folders if you're using Photoshop, or names to files if you're using Fireworks. In any case, these naming conventions are relatively similar for all situations.

The General Rules

The naming convention follows a few simple rules. The first part of the name is the component name—for example, Button, ComboBox, Panel, and so on. The name of the component is followed by an underscore (_) and the skin part or state name—for example, upSkin, upIcon, trackSkin, and so on. You can refer to Appendix A, "Skinning and Styling Diagrams," as a reference for these skin parts.

As an example, an asset for a Button component's upSkin would be named Button_upSkin. If an asset with that naming convention is used with the Skin Import Wizard, it would automatically be assigned to the button's `upSkin` property in CSS. To familiarize yourself with the different skinnable parts of a component, you may want to refer to the Flex 3 documentation, poke around in CSS Design View, or refer to Appendix A.

This same naming convention also can be used for custom components. For a custom component called MyComponent, you could specify a background image asset using the name of MyComponent_backgroundImage.

Naming for Class Selectors

When creating skins for components that will use a class selector, you also may consider a naming convention. For example, if you were creating a `Button upSkin` to be used with a class selector of `.blueButton`, you could name the graphical asset `Button_blueButton_upSkin`. Using this naming convention produces a CSS class selector with rules as in Listing 5-6. To learn more about class selectors, refer to Chapter 4, "Styling."

Listing 5-6   **Using a naming convention for a class selector**

```
Button.Bluebutton
{
    upSkin:    Embed(source="skins/assets/Button_blueButton_upSkin.png");
}
```

Naming for Sub-Components

Some components in Flex 3 are made up of other sub-components. For example, a `ComboBox` has a `dropdown`, a `DateField` uses a text input, an `HBox` has scrollbars, and so on. You can usually recognize components with sub-components because they'll have a style property ending with `StyleName`, like `dropdownStyleName`, `textInputStyleName`, and so on, as shown in Listing 5-7. Refer to Appendix A for more examples of other controls with sub-component styles.

Listing 5-7   **ComboBox drop-down sub-component styling**

```
ComboBox
{
    dropDownStyleName: 'myDropDown';
}

.myDropDown
{
    backgroundColor: #CCCCCC;
}
```

Notice in Listing 5-7 that a class selector of `myDropDown` is specified for the `dropDownStyleName` of `ComboBox`. This example sets the `backgroundColor` of the `ComboBox` drop-down to gray. After you understand how to style these sub-components, you'll be able to fine-tune the look of your Flex application.

Each of these sub-components can be styled by using a naming convention as well. However, the naming convention has a small variation depending on the application you're using to create your skins, as will be pointed out. To target these skinnable parts of a component, you specify the following, in order:

- Component name.
- Hyphen (-) *if you're using Photoshop, Illustrator, or Fireworks.*
- Dollar sign ($) *if you're using Flash.* (Flash uses a dollar sign because a hyphen gives errors when a SWF or SWC is compiled.)
- Sub-style part name.
- Underscore (_).
- The skin part.

As an example of this naming convention, a background image of a ComboBox drop-down created in Fireworks, you would name the asset `ComboBox-dropdown_backgroundImage`. The same example in Flash would be `ComboBox$dropdown_backgroundImage`. Here is a quick reference, the only difference being the dollar sign or hyphen:

- `ComponentName-subComponent_skinPart`. Fireworks, Illustrator, Photoshop
- `ComponentName$subComponent_skinPart`. Flash

You'll notice that `StyleName` is not included with `dropdown` as it appears in the CSS in Listing 5-7. This is because `StyleName` is automatically appended to `dropdown` when you use the Import Skin Artwork Wizard. In this case, the CSS rules in Listing 5-8 would be produced when using the Skin Import Wizard.

Listing 5-8   Using a naming convention for a sub-component style

```
ComboBox
{
    dropdownStyleName:   "myDropDownStyle";
}


.myDropDownStyle
{
    backgroundImage:   Embed(source="skins/assets/
                             ComboBox-dropdown_backgroundImage.png");
    backgroundSize:   "100%"
}
```

You'll see these naming conventions being used throughout the exercises that go along with this chapter, and it's really easy to implement after you know how it works. Granted, you don't have to use them, but it makes it easier to use the Import Skin Artwork feature of Flex Builder 3. It also keeps all your assets organized and helps to set standards that can carry through any project you may be a part of.

Using the Skin Import Wizard

When you're ready to import your skin assets, the Skin Import Wizard takes you through a step-by-step process to specify your skin assets and create the appropriate CSS code to have those skins applied correctly to your application components. You'll find that using this wizard saves you lots of time. This wizard can be accessed in Flex Builder 3 under File > Import > Skin Artwork.

The Skin Import Wizard is divided into two screens. The first screen of the wizard comprises several steps:

1. Select the type of skins you are importing—a folder of Bitmaps or a SWF/SWC— and specify their location (see Figure 5-9).

Figure 5-9   First step of the Skin Import Wizard

2. Specify where you would like to import your skin assets within your Flex project.

3. Specify which CSS file you would like to create the style rules in.

4. Specify the MXML file you would like to attach the CSS file to.

On the second screen of the Skin Import Wizard (see Figure 5-10), all you have to do is make sure each skin asset is assigned to the appropriate Style Selector and Skin Part. The wizard tries to assign your assets based on the file or symbol names as described in the section about naming conventions. If the Skin Import Wizard did not correctly assign the skin to the correct Style Selector and/or Skin Part, don't worry. The items listed in the Style Selector and Skin Part column are actually combo boxes that you can use to change the selector or part by clicking on them.

> **Note**
>
> The Skin Import Wizard doesn't assign 9-slice grid values to your skin embeds. After importing your skin assets, you can go into CSS Design View and assign the scale grid values or do it manually in the CSS code. If you set the 9-slice guides in Flash or Illustrator, the 9-slice grids will be retained through the import process. This is covered in more detail in the exercises that support this chapter.

Figure 5-10   Second step of the Skin Import Wizard

The wizard doesn't give the option to attach the CSS code in an `<mx:Style>` tag within an MXML file you specify. If that's something your project requires, you'll have to copy and paste the CSS from the external CSS file and paste it to the desired destination.

Using the Skin Import Wizard is a great way to quickly bring graphics assets into Flex. The ability to customize your components visually doesn't stop there. Flex Builder provides a CSS Design View where you can fine-tune the appearance of your Flex application.

Working with Skins in CSS Design View

After successfully bringing in your skins to Flex, you can further refine the way your components look using the CSS Design View in Flex Builder. This view is accessible when viewing a CSS file and by clicking on the Design button next to the Source button. CSS Design View allows you to visually see what's going on with your skins as they're applied to components. This view also contains a Skin Properties Palette, shown in Figure 5-11, which provides another option for bringing in skin artwork as well as the ability to fine-tune your skinned components.

You can apply skins to a selected Type or Class selector using the combo box in the Skin portion of the palette. Like the Skin Import Wizard, you have the option to embed Flash symbols from a SWF or SWC or specify bitmap assets to be used as skins. What you choose is a matter of preference that will probably be dictated by whether you choose to use vector or bitmap assets and what graphics application you feel most comfortable using.

Not only can you apply skins to components, but you can also fine-tune some of the style properties such as padding, font attributes, and icons. Padding can be very helpful for positioning the items within the skin area. Any of the changes you make in this palette will update the CSS file accordingly.

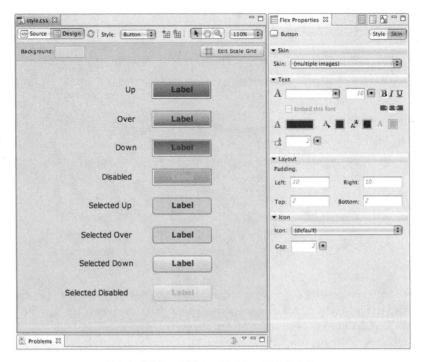

Figure 5-11   CSS Design View Skin Palette

> **Note**
>
> To use CSS Design View, you must be working within a CSS file. CSS Design View is inaccessible for trying to view styling specified using an `<mx:Style>` tag within MXML. For more information regarding the CSS Design View, see the section, "Working with Skins in CSS Design View."

Skin Templates

In the exercises that support this chapter, you will be guided through creating skins for your Flex application from scratch. Although this is a great way to learn the ins and outs of skinning, it is not entirely necessary. Adobe has provided Skin Design Extensions for Photoshop, Illustrator, Flash, and Fireworks that include skin templates for you to start with. These templates include skins for nearly every Flex component that you can edit in one master template or one component at a time (see Figure 5-12). All you have to do is change the artwork to your liking and export your skins to be used in your Flex application. In each of the exercises that support this chapter, you'll learn more about these templates.

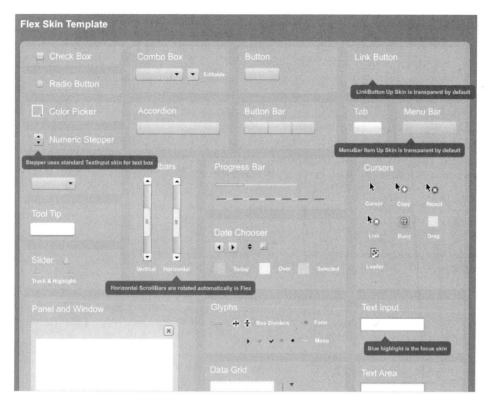

Figure 5-12   A skin template that comes with
the Skin Design Extension for Fireworks

Mixing Tools

One of the benefits of using Adobe Create Suite is that each application has integration
with another. For example, you could create comps of your Flex application design in Fireworks then copy and paste that artwork into Flash to create your skins. The immediate
benefit of this is that you can freely design your Flex application to meet a deadline and
then repurpose that same artwork for the skinning process. There are some quirks though,
and those quirks vary from application to application. Additionally, not every feature of an
application correctly translates to another.

You can copy and paste artwork from one application to another to leverage features
from the application you are pasting artwork into. For example, Illustrator does not support
transparency on gradient colors, but you can paste that artwork into Flash and use the support Flash has for transparency on gradient colors. Another example is leveraging an application that has support for "live" display of artwork that has 9-slice guides applied to it to
clearly see what your skin will do when it is scaled in Flex.

Summary

Graphical skinning allows you to truly customize the look of your Flex applications using graphics applications like Photoshop, Illustrator, Fireworks, and Flash. You learned about embedding graphics for skinning for Flex applications, how you can use naming conventions to smooth out the skinning process, and how 9-slice grids can help your skins prevent distortion. All that, coupled with Flex Builder's integration with Adobe Creative Suite, allows you to rapidly implement custom application designs.

Now that you have a general understanding of graphical skinning and the methods that are involved, you can follow the exercises to get in-depth detail on how to skin your Flex applications. Each of the tools that have been mentioned (Photoshop, Illustrator, Fireworks, and Flash) are supported with an exercise. The exercises involve skinning the same component, a Button, so that you may make a direct comparison between Photoshop, Illustrator, Flash, and Fireworks.

In the next chapter, you will learn about programmatic skinning, which requires the use of drawing methods through ActionScript to create skins. Skinning components programmatically is more complex, but it yields a number of benefits.

6

Programmatic Skinning

Like graphical skinning, programmatic skinning is the process of customizing a component by replacing its visual elements. However, programmatic skinning uses ActionScript classes to dynamically create artwork rather than attaching pre-made graphics. The artwork can be drawn based on various parameters, which makes programmatic skins very powerful. The default Flex component skins, which are programmatic, are extremely versatile because they expose many style attributes that allow you to influence the way the skin looks.

Programmatic skinning requires ActionScript knowledge to extend classes, create shapes with drawing functions, and define what is accessible via styling. For this reason, programmatic skinning has a steeper learning curve than graphical skinning and is often more time consuming. However, you may get more mileage out of the programmatic skins you create because you can repurpose them throughout your application. For example, both buttons in Figure 6-1 (from the Photoshop Express launch screen) could have the same skin but with different styles specified to alter their color.

Figure 6-1   Two variations of the same button
skin as used in Photoshop Express

This chapter will introduce you to the ActionScript drawing API and the framework for creating programmatic skins. After reading this chapter, you should understand the fundamentals of programmatic skinning, which will be applied in Exercise 6.1, "Creating a Programmatic Skin."

Introducing the Drawing API

Flex draws artwork in terms of fills and strokes. Fills are solid areas of color or patterns, and strokes are solid lines or borders around fills. Using ActionScript, graphics can be programmatically drawn by defining set of instructions using methods such as `beginFill`, `lineStyle`, `moveTo`, and `lineTo`. These methods comprise a set of functionality known as the drawing API and are available to most classes in Flex 3. Table 6-1 outlines the basic functionality of the drawing API methods. For more detailed information, refer to the Adobe Flex language reference.

Table 6-1   **Drawing API Methods**

Specifying line styles and fills	
`lineStyle()`	Defines a single-color stroke with the specified color, thickness, and alpha parameters.
`lineGradientStyle()`	Defines a multi-color stroke with the specified gradient parameters.
`beginFill()`	Begins a single-color fill using the specified color and alpha parameters.
`beginGradientFill()`	Begins a multi-color fill using the specified gradient parameters.
`beginBitmapFill()`	Begins a fill with a bitmap image as specified by the parameters.
Drawing lines and shapes	
`lineTo()`	Draws a straight line from the current drawing position to the specified x and y position.
`curveTo()`	Draws a curved line from the current drawing position to the specified `anchorX` and `anchorY` position, arcing as specified `controlX` and `controlY`.
`drawCircle()`	Draws a circle using the specified parameters.
`drawEllipse()`	Draws an ellipse using the specified parameters.
`drawRect()`	Draws a rectangle using the specified parameters.
`drawRoundRect()`	Draws a rectangle with rounded corners using the specified parameters. All corners are rounded with the same radius.
`drawRoundRectComplex()`	Draws a rectangle with rounded corners using the specified parameters. Each corner may have a unique radius or none at all.
Utility methods	
`clear()`	Removes all graphics drawn.
`endFill()`	Applies a fill previously started with one of the begin fill methods.
`moveTo()`	Updates the current drawing position to the specified x and y position.

Understanding How Strokes Are Drawn

Strokes drawn with the drawing API are centered over the path specified, meaning a 10-pixel stroke will actually extend 5 pixels on either side of the path. Because of this, a rectangle drawn 100 pixels wide and 100 pixels tall with a 10-pixel stroke will actually render at 110 pixels by 110 pixels, which may result in an undesired effect (see Figure 6-2).

Also, strokes with odd widths—for example, 5, 7, and so on—are split evenly on either side of a path, which means they're not drawn on whole pixels, which can appear blurry when rendered.

Because of these caveats, it's common to draw borders by "nesting" rectangles within other rectangles so that the artwork has crisp edges and fits within the desired dimensions.

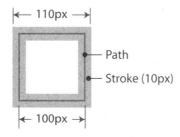

Figure 6-2   Strokes drawn with the drawing API extend on either side of the specified path.

Creating a Programmatic Skin

Creating a programmatic skin is like creating a simple ActionScript component. Your programmatic skin will extend a base-class, implement a couple of interfaces, and override a few methods. If that sounds scary, don't worry; you don't need to be an expert in object-oriented principles and you'll learn everything you need to know in this chapter.

Choosing a Base-Class

Rather than rewriting common logic over and over again, or completely rolling your own skin, you'll want to extend an existing class that has already done some of the work for you. There are three light-weight classes in the Flex 3.0 framework that are typically extended to program a skin: ProgrammaticSkin, Border, and RectangularBorder. Choosing the correct one is a matter of deciding what functionality your skin requires.

> **Note**
>
> These classes do not have any appearance, but rather define small sets of functionality useful for creating a programmatic skin. If you're familiar with abstract classes in other programming languages, it's useful to think of these classes as abstract classes.

mx.skins.ProgrammaticSkin

ProgrammaticSkin is the most simple and lightweight of the three base-classes. It provides the minimum functionality necessary to be attached to a component as a skin and to support CSS styling. Additionally, ProgrammaticSkin defines a few utility methods such as `drawRoundedRectangle()`, `horizontalGradientMatrix()`, and `verticalGradientMatrix()` that simplify using the drawing API. ProgrammaticSkin is typically extended to create simple graphics without borders, such as the icon for a PopUpButton or the small rectangle that indicates the selected date in the DateChooser component.

mx.skins.Border

Border extends ProgrammaticSkin and is used to skin controls that have borders, like Buttons or Tabs. The Border base-class introduces the notion of border metrics, which are used to communicate the dimensions of the border being drawn to other classes. This is useful because it can inform a component about how much space is available when it uses this skin.

mx.skins.RectangularBorder

RectangularBorder extends Border and adds support for background images. This functionality can be leveraged to incorporate graphic assets into programmatic skins. It is common to extend this class to create backgrounds and borders for containers.

Using a Nonstandard Base-Class

Because many instances of skin classes often exist in an application, it is recommended that one of the standard programmatic skin base-classes are extended because they are very lightweight and optimized. However, one drawback to the standard base-classes is that other components cannot be added to them as children—that is, it is not possible to composite several components to create a programmatic skin. Although such functionality should be used judiciously, and is not often needed, it is possible to extend a nonstandard base class that *does* support child components. For example, you might extend UIComponent and create a skin that contains several other classes that draw various bits of artwork.

Again, this is not recommended, and it's encouraged that you try to create the same artwork within a single object. Should you decide to extend a nonstandard base-class, consider implementing the IBorder and IProgrammaticSkin interfaces (discussed in the next section) so that your skin behaves more like a standard programmatic skin.

Implementing Interfaces

In object-oriented programming, an interface is something that acts as a contract for functionality, meaning that if a class implements a certain interface, other classes can make assumptions about what that class can do. In context of programmatic skinning, skins can implement an interface that tells other classes that the skin provides information about some of its dimensions or other properties.

If you extend one of the base-classes described earlier, you don't have to worry about implementing the skinning interfaces because the base-classes already do this for you. If you're not extending a base-class, read on. Implementing the interfaces described in this section will help your custom skin play nicely with the rest of the component framework.

> **Note**
> Implementing an interface does not actually add any functionality to your class as it does when you extend a class. It simply tells other classes that you agree to implement certain functionality.

IProgrammaticSkin

The IProgrammaticSkin interface ensures that any implementing class has an accessible `name` property. This is important because often the `name` is used to determine which state of a skin to draw. For example, you might create a single skin class that has instructions for drawing a button in all of its various states. When the button is in its *over* state, it attaches an instance of your skin and gives it a name of "overSkin". When it comes time to draw the skin, you can check the value of the `name property`, and if name is "overSkin", you know you want to draw a representation of the button's *over* state.

IBorder

The IBorder interface ensures that any implementing class has an accessible `borderMetrics` property. Throughout the Flex 3.0 framework, many controls and containers evaluate whether their skins implement IBorder, and respond accordingly. This usually means taking the size of the border into consideration while performing measurement and layout. See the upcoming section, "Understanding Measurement and Programmatic Skinning," for more information.

Overriding Methods

Extending a base-class makes it so that all you have to do to create a programmatic skin is simply override a few key methods, namely `styleChanged()` and `updateDisplayList()`. When overriding methods, you can choose to completely replace the functionality provided by the base-class, or more commonly, you can extend it by first making a call to the method in the base-class using the `super` keyword, and then writing your own logic (see Listing 6-1).

Overriding the styleChanged Method

As the name implies, overriding `styleChanged()` allows you to respond when one or more style properties have changed on the component that is being skinned. Overriding this method is useful if you need to calculate `borderMetrics` based on styles or if you're deriving color variations from style attributes. For example, mx.skins.HaloBorder exposes attributes such as `borderThickness` and `borderSides`, which when changed invalidate the current border dimensions (see Listing 6-1).

Listing 6-1   **The styleChanged override in mx.skins.HaloBorder**

```
/**
 *  If borderStyle may have changed, clear the cached border metrics.
 */
override public function styleChanged(styleProp:String):void
{
    if (styleProp == null ||
        styleProp == "styleName" ||
        styleProp == "borderStyle" ||
        styleProp == "borderThickness" ||
        styleProp == "borderSides")
    {
        _borderMetrics = null;
    }
    ...
}
```

Overriding the updateDisplayList Method

Overriding `updateDisplayList()` is the key step in creating a programmatic skin. Any time the component being skinned changes visually—changes states, resizes, and so on—the `updateDisplayList()` method of the skin is called and passed `width` and `height` parameters. In your override, you use drawing API methods to dynamically create artwork at the specified size (see Listing 6-2).

Listing 6-2   **The basic structure of an updateDisplayList override**

```
override protected function updateDisplayList(w:Number, h:Number):void
{
  super.updateDisplayList(w,h);

  // draw your artwork here
  ...
}
```

A single programmatic skin can be used to draw the various states of a control. When overriding updateDisplayList in this kind of skin, you conditionally draw artwork for the current state of the control. Listing 6-3 shows an updateDisplayList override that might be used to create a button skin. Notice that using a switch statement on the `name` property allows you to draw different artwork depending on whether the button is selected.

Listing 6-3   **The basic structure of an updateDisplayList override**

```
override protected function updateDisplayList(w:Number, h:Number):void
{
    super.updateDisplayList(w,h);

    switch (name)
    {
        case "selectedUpSkin":
        {
            // draw artwork for when the button is
            // up and selected
            ...
            break;
        }

        case "upSkin":
        {
            // draw artwork for when the button is
            // up and not selected
            ...
            break;
        }
    }
}
```

The width and height values that are passed to the updateDisplayList method represent the size of the component being skinned. If you draw artwork bigger than these bounds, your skin may overlap other components or may appear "cut off." You can, however, use this to your advantage—for example, if might want to create a skin for a scroll-bar button that extends into part of the area reserved for the scroll-track, as shown in Figure 6-3. In this case, you would draw the "wings" below the button outside of the specified boundaries.

Tip

The `updateDisplayList` method may be executed several times throughout the life of the skin. As such, it's important to clear out any previously drawn graphics before drawing new artwork. If you don't, you may end up with extra lines and strokes, which create an undesired effect. To clear graphics, use the `clear()` drawing API method.

Figure 6-3   The "wings" below this scroll button are drawn
beyond the bounds specified in updateDisplayList and overlap
part of the scroll track. The orange line represents the width
and height passed to updateDisplayList.

Understanding Measurement and Programmatic Skinning

When visual components are being laid out on the screen, Flex 3 invokes a measurement routine to determine the size of each component. Some components may have an explicit size specified, whereas others attempt to calculate an ideal size. When measuring a component with a programmatic skin, the skin can actually affect the size of the component. For example, the default Flex Button skin (mx.skins.Button) specifies that it should not be smaller than 40 pixels wide by 22 pixels tall. This means that a Button component left to determine its size will measure at least 40 pixels by 22 pixels. To specify the size of a skin, override the `measuredWidth` and `measuredHeight` properties as shown in Listing 6-4.

Listing 6-4   **Overriding measuredWidth and measuredHeight to specify 40 pixels by 22 pixels**

```
//------------------
//  measuredWidth
//------------------

override public function get measuredWidth():Number
{
    return 40;
}


//------------------
//  measuredHeight
//------------------
```

Listing 6-4   Continued

```
override public function get measuredHeight():Number
{
    return 22;
}
```

Similarly, a skin that implements IRectangularBorder can provide information about how much space is available inside of the component after taking the dimensions of the border into consideration. Consider a button that is 100 pixels wide and 22 pixels tall. With a 4-pixel border on all sides, the available internal width will be 92 pixels (100 pixels minus 4 pixels left border minus 4 pixels right border). The available height will be 14 pixels (22 pixels minus 4 pixels top border minus 4 pixels bottom border). To specify border dimensions, override the `borderMetrics` property as shown in Listing 6-5.

Listing 6-5   Overriding borderMetrics to specify a 4-pixel border on all sides

```
import flash.geom.Rectangle;

//------------------
// borderMetrics
//------------------

override public function get borderMetrics():Rectangle
{
    return new Rectangle(4,4,4,4);
}
```

Summary

Nobody said programmatic skinning is easy. It is typically more challenging and time consuming than graphical skinning, but it has its advantages. After a skin has been programmed, you can easily change the colors or other attributes using style parameters. This enables you to create incredibly robust components that you can repurpose throughout one or more of your applications.

This chapter has covered the fundamentals of drawing with ActionScript and programmatic skinning. See Exercise 6.1, "Creating a Programmatic Skin," to apply these topics.

7

Lists and Navigation Components

You've already learned about customizing controls and containers; however, there are other components that are somewhat of a hybrid. These are components that act like containers, but are dynamically populated with controls based on a data source. Components with this type of behavior include list-based components like List, Tree, TileList, and so on, and navigation components like ButtonBar, and TabBar. The benefits of using data-driven components include standardized structure of common elements, ability to be updated dynamically, and opportunities for advanced customization. After you gain an understanding of the extent to which you can customize these components, you may find you can leverage them in many ways throughout your application.

Customizing list-based components not only makes the data of your application more visually pleasing, but can also be used to greatly enhance functionality. Consider the image browser feature in a program like Scrapblog (shown in Figure 7-1). The TileList used to show images has been stylized to match the rest of the interface, but has also been customized to provide a zoom button the user can click to gain additional detail on a selected photo before adding it to her project. Additionally, you can see that the view of the application is kept rather clean by only showing options for a particular photo when a user is focused on it. That can be a valuable concept to take advantage of, as it can prevent unnecessary clutter as the user navigates through your application.

Figure 7-1   A custom TileList gives users a way to
zoom in on a photo before adding it to the project

Similar to list-based controls, the elements of a navigation control are created based on a data source. Navigation controls, like a ButtonBar, allow you to create sets of logically related buttons and give them a common appearance. Each navigational control provides its own set of functionality. For example, components like ToggleButtonBar and TabBar save you from having to write code to toggle selections because that functionality is part of the component. A perfect example of a ToggleButtonBar can be found in Photoshop Express's view mode selector (shown in Figure 7-2). A developer could have built this widget by placing three Buttons in an HBox container and writing the necessary logic to get the buttons to toggle appropriately. However, he or she would have to stylize each button individually, and that solution does not provide for rapid scalability for adding buttons.

Figure 7-2   A customized ToggleButtonBar component

Because navigation controls are driven by data, they can be dynamically generated. Consider a scenario where the available navigation options are based on the current user's permissions. The data structure that drives the component could be generated based on some sort of business logic that only shows certain buttons to certain users. Needless to say, utilizing data-driven components is very powerful and customizing them is a key part of creating a great visual experience.

List-Based Components

List-based components represent a series of data-items in individual cells, or rows of cells in the case of DataGrid. By default, each item is displayed by showing the value of its `label` property as text. However, using *item renderers*, it is possible to control how the data in each cell is represented. List-based components can be stylized in a number of ways by specifying attributes such as `themeColor`, `rollOverColor`, `alternatingItemColors`, and so on. Also, just like other components you've learned about, list-based components have skinnable elements. Refer to Appendix A's "Skinning and Styling Diagrams" to see what can be stylized and skinned for each component.

> **Note**
>
> Setting padding does not affect the inner spacing of a list-based component; however, it does affect the inner spacing surrounding each of the data items. This can be a great way of setting the spacing in between data items.

> **Note**
>
> Adobe Flex 3 Professional comes with additional data-driven components, including OLAP Data Grid and Advanced Data Grid. For more information, navigate to http://www.adobe.com/products/flex/.

> **Tip**
>
> As you add, update, or delete items within a list-based component, you can add dynamic visual effects to animate the changing of data. These effects are called *data effects* and are discussed in detail in Chapter 11, "Effects and Transitions."

List, HorizontalList, and TileList

List, HorizontalList, and TileList are all used to display a flat data structure. List arranges items vertically, HorizontalList arranges items horizontally, and TileList arranges items in a grid formation using columns and rows (see Figure 7-3). The size and position of the items can be fine-tuned using properties including `rowCount`, `columnWidth`, `direction`, and so on. Using these properties along with `padding` and `gap`, you can achieve pixel-perfect positioning of data items. Additionally, if you are using *item renderers*, which will be discussed in the next section, you can achieve finer-grain control over the positioning and function of items. Refer to the Flex documentation for all available properties.

> **Note**
>
> The drop-down that appears when you open a ComboBox is a List component. To customize it, specify a `dropdownStyleName` style property.

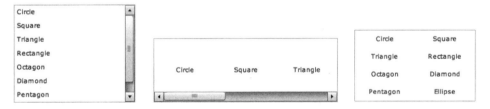

Figure 7-3   From left to right: List, HorizontalList, TileList

Tree

Tree is a special list used to display a hierarchical (nested) data structure. Items are represented similarly to items in a list; however, a tree allows a user to expand an item to display its child items, or nodes. An item with children is called a branch, and one without is called a leaf. Branches can contain other branches and/or leaves, making it possible to display an indefinitely deep nested structure. Figure 7-4 is a representation of a Tree component.

Figure 7-4   A Tree component

The button used to expand or collapse an item, and the icons representing branches and leaves can be skinned to achieve a custom appearance. Refer to the Tree section of the diagrams in Appendix A.

DataGrid

A DataGrid can display tabular data. Items are displayed in rows, just like in a list, except DataGrid also has columns that represent other properties of the item, as shown in Figure 7-5. By default, the name of the property is displayed as a header at the top of each column, and the data set can be sorted on a particular column by clicking the header. Columns can be rearranged and resized as the user sees fit.

Name	Phone	Email	
Christina Coenraets	555-219-2270	ccoenraets@fictitious.com	
Joanne Wall	555-219-2012	jwall@fictitious.com	
Maurice Smith	555-219-2012	maurice@fictitious.com	
Mary Jones	555-219-2000	mjones@fictitious.com	

Figure 7-5   Data grid component

Among other things, the header background can be skinned, and the colors of the alternating rows can be specified. Custom cursors denote the resizing of columns as the user clicks and drags between headers. Refer to the DataGrid section of the diagrams in Appendix A.

Menu

Similar to a tree, a menu can display a hierarchical data structure. Rather than an item expanding or collapsing to expose its children, items are displayed in a fly-out menu as shown in Figure 7-6. Menus are typically not created directly, but instead are displayed as pop-ups from either PopUpMenuButton or MenuBar components. A bonus feature of menu is that it supports separators. Any object in the data source that has its `type` property set to "`separator`" will display as a dividing line instead of a label. The line can be customized by specifying a `separatorSkin` style property.

Figure 7-6   An expanded menu displayed with a PopUpMenuButton

Item Renderers and Editors

Item renderers and editors give you control of how a data item is represented and interacted with within a cell of a list-based components. They comprise elements such as graphics, text, and visual components, and can define additional logic for customizing data visualization. Think of an item renderer/editor as a mini-component whose purpose is to display data or define interaction for each data item.

Item renderers and editors are specified by setting the `itemRenderer` or `itemEditor` properties on a list-based component. Item *renderers* typically show data in a read-only way, usually in the form of text and/or images. In contrast, item *editors* are used to modify data and often present the user with an interactive control such as a CheckBox or TextInput. It is possible to use the same component for the item renderer and editor by setting `rendererIsEditor` to `true`.

For performance, item renderers/editors are "recycled." Think of a list that is 100 pixels tall with a `rowHeight` of 20 pixels. Only 5 rows are visible at once, so only 5 item renderers/editors are created. As the visible data items change (usually through scrolling), each of the item renderers/editors is passed new data, and updates accordingly. In some cases, this may cause adverse effects where newly displayed data appears to take on properties of a formerly displayed item renderer, especially when the dimensions of the renderer change.

> **Note**
>
> When using item renderers, you must explicitly define changes between each data item. Otherwise, you run the risk of a data item "inheriting" set data from another data item. For example, if you set the background color of an item renderer of a data item to blue, but do not explicitly set the background color of other data items, you run the risk of other data items "magically" setting themselves to the blue background color as you scroll. In this case, this could be prevented by setting the background colors of the other item renderers of data items to the desired color.

Using a Drop-In Item Renderer or Editor

Using a drop-in item renderer simply means referencing an existing control as an item renderer. Many of the controls in the Flex 3 framework have been designed to be used directly as item renderers or editors. For example, if each of your data items has a `selected` property and you specify CheckBox as the itemEditor for a list, each row will show a

CheckBox control that allows you to toggle the value of the selected property between true and false. Listing 7-1 shows an example of using a CheckBox drop-in item renderer as it might be used in a simple to-do list.

Listing 7-1   Using a CheckBox as a drop-in item renderer to create a simple to-do list

```
<mx:DataGrid>
    <mx:dataProvider>
        <mx:Object completed="false" title="email publisher"/>
        <mx:Object completed="true" title="contact Adobe"/>
        <mx:Object completed="false" title="finish Book"/>
        <mx:Object completed="true" title="call EffectiveUI"/>
        <mx:Object completed="false" title="cancel vacation"/>
        <mx:Object completed="true" title="move to denver"/>
    </mx:dataProvider>
    <mx:columns>
        <mx:DataGridColumn
            editorDataField="completed"
            dataField="completed"
            headerText=""
            itemRenderer="mx.controls.CheckBox"
            rendererIsEditor="true"/>
        <mx:DataGridColumn
            dataField="title"
            headerText="Task"/>
    </mx:columns>
</mx:DataGrid>
```

Tip

You can design your own components to work as drop-in item renderers/editors by implementing the IDropInListItemRenderer interface. This lets you define a default property for your control to represent when it is used as an item renderer/editor.

Creating an Inline Item Renderer or Editor

For more control over how a data item is displayed, you can create an inline item renderer/editor. Within a component's tag, you can specify a component to be used as the item renderer/editor as shown in Listing 7-2.

Listing 7-2   Using an inline renderer to show icons with labels

```
<mx:List>
    <mx:dataProvider>
        <mx:Object
            url="http://www.scalenine.com/images/icons/photoshopIcon20.gif"
            label="Photoshop"
            />
```

Listing 7-2   **Continued**

```
        <mx:Object
            url="http://www.scalenine.com/images/icons/apolloIcon20.gif"
            label="AIR"
            />
        <mx:Object
            url="http://www.scalenine.com/images/icons/flashIcon20.gif"
            label="Flash"
            />
        <mx:Object
            url="http://www.scalenine.com/images/icons/flexIcon20.gif"
            label="Flex"
            />
    </mx:dataProvider>
    <mx:itemRenderer>
        <mx:Component>
            <mx:HBox>
                <mx:Image source="{data.url}"/>
                <mx:Label text="{data.label}" />
            </mx:HBox>
        </mx:Component>
    </mx:itemRenderer>
</mx:List>
```

This bit of MXML produces an item renderer that has an HBox with an image and label inside. Each one of those components within the item renderer can connect to its own data properties and has different functionality. The Image component displays a GIF icon for an Adobe product, and the Label component displays the name of the product.

Using inline item renderers/editors is most suitable for quick mockups or one-off cases because of the embedded nature of the implementation. With an inline item renderer, you need to open up a potentially large MXML file just to edit the item renderer. This can sometimes be cumbersome, so in most cases you want to create your item renderers as separate components.

Creating an Item Renderer as a Separate Component

Creating an item renderer as a separate component makes it easier to manage and repurpose throughout your application. Consider the previous example (see Listing 7-2); to create this as a separate component, you would put the same tags previously wrapped in the `<mx:Component>` tag into a separate MXML file as shown in Listing 7-3.

Listing 7-3   **External MXML item renderer, created in a separate MXML file**

```
<!— CustomRenderer.mxml —>
<?xml version="1.0" encoding="utf-8"?>
<mx:HBox>
```

Listing 7-3   **Continued**

```
    <mx:Image source="{data.url}"/>
    <mx:Label text="{data.label}" />
</mx:HBox>
```

Once created, this MXML component can serve as the item renderer for any number of List components by specifying it as shown in Listing 7-4, assuming you saved your file as CustomRenderer.mxml in a cve package.

Listing 7-4   **List specifying a separate component to use as an item renderer**

```
<mx:List itemRenderer="cve.CustomRenderer"/>
```

Tip

Since item renderers can be full components, you can use view states or show/hide controls and containers as a user interacts with the renderer. This is a great way to maintain a clutter-free view and only show information pertinent to a specific task.

Note

An inline item renderer displays in Design View, whereas an item renderer created as a sepa-rate component does not. You may want to create the item renderer inline to get it looking the way you want and then externalize it into a separate MXML file.

Note

Creating item renderers/editors as separate components can be done using ActionScript instead of MXML. To do this, make sure your ActionScript class implements the IListItemRenderer inter-face so it can access the data item for which it represents.

Creating an Item Renderer for a Tree or Menu

There are special considerations you must make when creating an item renderer for a Tree or Menu component. Because the default item renderers for these components define interaction that allows you to navigate through the data structure, your custom item ren-derers must do the same. For example, if you create an item renderer for a Tree component, a data item that has children should display a control for expanding this item and showing its children. To implement this, you would have a Button component in your item renderer that dispatches the appropriate events such as `TreeEvent.ITEM_OPEN` or `TreeEvent.ITEM_CLOSE`. Refer to TreeEvent in the Adobe Flex Language Reference for more information.

Navigation Controls

Navigation controls create and arrange several instances of a single button-like control (Buttons or LinkButtons) based on a data source. Using navigation controls allows you to group related buttons together and give them a common appearance, and it allows you to handle user interaction in one place (see Listing 7-5) rather than on each individual control. Some navigation controls, like ToggleButtonBar and TabBar, automatically manage selection and cause the buttons to behave like radio buttons with a selection state.

Listing 7-5   **Handling a user's interaction with a button within a navigation component**

```
<mx:Script>
    <![CDATA[
        import mx.controls.Alert;
        import mx.events.ItemClickEvent;

        protected function myButtonBar_clickHandler(event:ItemClickEvent):void
        {
            Alert.show("You clicked a button labeled "+event.item.label+".");
        }

    ]]>
</mx:Script>

<mx:ButtonBar
    id="myButtonBar"
    itemClick="myButtonBar_clickHandler(event)"
    >
    <mx:dataProvider>
        <mx:Object label="one" />
        <mx:Object label="two" />
        <mx:Object label="three" />
    </mx:dataProvider>
</mx:ButtonBar>
```

It is typical to use a navigation control to switch between views contained in a View-Stack component (described in Chapter 3). As such, an instance of a ViewStack can be used as the data source for a navigation control shown in Listing 7-6. In this scenario, clicking a button in the navigation control automatically changes the `selectedIndex` property of the ViewStack. Alternately, an Array or ArrayCollection can be also be used as the data source. In either case, navigation controls employ the field/function mechanism, described in the upcoming "Specifying Labels and Icons" section, to resolve the values for the `label` and `icon` properties of each Button or LinkButton.

Listing 7-6   **A reference to a ViewStack can be specified as**
                the dataProvider for a navigation control

```
<mx:ViewStack id="views" width="100%" height="100">
    <mx:Canvas width="100%" height="100%" label="One" icon="viewOneIcon.png">
        <mx:Label
            text="View One"
            verticalCenter="0"
            horizontalCenter="0" />
    </mx:Canvas>
    <mx:Canvas width="100%" height="100%" label="Two" icon="viewTwoIcon.png" >
        <mx:Label
            text="View Two"
            verticalCenter="0"
            horizontalCenter="0" />
    </mx:Canvas>
    <mx:Canvas width="100%" height="100%" label="Three" icon="viewThreeIcon.png" >
        <mx:Label
            text="View Three"
            verticalCenter="0"
            horizontalCenter="0" />
    </mx:Canvas>
</mx:ViewStack>

<mx:LinkBar dataProvider="{views}" />
```

There are several variations of navigation controls in the Flex 3 framework, but they all extend from an abstract class called NavBar, which manages layout and selection and encapsulates the label and icon field/function mechanism. All navigation controls can be directed to arrange their buttons either vertically or horizontally using the `direction` property; the space between the buttons can be specified using the `horizontalGap` or `verticalGap` styles.

Note

Even though NavBar extends the Container class, you should not attempt to directly add or remove children usingaddChild/addChildAt or removeChild/removeChildAt on any of the navigation controls. Because the buttons within navigation controls are dynamically created, you do not stylize them individually. Instead, they are passed styles when they're created as specified in style properties such as `buttonStyleName` or `linkButtonStyleName`. Most navigation controls allow you to specify unique styles for the first and last buttons that are different from the rest of the buttons using style properties like `firstButtonStyleName` or `lastButtonStyleName` as shown in Listing 7-7. The exception is LinkBar, which does not have separate styles for the first and last buttons, but does expose style properties for customizing the separator shown between the individual LinkButton instances. Assigning this CSS to the button style names of a ButtonBar would produce a result shown in Figure 7-7.

Listing 7-7   **Specifying unique styles for the first and last buttons in a navigation control**

```
<mx:Style>
    .snazzyButton
    {
        color: #00CC00;
    }

    .snazzyFirstButton
    {
        color: #CC0000;
    }

    .snazzyLastButton
    {
        color: #0000CC;
    }
</mx:Style>

<mx:ButtonBar
    id="myButtonBar"
    buttonStyleName="snazzyButton"
    firstButtonStyleName="snazzyFirstButton"
    lastButtonStyleName="snazzyLastButton"
    >
    <mx:dataProvider>
        <mx:Object label="first" />
        <mx:Object label="middle a" />
        <mx:Object label="middle b" />
        <mx:Object label="last" />
    </mx:dataProvider>
</mx:ButtonBar>
```

Figure 7-7   A ButtonBar with the first and last buttons styled uniquely

ButtonBar

ButtonBar is a direct descendent of NavBar. For each item in the data source, a standard Button control is created and positioned after the button attached for the previous item, either to the right of or below, depending on the `direction` property. The buttons are not toggle enabled, and ButtonBar provides no logic around selection state. When a button is clicked, an `ItemClickEvent` is dispatched, carrying information about the data item for which the button represents. The buttons are styled using the `buttonStyleName`, `firstButtonStyleName`, and `lastButtonStyleName` style properties as shown in Listing 7-7. Figure 7-8 shows an example of a ButtonBar component.

Figure 7-8   A ButtonBar component

ToggleButtonBar

ToggleButtonBar extends ButtonBar and adds logic for maintaining selection state. By default, when a button is clicked, it remains selected until another button in the bar is clicked (see Figure 7-9). This behavior can be changed by setting the `toggleOnClick` property to `true`. This allows a user to click the selected button to deselect it. ToggleButtonBar adds a style property called `selectedButtonTextStyleName` that allows you to customize the text of the selected button.

Figure 7-9   A ToggleButtonBar component with the third button selected

TabBar

TabBar extends ToggleButtonBar to attach instances of tabs instead of a button (see Figure 7-10). To customize the tabs, use style properties such as tabStyleName, firstTabStyleName, lastTabStyleName, and selectedTabStyleName. A TabBar can be used by itself or as part of a TabNavigator. A TabNavigator is a special container that serves as a pre-coupled TabBar and ViewStack.

Figure 7-10   A TabBar component with the third tab selected

> ### Note
>
> In some cases, it may also be necessary to specify styling for `buttonStyleName` in order to get the TabBar to take on the desired appearance. However, you can just use the class selectors defined for the `tabStyleName`. As a default, you might want to just specify styling for Tab and Button styles.

LinkBar

LinkBar is a direct descendent of NavBar, and it functions similar to the ToggleButtonBar. However, instead of Buttons, LinkButtons are displayed with separators (see Figure 7-11). If a ViewStack is specified as the data source for a LinkBar, the link corresponding with the visible view stack is selected. Otherwise, selection state is not managed by the LinkBar. The first and last links cannot be styled separately as with the other navigation controls, but the separators can be stylized using properties such as `separatorSkin` and `separatorColor`.

Figure 7-11   A LinkBar component

Navigation Containers

There are two components in the Flex framework that function as containers with built-in navigation. They are the TabNavigator and Accordion components shown in Figures 7-12 and 7-13. Both are used to wrap two or more other containers and provide a way to switch between them. For example, TabNavigator functions as a ViewStack, pre-coupled with a TabBar. Clicking a Header in an Accordion reveals a single view and hides the others, similar to how clicking a tab in the TabNavigator switches which view of the ViewStack is shown. Accordions are often used to present views that represent sequential steps. The markup for creating an Accordion component and a TabNavigator component is almost identical (see Listings 7-8 and 7-9).

Figure 7-12   A TabNavigator that wraps three views,
with the second tab selected

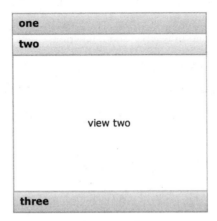

Figure 7-13   An Accordion component that wraps three views,
with the second view selected

Listing 7-8   Creating an Accordion component with three contained views

```
<mx:Accordion id="myAccordion" width="300" height="200">
    <mx:Canvas width="100%" height="100%" label="one">
        <mx:Label
            text="View One"
            verticalCenter="0"
            horizontalCenter="0" />
    </mx:Canvas>
    <mx:Canvas width="100%" height="100%" label="two">
        <mx:Label
            text="View Two"
            verticalCenter="0"
            horizontalCenter="0" />
    </mx:Canvas>
    <mx:Canvas width="100%" height="100%" label="three">
        <mx:Label
            text="View Three"
            verticalCenter="0"
            horizontalCenter="0" />
    </mx:Canvas>
</mx:Accordion>
```

Listing 7-9   Creating a TabNavigator component with three contained views

```
<mx:TabNavigator id="myTabNavigator" width="300" height="200">
    <mx:Canvas width="100%" height="100%" label="one">
        <mx:Label
            text="View One"
```

Listing 7-9   **Continued**

```
                verticalCenter="0"
                horizontalCenter="0" />
    </mx:Canvas>
    <mx:Canvas width="100%" height="100%" label="two">
        <mx:Label
            text="View Two"
            verticalCenter="0"
            horizontalCenter="0" />
    </mx:Canvas>
    <mx:Canvas width="100%" height="100%" label="three">
        <mx:Label
            text="View Three"
            verticalCenter="0"
            horizontalCenter="0" />
    </mx:Canvas>
</mx:TabNavigator>
```

A TabNavigator can be customized by specifying container-related styles such as borderColor, borderThickness, backgroundColor, and so on, as well as the styles described in the earlier "TabBar" section. It is not possible to specify a direction property for a TabNavigator component. That means if you want to use horizontal tabs to switch views, you have to manually couple a TabBar and ViewStack.

Likewise, in addition to standard container-related styles, the headers used in an Accordion can be customized by specifying a headerStyleName style property. Several header-related style properties, such as fillColors and fillAlphas, can be applied directly to the Accordion. However, these properties have been deprecated in Flex 3, and it's recommended that you use headerStyleName (see Listing 7-10).

Listing 7-10   **Style properties for the Accordion headers should be specified in a separate class selector**

```
<mx:Style>

    /* do this */

    Accordion
    {
        headerStyleName: "snazzyHeader";
    }

    .snazzyHeader
    {
        fillColors: #CC0000, #990000;
    }
```

Listing 7-10   **Continued**

```
    /* do NOT do this */

    Accordion
    {
        headerStyleName: "snazzyHeader";
        fillColors: #CC0000, #990000;
    }

</mx:Style>
```

Specifying Labels and Icons

For both list-based components and navigation controls, there exists a mechanism to determine the label and icon displayed for each item in the data source. If the data items are strings, they are used directly as the label, and no icon is displayed. If the data items are objects with a `label` property, the value of that property is displayed. Likewise, if the objects have an `icon` property, that is used (if possible) to create an icon for the control.

Using the `labelField` and `iconField` properties available on both list-based components and navigation controls, you can instruct the component to use the value of any property for the label and/or icon. For example, if you have a list populated with objects representing employees, you could specify to use the `firstName` of the Employee object as the label in each cell. In some cases, you may want to combine the value of two or more fields to use for the label, or execute some logic to determine which icon to use. You can do this by specifying a `labelFunction` or `iconFunction.` The function you specify for either property is called for each item and passed a reference to the item so you can return an appropriate value. For example, Listing 7-11 uses a function called `concatenateName` to combine the first and last name of each person in the List's data provider, and show the results as the label.

Listing 7-11   **Using a label function to combine a person's first and last names to show in a list**

```
<mx:Script>
    <![CDATA[

        public function concatenateName(item:Object):String
        {
            var person:Person = item as Person;
            return person.firstName + " " + person.lastName;
        }
```

Listing 7-11   **Continued**

```
    ]]>
</mx:Script>
<mx:List width="300" labelFunction="{concatenateName}">
    <mx:dataProvider>
        <local:Person firstName="Patrick" lastName="Hansen"/>
        <local:Person firstName="Rick" lastName="Atsley"/>
        <local:Person firstName="Chuck" lastName="Toporek"/>
        <local:Person firstName="Ted" lastName="Patrick" />
    </mx:dataProvider>
</mx:List>
```

Using a List-Based Component for Navigation

List-based components are not only good for displaying data, they can also facilitate inter-activity, including navigation throughout your application. For example, take the tool palette in Photoshop Express shown in Figure 7-14. It's basically a simple Tree component (see Figure 7-15) with custom icons. The only additional customization needed is to create an item renderer that colors the selected item and override the default selection behavior. Scalability is a key benefit of taking this approach to navigation. If at any point an additional tool is available, to add that tool to the view, you simply need to update the data provider.

Figure 7-14   The tool palette in Photoshop
Express is a customized Tree component

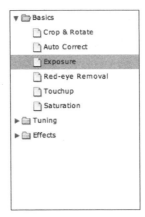

Figure 7-15   A standard Tree component populated
with Photoshop Express's tool palette structure

Summary

In this chapter, you learned about list and navigation components. These components provide unique challenges for customization, but offer opportunities for presenting content based on a data source. Because the contents of these components are data-driven, you do not directly style the elements that comprise them; instead, you specify styles that will be applied to each element as it is created.

You also learned that the items in list-based controls can be customized by way of specifying an item renderer, which serves as a template for each item; and navigation controls expose a common style for the controls within. Customizing lists and navigation controls not only adds to the aesthetics of your application, but also can be used to add functionality and reduce visual clutter.

List components include additional functionality (like drag-and-drop) that is not immediately apparent to a user. In the next chapter, you'll learn about ways of guiding your user through interactions within your applications by using indicators and cursors.

Indicators and Cursors

Using any application can be an adventure, but it must be easy to navigate in order to be successful. One way to guide the user through your application is to use indicators. Indicators can be a variety of things including icons and cursors that act as experience "road signs" and promote discoverability of workflows and features. In this chapter, you will learn techniques for incorporating indicators like icons, cursors, and tool tips into a Flex application.

What is the value in guiding the user? Well, have you ever been working within an application and not know where to go? Clicked on something only to discover that it does something completely unexpected? Things like that create stumbling blocks and can kill user adoption. By guiding a user through an application, you provide an experience that successfully allows him to accomplish tasks and access content that is most important to him.

A successful indicator doesn't have to be something that slaps the user in the face. It can be a subtle color change, a descriptive icon, or a pulsing button. However, it is always important to consider the rules of hierarchy to ensure that the most important areas of your application get the attention they deserve. Giving equal importance to every object presented to the user can cause confusion.

Note
For ideas on how to use motion as an indicator, see Chapter 11, "Effects and Transitions."

Understanding by Example

Before you dive into the various opportunities available in Flex for guiding your users, let's take a look at a few examples of where you might want to use indicators and cursors. You may recognize some of the mechanisms that are shown in the following examples. Each works for various reasons and in ways that may not be immediately obvious. Hopefully, these examples will get you thinking about how you may better guide your users in your own application.

One of the most common elements in an application can be a toolbar. Usually toolbars have a lot of controls that serve their own unique purpose. Additionally, vertical or horizontal space can be a premium, so these tools may end up being represented by only an icon. An icon has to do a lot of work to communicate a function, but that's not a bad thing. It just means it has to be as descriptive as possible. Figure 8-1 is an example of a toolbar. Just by looking at the icons, you can tell it is part of a word processor. Just by looking at the icons, without any labels, you know what you need to do to change the properties of the text.

Figure 8-1   Icons used to represent tools. (Adobe product screenshot(s) reprinted with permission from Adobe Systems Incorporated.)

Drag and drop is a feature that can be implemented in your Flex application as a means of transferring content or configuring the user interface. As a default, Flex changes the cursor during a drag-and-drop operation to indicate where the item that is being dragged can be dropped. As an item is dragged over an area where it can be dropped, the cursor shows a plus sign within a green circle. If the item is dragged over an area where it can't be dropped, the cursor shows a red circle with an x (see Figure 8-2). Just by changing the cursor, a user can immediately get an indication of what may or may not happen as she carries through with the interaction.

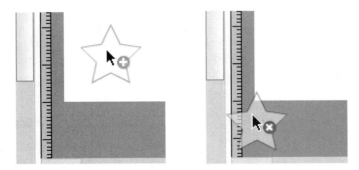

Figure 8-2   Using cursors to indicate drop areas

These examples are just the tip of the iceberg. Every application serves a different purpose, so the indicators, cursors, and other guiding vehicles must support that purpose. Always use indicators that make the most sense for the application you are working on rather than trying to make things from other applications work. Let's take a look at what Flex has available for you to guide your users and promote usability, so you can decide what may work best for your application.

Icons

We all run across symbols as we interact in our everyday environments. Some are more recognizable and universal than others, but the most powerful ones can be easily understood. For example, a symbol of a male figure on a door could be easily recognized as a men's restroom without needing any text to say so.

Icons in an application play the same role as these symbols we encounter and are a great way to reinforce messaging to a user. For example, instead of a button that says "Download," an icon of a downward pointing arrow could be used, as in Figure 8-3. With the addition of something as simple as an icon, you have a better chance of drawing a user's attention as well as making a user interface feel more friendly and approachable. Icons also have the capability to transcend language barriers.

Figure 8-3   Example of an icon

> **Tip**
>
> If you're planning on only using an icon as an interactive point within an application, consider reinforcing that icon with a tool tip. You learn more about those later in the "Tool Tips" section of this chapter.

Implementing an Icon

An icon in Flex either is a vector or bitmap image embedded in your application and applied to a component via CSS or inline. By following similar steps used to skin your components, you can add icons as well. The CSS code snippet in Listing 8-1 shows how you would embed bitmap icons for different states of a button. You can also use symbols in a SWF (pronounced "swif") file as icons, as in the CSS shown in Listing 8-2.

> **Note**
>
> Not every component accepts an icon. In some cases, it is necessary to create a custom component to support an icon. The Flex community has already extended many of the standard Flex components to support icons, so you might search for one before creating your own. For example, Accordions do not typically support icons in the Accordion Header, but a quick search on the Internet will reveal some solutions.

Listing 8-1   **Assigning bitmaps as icons**

```
.myButton
{
    upIcon:       Embed(source="upIcon.png");
    overIcon:     Embed(source="overIcon.png");
```

Listing 8-1   **Continued**

```
        downIcon:     Embed(source="downIcon.png");
        disabledIcon: Embed(source="disabledIcon.png");
}
```

Listing 8-2   **Assigning SWF symbols as icons**

```
.myButton
{
        upIcon:       Embed(source="skins.swf",
                            symbol="upIcon");
        overIcon:     Embed(source="skins.swf",
                            symbol="overIcon");
        downIcon:     Embed(source="skins.swf",
                            symbol="downIcon");
        disabledIcon: Embed(source="skins.swf",
                            symbol="disabledIcon");
}
```

Positioning an Icon

When adding an icon to a component, you can use padding, alignment, gap, and other style properties to position an icon within a component. By using the `labelPlacement` property, you can set the label to be to the left, right, top, or bottom of the icon as in Listing 8-3 to produce a button that looks like Figure 8-4. Refer to Appendix A, "Skinning and Styling Diagrams," for diagrams that show the properties you can use to position an icon within a component.

> **Note**
> The `labelPlacement` property is *not* a style property, so it can't be assigned via CSS.

Listing 8-3   **Button label placed above an icon**

```
<mx:Button label="Button" labelPlacement="bottom">
      <mx:icon>@Embed(source="myIcon.png")</mx:icon>
</mx:Button>
```

Figure 8-4   Button with icon and bottom label placement

Focus Border

Most every control within the Flex framework has something called a focus border that is visible whenever a user focuses on the control using his cursor or by tabbing. When a control is in focus, it is apparent that the user is working with that control and an outer border appears around the control. For example, if a user clicks on a TextInput, the focus border appears around the input to signify focus, as in Figure 8-5.

Figure 8-5   Focused text input

There are a number of properties that can be adjusted to create a custom appearance for a focus border. For different controls, you can adjust the properties shown in Table 8-1 for a focus skin.

Table 8-1   **Focus Skin Properties**

Property	Description
focusAlpha	The alpha of the focus border.
focusBlendMode	The blend mode of the focus. Refer to Chapter 10, "Filters and Blends," for a list of the available blend modes.
focusRoundedCorners	The corner radius of each corner of the focus border.
focusSkin	Specify a graphic asset or programmatic class as a skin for the focus border. For more information on creating a skin, refer to Chapter 5, "Graphical Skinning."
focusThickness	The thickness of the focus border.

> **Note**
>
> You can use the `themeColor` style property to set the color of the focus border. However, depending on the component, changing the theme color may also affect the appearance or other aspects of a control. Theme color is used throughout the Flex framework as a default accent color for things like highlights, focus, selection, rollover, and more. It makes the default skins in Flex have a consistent appearance.

> **Tip**
>
> Consider setting a `themeColor` using the `global` selector so that all other components take on the same color. This helps reinforce consistency. For more information, refer to Chapter 4, "Styling."

Simply by adjusting some of the style properties, you can achieve a custom look. The MXML code snippet in Listing 8-4 is an example of using inline style properties to adjust the appearance of a focus border on a text input. These values create a focus skin that looks like Figure 8-6.

Listing 8-4   **Styling the focus border**

```
<mx:TextInput
        focusAlpha=".5"
        focusRoundedCorners="0"
        focusThickness="3"
        themeColor="#C50000"
        focusBlendMode="multiply"/>
```

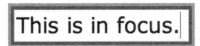

Figure 8-6   Styled focus skin

> **Tip**
>
> You can use a button's `emphasized` property to draw further attention to it. This is a great way to help a button that has special importance stand out from other controls that may surround it. For example, Figure 8-7 shows the Submit button of a form.

Figure 8-7   Submit button set as emphasized

Tool Tips

Tool tips are a quick and easy way to give a user additional information about a control or interactive touch point and are used in many Web-based or desktop applications. Tool tips help an interface stay clean without sacrificing necessary information to the user by hiding that information when it's not needed. Generally, a tool tip is shown when a user hovers his cursor over an object; a tool tip is removed when the user moves his cursor out of the target area or when the tool tip has been displayed for a default amount of time.

Although all components are capable of having tool tips, most are not assigned them by default and thus they do not show up on normal mouse interactions. Other components have tool tips enabled only under certain conditions by default, such as when a button's text is too long. Figure 8-8 shows an example of a tool tip that has been applied to a button to give the user extra explanation about its purpose.

Figure 8-8   Default tool tip

Creating Tool Tips

Creating a tool tip for an object within Flex is fairly simple. All you have to do is specify the text for your tool tip using the `toolTip` property of the target control or container. For example, Listing 8-5 shows MXML for a button that has a tool tip of "Click Me."

Listing 8-5   **Sample MXML of a tool tip**

```
<mx:Button toolTip="Click Me." label="Button"/>
```

As with many properties of MXML components, the value of the `toolTip` property can be bound to a variable, making it dynamic. Listing 8-6 shows a tool tip on a button that is bound to the label of the panel that contains it. This code snippet produces a tool tip as shown in Figure 8-9.

Listing 8-6   **Tool tip bound to a Panel title**

```
<?xml version="1.0" encoding="utf-8"?>
<mx:Application
      xmlns:mx="http://www.adobe.com/2006/mxml"
      layout="absolute"
      >
      <mx:Panel
          id="myPanel"
```

Listing 8-6   **Continued**

```
            layout="vertical"
            title="Sign Up Now"
            borderColor="#3C3C3C"
            color="#1C1C1C"
            horizontalAlign="center"
            paddingTop="10"
            paddingBottom="10"
            >
            <mx:Button
                label="Button"
                toolTip="{myPanel.title}"
                />
        </mx:Panel>
</mx:Application>
```

Figure 8-9   Tool tips can be bound to other values.
In this case, the tool tip is bound to the Panel title.

Error Tips

There are standard tool tips that can be applied to any control or container (see Figure 8-9), but there are also error tips that appear when using validation on a text input, combo box, and so on. Error tips have a different appearance that allows you to alert a user that she hasn't completely filled in a form or filled out the form incorrectly. Figure 8-10 shows an error tip with default styling, which was created using the code snippet in Listing 8-7.

Despite the name, error tips can be used for a variety of situations besides errors. Consider using error tips to guide a user through steps, point out important controls, or display information that is pertinent to a current task. However, it's not a good idea to leave them red unless they denote errors. See the "Using the Tool Tip Manager" section in this chapter to learn more. Refer to the Flex 3 documentation for more information on form validation and integrating error tips.

Figure 8-10   Default error tip

Listing 8-7   **Creating a default error tip**

```
<mx:Script>
<![CDATA[
      import mx.controls.ToolTip;
      import mx.managers.ToolTipManager;

      private var errorTip:ToolTip;
      private var myMessage:String;

      private function validateEntry(type:String, event:Object):void
      {
            switch(type) {
            case "numbers" : myMessage="Wrong numbers. Sorry.";
            break;
      }

      numbers.errorString = myMessage;
      }
]]>
</mx:Script>

<mx:TextInput
      id="numbers"/>
<mx:Button
      label="Submit"
      click="validateEntry('numbers',event)"/>
```

Data Tips

Data tips are tool tips that display information based on user interaction with data items. Using data tips, you can display additional information that would otherwise take up a lot of space. This is a great way to keep your application clean and prevent information overload. By default, data tips show text that is too long to be displayed in the view of the list. By setting `showDataTip` to `true`, a data tip is displayed to show the full text as a data tip (see Figure 8-11).

Figure 8-11   Data tips can show full text of an item

You can expand upon the default functionality of a data tip to display custom information using the `dataTipFunction`. For example, you could show a description of an item as a data tip, as shown in Figure 8-12. This functionality was implemented using the code snippet in Listing 8-8.

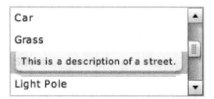

Figure 8-12   Show custom information with data tips—
in this case, a description for each item

Listing 8-8   **Customizing the data tip of an item to show a description**

```
<mx:Script>
    <![CDATA[
        public function getItemDescription(item:Object):String
        {
            return item.description;
        }
    ]]>
</mx:Script>

<mx:List
    id="itemList"
    width="200"
    rowCount="4"
    dataProvider="{itemsData}"
    showDataTips="true"
    dataTipFunction="getItemDescription"
    />
```

Scroll Tips

Scroll tips provide additional feedback to users as they scroll through a list. By default, scroll tips display the index number of the topmost item shown in the current view of a list, as shown in Figure 8-13. To set a scroll tip to be displayed, you simply set the `showScrollTips` property to `true`.

Similar to a `labelFunction` used in a List, scroll tips can display custom information by using the `scrollTipFunction`. This feature is helpful for providing contextual information as a user scrolls through large data sets. For example, if there is a long list of alpha-

Figure 8-13   Default scroll tip

betically organized names, you could display the first item label and last item label as a user scrolls. This provides a range to let the user quickly know whether she has scrolled to the right area within the list of data, as shown in Figure 8-14. This List uses a custom `scrollTipFunction` that displays the first and last label of the visible data items, as shown in Listing 8-9.

Figure 8-14   Setting the scroll tip to display custom text—
in this case, specifying a range of items

Listing 8-9   **Creating a custom scrollTipFunction to display a range of items**

```
<mx:Script>
    <![CDATA[
    public function getScrollInfo(dir:String, pos:Number):String
    {
    var rowCount:Number = colorList.rowCount;
    var firstItem:Object = colors.getItemAt(pos);
    var lastItem:Object = colors.getItemAt(pos+rowCount-1);
    return firstItem.label + " - " + lastItem.label;
    }
    ]]>
</mx:Script>

<mx:List
    id="colorList"
    width="200"
    rowCount="4"
    dataProvider="{colors}"
```

Listing 8-9   **Continued**

```
        scrollTipFunction="getScrollInfo"
    />
```

Customizing the text with a tool, data, or scroll tip can add context, but you can also change the look of these tips to match the application design or support usability.

Styling and Skinning a Tool Tip

Like many other aspects of Flex, a tool tip can be styled and/or skinned to customize its appearance. To do this, you can use CSS and the same methods as outlined in Chapters 4 and 5. The CSS in Listing 8-10 is an example of a tool tip being customized to look like Figure 8-15. To see what other style properties can be manipulated for a tool tip, see Appendix A, "Skinning and Styling Diagrams."

Listing 8-10   **Sample CSS of a customized tool tip**

```
ToolTip {
        color:              #222222;
        backgroundColor:    #91B63A;
        cornerRadius:       0;
}
```

Figure 8-15   Custom tool tip

Error tips are derived from `ToolTip` and can be styled using the `errorTip` class selector in CSS. The CSS in Listing 8-11 shows custom styling for an error tip and creates an error tip that looks like Figure 8-16. Notice that with an error tip you also have the ability to define the direction of the error tip by specifying `errorTipAbove`, `errorTipRight`, or `errorTipBelow` for the border style.

Listing 8-11   **Sample CSS of a customized error tip**

```
.errorTip {
        color:        #FFFFFF;
        fontSize:     12;
        shadowColor:  #666666;
        borderColor:  #62ABCD;
        borderStyle:  "errorTipBelow";
}
```

Figure 8-16   Custom error tip

> **Note**
>
> Using the type selector of `ToolTip` to customize the appearance of your tool tips may affect some style properties of your error, data, and scroll tips. If you see these changes affecting your error tips, you can fix this by adjusting the styling for that particular instance or adjust the `errorTip` class selector.

Using the Tool Tip Manager

The tool tip manager is the mechanism in Flex that controls the display of tool tips within a Flex application, including appearance and animation. You can use the tool tip manager to display tool tips programmatically and even have a tool tip display as an error tip in any given situation.

Creating a Tool Tip Programmatically

Using the Tool Tip Manager, you have complete control of the tool tips within an application. The MXML in Listing 8-12 creates a tool tip with the appearance of an error tip positioned underneath a button. The tool tip is shown when the button is rolled over by explicitly making a call to the Tool Tip Manager's static `createToolTip` method. Notice that the fourth parameter in this method call is `errorTipBelow`. This is how you define the style of the tool tip that is about to be displayed.

Listing 8-12   Sample MXML of a created error tip

```
<?xml version="1.0"?>
<mx:Application xmlns:mx="http://www.adobe.com/2006/mxml"
backgroundGradientColors="[#FFFFFF,#FFFFFF]">

    <mx:Script>
    <![CDATA[
    import mx.managers.ToolTipManager;        import mx.controls.ToolTip;

    public var customTip:ToolTip;
        private function showTip(event:Event):void {
    var myMessage:String = "This is a custom error tip.";
        customTip = ToolTipManager.createToolTip(
    myMessage,
    event.currentTarget.x + event.currentTarget.width/2,
```

Listing 8-12   **Continued**

```
        event.currentTarget.y + event.currentTarget.height*.75,
        "errorTipBelow") as ToolTip;
        }
            private function removeTip():void {
ToolTipManager.destroyToolTip(customTip);
        }
            ]]>
        </mx:Script>
        <mx:Button label="Show Error Tip"
        rollOver="showTip(event)"
        rollOut="removeTip()"/>
</mx:Application>
```

Timing and Motion of Tool Tips

When customizing tool tips, you're not limited to the visual aspects, but you can also customize other aspects such as how long a tool tip is displayed and which effects are used to display it. Remember that you need to import the `ToolTipManager` into your MXML file to use it. Doing this gives you access to additional properties for customizing tool tips. The properties in Table 8-2 allow you to set the timing and effects for tool tips.

Table 8-2   **Tool Tip Properties**

Property	Description
showDelay	The amount of time, in milliseconds, that is delayed before a tool tip is shown.
hideDelay	The amount of time, in milliseconds, that is delayed before a tool tip is hidden.
scrubDelay	The amount of time, in milliseconds, that is delayed between when a user moves his cursor from one control to another before a new tool tip is shown.
showEffect	An effect that is played when a tool tip is shown.
hideEffect	An effect that is played when a tool tip is hidden.

> **Note**
> For the tool tip show and hide effects, you can use the effects covered in Chapter 11.

The MXML in Listing 8-13 produces a button with a tool tip that has custom effects and duration applied to it. To get the full effect, you have to compile the example.

Listing 8-13 **Tool tip with custom timing and effects**

```
<?xml version="1.0" encoding="utf-8"?>
<mx:Application xmlns:mx="http://www.adobe.com/2006/mxml"
backgroundGradientColors="[#FFFFFF,#FFFFFF]" creationComplete="setToolTip()">

    <mx:Script>
        <![CDATA[
        import mx.managers.ToolTipManager;

        private function setToolTip():void {
        ToolTipManager.showEffect = showTipEffect;
        ToolTipManager.hideEffect = hideTipEffect;
        ToolTipManager.showDelay = 500;
        ToolTipManager.hideDelay = 1000;
        }
        ]]>
    </mx:Script>

    <mx:Parallel id="showTipEffect">
    <mx:Zoom zoomHeightFrom=".2"
        zoomHeightTo="1"
        zoomWidthFrom=".25"
        zoomWidthTo="1"/>
    <mx:Fade alphaFrom="0"
        alphaTo="1"/>
    </mx:Parallel>

    <mx:Parallel id="hideTipEffect">
    <mx:Move xBy="-30" />
    <mx:Fade alphaFrom="1"
        alphaTo="0"/>
    </mx:Parallel>

    <mx:Button  label="Show Tool Tip"
        toolTip="That was a custom tool tip effect." />

</mx:Application>
```

Cursors

When working within a desktop application, you may come across instances where your cursor changes to reflect a tool change or to signify an action that may take place when you interact with a control. With Flex, you have the capability to customize the cursor too. Changing the cursor based on requirements or interactions within your application is another way to help guide a user, especially if your application involves different tools for a user to interact with.

The cursor within a Flex application can be changed a few different ways within Flex. There are default cursors, shown in Figure 8-17, that show up when performing drag-and-drop operations or whenever a Flex application is processing a task.

Figure 8-17   Default cursor set, including drop, link, and busy cursors

These default cursors can be customized using CSS, which affect the way they are shown throughout the entire application. The MXML in Listing 8-14 styles a `BusyCursor` to use the specified `myBusyCursor.png` rather than the default clock shown in Figure 8-17.

Listing 8-14   **Sample CSS skinning the busy cursor**

```
CursorManager
{
    busyCursor: Embed(source="myBusyCursor.png");
}
```

In the case of Listing 8-14, the Busy Cursor skin is assigned within the Cursor Manager type selector. However, not all cursors are assigned the same way. Different components including Data Grid, Lists, DividedBoxes, and so on have their own cursors to support functionality within them. Listing 8-15 shows the CSS you can use to customize the cursors in various components. You can also refer to the diagrams in Appendix A. If you want to change the skin artwork, you can use the Skin Templates covered in the exercises for Chapter 5.

Listing 8-15   **CSS for skinning**

```
CursorManager
{
    busyCursor: Embed(source="myBusyCursor");
    busyCursorBackground: Embed(source="myBusyCursor");
}


DataGrid
{
    columnResizeSkin: Embed(source="myDataGridColumnResizeSkin");
    stretchCursor: Embed(source="mycursorStretchCursor");
}


DividedBox
```

Listing 8-15   **Continued**

```
{
    horizontalDividerCursor: Embed(source="myHBoxDividerCursor");
    verticalDividerCursor: Embed(source="myVBoxDividerCursor");
}

DragManager
{
    copyCursor: Embed(source="myDragCopyCursor");
    defaultDragImageSkin: Embed(source="myDragImage");
    linkCursor: Embed(source="myDragLinkCursor");
    moveCursor: Embed(source="myDragMoveCursor");
    rejectCursor: Embed(source="myDragRejectCursor");
}

PrintDataGrid
{
    columnResizeSkin: Embed(source="myDataGridColumnResizeSkin");
    stretchCursor: Embed(source="mycursorStretchCursor");
}
```

Tip

Because the busy cursor represents a process, you may want to use an animated cursor. You can create an animated cursor in Flash CS3 and reference it in your CSS. Refer to Chapter 5 for more information.

The Cursor Manager

You can trigger a custom cursor to be displayed whenever necessary. To do this, you import and use the Cursor Manager. This manager allows you to perform events that directly influence the cursor within an application. For example, if your application has a pencil tool, you could switch the cursor to a pencil when the user selects it.

The MXML snippet in Listing 8-16 switches the cursor when a user rolls over the button to give the user a hint as to what action will be performed (see Figure 8-18). For more information regarding the Cursor Manager, refer to the Flex 3 documentation.

Listing 8-16   **Switching the cursor**

```
<?xml version="1.0" encoding="utf-8"?>
<mx:Application xmlns:mx="http://www.adobe.com/2006/mxml" layout="absolute">

    <mx:Script>
        <![CDATA[
            import mx.managers.CursorManager;
```

Listing 8-16   **Continued**

```
        [Embed(source="myCustomCursor.png")]
        private var myCustomCursor:Class;
        ]]>
    </mx:Script>

    <mx:Button
        label="Roll Over Me."
        rollOver="CursorManager.setCursor(myCustomCursor);"
        rollOut="CursorManager.removeCursor(CursorManager.currentCursorID)"/>

</mx:Application>
```

Figure 8-18   Switching the cursor to a custom one

Summary

Indicators are a great way to guide users, add context to a given control or data set, and add extra details throughout an application. In this chapter, you learned how to add indicators like cursors, icons, and tool tips into a Flex application. With a base understanding of these concepts, you can begin to add bits of guidance to your Flex applications to help your users accomplish their most important tasks.

In the next chapter, you will learn about using fonts and text styling to further customize and add content clarity to Flex applications.

Fonts and Text

One of the easiest things you can do to customize an application is to introduce a custom font and text styling. Fonts, just like colors, can help establish or reinforce a brand, evoke an emotion, or promote legibility. It is important to understand that just because you *can* use a certain font doesn't mean that you *should*. The most important thing when working with text is legibility. Also, be considerate of your audience and what they would feel comfortable reading on the screen. Formatting text can be tedious, but when executed properly, it can make your application look polished and professional. In this chapter, you will learn how to work with fonts and style text in Flex.

When working with Flex, you may find the need to mix and match fonts, but try to find fonts that compliment each other. For example, it is not the best idea to use a script font as the primary font; however, you can use a stylized font as an accent font throughout an application. Don't go overboard with the number of fonts you use either. The most important thing is to not distract a user from consuming the information he needs or prevent him from achieving a goal.

> **Note**
>
> Unlike other components in Flex that rely on pixel values for sizing, text can be sized using other measurement increments like points, centimeters, inches, picas, and so on. Refer to Chapter 4, "Styling," for more information.

Attention to Text

Paying special attention to text layout, color, size, and font selection can play an important role in how your users take in information. As you compare applications on a day-to-day basis, look at how large bodies of text are handled. Do some feel more "clean" or easier to understand just by the way the text is handled? Are there cases when you don't even want to read the text? This is probably not the way you want your users to feel.

Rather than get into a dialogue about typography, the primary thing to understand is that text matters. When you look at a body of text that "feels right" to you, ask yourself

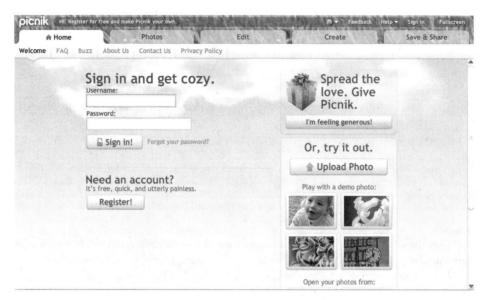

Figure 9-1   Picnik uses color, size, and grouping to create a clean read for
the user. You can experience the application at http://www.picnik.com.

why. Asking that question will help you be more perceptive to the importance of font and text usage. There are plenty of books surrounding the topic of typography, but here you will find plenty of examples of Flex applications that pay attention to this extra level of detail.

One example is a photo editing application called Picnik, shown in Figure 9-1. Picnik uses color, size, grouping, and white space to create focus and provide the user with a clean read. It isn't uncommon to see people try to cram as much information into one spot as possible, but that isn't the case here. Notice the consistent use of text treatments and the unique font used specifically for this application. These bits of detail add to the fun and colorful nature of the application.

Customizing Fonts

There are a few different ways you can customize a font in a Flex application. You can use device fonts, system fonts, or embed fonts. By relying on device and system fonts, you will not add to the file size of your Flex application; and because they are not embedded, the font will be rendered by the operating system, making text appear clearer and more crisp. The other method of embedding fonts compiles a font into your Flex application, making the file size of the Flex application larger, but that font will successfully render on any user's machine. It is possible to mix and match the following methods of customizing the text within your application.

Device Fonts

If the specific font face is not important and you can get away with specifying just the general style of the font, you can use device fonts, which are _sans, _serif, and _typewriter (see Listing 9-1).These fonts are dependent on the device they are running on, and so they can vary depending on the setting or preferences of the device. For example, one user may have her _sans device font set to Arial and someone else may have it set to Helvetica.

Listing 9-1   **Specifying a device font**

```
<mx:Button fontFamily="_sans"/>
```

Using a System Font

Another option is to specify an actual font name for the **fontFamily** property, as shown in Listing 9-2. Doing this means that each of your users must have this exact font installed on his or her computer. If the user does not have the correct font, an alternative is displayed. Some common system fonts include Arial, Times Roman, Helvetica, Trebuchet, and Courier.

Listing 9-2   **Specifying a system font**

```
<mx:Button fontFamily="Times Roman"/>
```

With CSS, you can specify multiple **fontFamily** names by separating them with a comma, as shown in Listing 9-3. If a user doesn't have the first font, Flex moves to the next one until it finds a font that matches, similar to CSS with HTML.

Listing 9-3   **Specifying a set of system fonts**

```
.myLabel
{
    fontFamily: "Trebuchet MS", "Verdana", "Arial", "Helvetica";
}
```

Embedding Fonts

Just like any other embedded asset you use in your Flex application, using a custom font adds to your final application's file size. Beyond the design considerations for using a custom font, you also want to evaluate what using a custom font means to your application's final file size.

When embedding with fonts, you have a few options to consider. You can embed a font installed on your local system, from a font file in your Flex Project, or from a Flash file with a font embedded within it. Currently, Flex only allows for the embedding of TrueType (TTF) and OpenType (OTF) fonts directly or from a SWF (pronounced "swif") with an embedded font. In each case, you also have the option to embed specific character ranges.

A font embed statement uses @font-face and is specified within an <mx:Style> tag or external CSS file. The embed statement includes the name or location of a font, font family name, font weight, character ranges, and display preferences, as shown in Listing 9-4.

Listing 9-4   Font-face embed syntax

```
@font-face
{
    src:        url("location") | local("name");
    fontFamily: alias;
    fontStyle:  italic | oblique | normal;
    fontWeight: bold | heavy | normal;
}
```

Depending on the font you embed, you may need to specify values other than those listed in Listing 9-4. For example, you may need to specify medium for fontWeight if the font you're embedding has a medium-weight font description.

Here are the pros and cons of embedding fonts:

Pros
Ensures that a user will see fonts as you intended
Fonts will act accordingly with effects, transitions, or rotation

Cons
Increases file size
Lower legibility at smaller point sizes

Embedding a Local Font

A local font is a font that is installed on your computer. You can embed these fonts into an application just by specifying a font by name in the embed statement. Although it may be convenient to simply specify a font name, local fonts may not be embedded if they are not on the local system. Consider embedding fonts by specifying src as a url rather than referencing local. Listing 9-5 is an example of embedding a local font.

Note
In some cases, you get an error if you assign a fontFamily name that is the same name as the font you're embedding. Try specifying a custom fontFamily name to correct this.

Listing 9-5   Embedding a local font

```
@font-face
{
    src:        local("Arial");
    fontFamily: MyArial;
    fontStyle:  normal;
    fontWeight: normal;
}
```

Embedding a TTF File

Flex 3 allows you to embed a font file directly, rather than specifying a font by name from your local system. Currently, Flex only allows for the embedding of TrueType and Open-Type fonts using this method. Embedding from a referenced TTF or OTF file enables you to add a font file into your Flex project so that anyone working with it will have the appropriate font to compile the application. Listing 9-6 is an example of a font referenced in a fonts folder within a Flex Project.

Listing 9-6   **Embedding a TTF file**

```
@font-face
{
    src:        url("assets/fonts/Comic Sans.ttf");
    fontFamily: Comic Sans;
    fontStyle:  normal;
    fontWeight: normal;
}
```

Using Fonts from SWFs

The most versatile method of embedding a font in your Flex application is to embed a font inside a SWF. You can do this a couple of ways: in a SWF file generated with Flash or by compiling a CSS file with embedded fonts into a SWF. The benefits of using Flash are that you can embed any font supported by Flash, easily specify character ranges, and include multiple fonts using a visual tool set. Exercises 9.1 and 9.2 walk through these two methods of packaging a font as a SWF to use in your Flex application.

The capability to embed multiple fonts allows you to embed each font variation that might be used in your Flex application, including `plain`, `bold`, `italic`, and `bold-italic`. As a rule, you may want to embed these four font variations because some Flex components use font faces that are not `plain`. For example, a Link Button component uses a bold typeface, so if you didn't embed a bold typeface, that font wouldn't show up. Using fonts embedded in a SWF is covered in more detail in Exercise 9.1.

> **Tip**
>
> You can change the `fontWeight` and/or `fontFamily` style property of a component so it doesn't use a bold typeface or other font variation.

Advanced Anti-Alias Properties

When embedding fonts, there are other properties you can specify to improve legibility. These properties include `fontAntiAliasType`, `fontSharpness`, `fontThickness`, and `fontGridFitType`. You may want to try different values to get your font to display the way you want. These properties are described in Table 9-1.

Table 9-1   **Anti-Alias Properties**

`fontAntiAliasType`	Specify `normal` or `advanced` to adjust an embedded font's anti-alias properties. The default is `advanced`.
`fontSharpness`	Assign values between –400 and 400 to adjust the sharpness of an embedded font. The lower the number, the softer it becomes. The higher the number, the sharper.
`fontThickness`	Assign a value between –200 and 200 to thin or thicken the weight of an embedded font.
`fontGridFitType`	Specify `none`, `pixel`, or `subpixel`.

Specifying Character Ranges

Every font is made up of a variety of characters; some have more than others. In many cases, there is no need to embed every character, whether it's to reduce file size or because you only need certain ones.

There are a couple ways to specify a character range for an embedded font. One method is to specify the character range in the `@font-face` embed statement, or if you're using a SWF font, you can specify the character range in Flash.

Character Ranges in an @font-face Declaration

To embed a character range within a font-face declaration, you use the `unicodeRange` attribute. Listing 9-7 shows a character range specified for the font `Helvetica`, which can be implemented via an external CSS file or `<mx:Style>` tag.

Listing 9-7   **Character ranges in a font-face declaration**

```
@font-face
{
    src:            url("assets/fonts/Helvetica.ttf");
    fontFamily:     MyHelvetica;
    fontStyle:      normal;
    fontWeight:     normal;
    unicodeRange:   U+0041-U+005A, /* Upper-Case [A..Z] */
                    U+0061-U+007A, /* Lower-Case a-z */
                    U+0030-U+0039, /* Numbers [0..9] */
                    U+002E-U+002E; /* Period [.] */
}
```

Character Ranges in Flash

If you're working with a font embedded through Flash, you can also specify the character ranges. In Flash, there is a panel that easily allows you to specify a character range without needing to know any unicode values. You can access this panel in Flash when working with a Dynamic Text area and clicking the Embed button in the Properties Inspector, as in Figure 9-2.

Figure 9-2   Flash Properties Inspector

As you can see in Figure 9-3, the Character Embedding panel is much easier to work with, letting you select the character ranges you want to use. The selected character ranges are embedded when you publish the SWF.

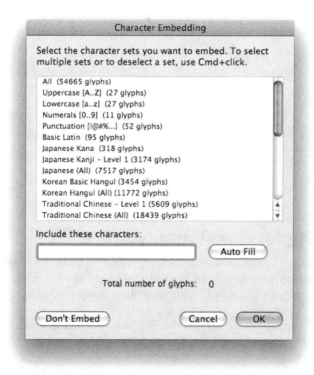

Figure 9-3   Character Embedding panel

Working with Fonts in CSS Design View

With the new CSS Design View in Flex 3, it is much easier to assign and embed fonts for components. When creating CSS styling for a component that requires a specific font, you now have the option to embed a font with the selection of a check box.

In CSS Design View, there is a Flex Properties panel for styles that includes an area for text (see Figure 9-4). When styling a component, if you select a custom font, you can simply select the *Embed this font* check box and Flex automatically writes out the proper `@font-face` declaration so you don't have to. Keep in mind that Flex embeds a font from your system and does not give you the option to specify character ranges.

> **Note**
>
> If you embed a font and later decide you don't want to use that font, you must manually delete the `@font-face` declaration from the CSS file. This also means that each time you change the font for a styled component, that font is embedded. Make sure that you don't embed more fonts than you need to, as each embedded font adds to the final file size of your SWF.

Figure 9-4   CSS Properties panel

Text Styling for Consistency

Maintaining consistency throughout your application is always something you should strive for, especially when working with fonts. Too many varieties of fonts and text styles can confuse a user or fragment his focus. One method of maintaining consistency when working with text is by creating text styles using an external CSS file or `<mx:Style>` tag.

By creating text styles, you can easily maintain consistency and at any time change the way your text looks throughout your application. This can be helpful when you need to change the font, text size, or any other text property for the text in your application. Listing 9-8 shows a few examples of text styling applied to text in MXML in Listing 9-9 and Figure 9-5 shows what that text looks like with applied styling.

Listing 9-8   **Text styling in CSS**

```
.titleText
{
    fontFamily: Arial;
    color:      #666666;
    fontSize:   24;
}


.instructionsText
{
    fontFamily: Arial;
    color:      #000000;
    fontSize:   11;
}
```

Listing 9-9   **Text styling applied to a label in MXML**

```
<mx:Label
      text="Title Text"
      styleName="titleText"/>

<mx:Label
      text="Instructions Text"
      styleName="instructionsText"/>
```

Figure 9-5   Text with styling

For more information about working with CSS styling, see Chapter 4.

Working with Text

Nearly every visual component within the Flex 3 framework displays text. The functionality of some components is solely to display text. Regardless of the component, you most likely need to spend a little time working with text-specific properties to get text positioned or to appear the way you want. This is especially the case if you have embedded a custom font because each font has different characteristics.

Positioning Text

Each component that uses text has a number of properties that help you fine-tune how text is positioned. In addition to the text-specific positioning properties, you can also use `paddingTop`, `paddingLeft`, `paddingRight`, and `paddingBottom` to add space around text areas. Descriptions of these available properties are pointed out in Table 9-2.

Table 9-2   **Properties for Positioning Text**

Property	Description
leading	Leading is the vertical space between lines of text that can be specified with a numeric value. The term "leading" is derived from the lead that was used to create the vertical spacing between lines on older printing presses.
	This text has a value of 20 for the leading, which creates vertical spacing between lines of text. *leading*
kerning	Kerning is the space between individual characters without influencing the space between other characters within the same block of text.
letterSpacing	Letter spacing is the space between *all* characters in a block of text and can be specified with a numeric value.
	This text has a value of 15 for the letterspacing.
textIndent	Text indent specifies the amount of space on the left side of the text and can be specified with a numeric value.
	text indent This text has a value of 20 for the text indent, which indents the first line of text.
truncateToFit	Setting your text to truncate to fit means that text will be "clipped" and an ellipsis (...) added if the text is larger than the text area or holding container in which it is held. Specify a `true` or `false` value.
	Truncated ...
wordWrap	Specify a `true` or `false` value.

> **Tip**
>
> When working with a `Button`, you might try using `leading` to position text in relationship to an icon.

Working with HTML Text

If you want to have text with multiple attributes within a single text area, you can use HTML text. With HTML text, you can have text with multiple size, colors, weights, and breaks, creating a sense of visual hierarchy within a body of text.

Although the HTML syntax is similar to what you might work with when creating an HTML Web site, it is not the same. Similarly, creating and assigning text styles is a more involved process than working with typical HTML and CSS.

HTML text can be used within any `text` property within a component. This does not include the `label` property within components like Button, CheckBox, LinkButton, TitleWindow, and so on.

Assigning HTML Text

HTML text can be assigned within a `text` property using the `<mx:htmlText>` tag. Inside the `<mx:htmlText>` tag, you must specify text within **CDATA** block. Listing 9-10 shows HTML text being used in a **Text** component.

Listing 9-10   **HTML text**

```
<mx:Text>
     <mx:htmlText>
          <![CDATA[This is some <b>HTML</b> text.]]>
     </mx:htmlText>
</mx:Text>
```

Styling Characters within HTML Text

When using HTML text, there are a number of HTML tags you can use to customize the appearance of the text. These tags can be used inline of the text. Table 9-3 describes the available HTML tags that are available.

Table 9-3   **HTML Tags**

HTML Tage	Description
`<font>`	Within a Font tag, you can specify `size`, `color`, etc. Any text within the `<font>` tag takes on the specified attributes.
`<b>`	Bolds text within the tag set.
` `	Creates a line break.
`<p>`	Creates a new paragraph.
`<i>`	Italicizes text within the tag set.
`<u>`	Underlines text within the tag set.

Table 9-3   **Continued**

HTML Tage	Description
`<a>`	The Anchor tag creates a hyperlink when used with text and supports the `href` and `target` attributes. • `href`: The URL of the page you're linking to. • `target`: The window you want the linked destination to load into. You can also specify link events that can call custom functions when a user clicks on text wrapped in an Anchor tag.
`<img>`	The Image tag allows you to display an image by specifying a source using the `src` attribute. Other attributes that can be specified include • `align`, `height`, `hspace`, `id`, and `vspace`. • `src`: Specify the URL of a GIF, JPG, PNG, or SWF. • `align`: Positions the image in relationship to the text. • `height`: Vertical dimension of the image. • `hspace`: The horizontal space the image occupies. • `id`: Assign an id to the image. • `vspace`: The vertical space the image occupies.
`<li>`	Specifies a list item.
`<textformat>`	Allows for subparagraph formatting, including `indent`, `blockindent`, `rightmargin`, `leftmargin`, `leading`, and `tabstops`. `indent`: Applies a left indent to the first line of text using the value specified.

> This is text with an indent value specified within a textformat tag.This is text with an indent value specified within a textformat tag.

`blockindent`: Applies a left indent to the entire block of text using the value specified.

> This is text with an blockindent value specified within a textformat tag. This is text with an blockindent value specified within a textformat tag.

`rightmargin`: Applies a right margin to the entire block of text using the value specified.

> This is text with an rightmargin value specified within a textformat tag. This is text with an rightmargin value specified within a textformat tag.

Table 9-3   **Continued**

HTML Tage	Description
`<textformat>`	`leftmargin`: Applies a left margin to the entire block of text using the value specified.

> This is text with an leftmargin value specified within a textformat tag. This is text with an leftmargin value specified within a textformat tag.

`leading`: Sets the vertical spacing between each line of text using the value specified.

> This is text with an leading value specified
>
> within a textformat tag. This is text with an
>
> leading value specified within a textformat tag.

`tabstops`: Positioning of tabs.

With all these available HTML tags, you can really manipulate format text to enhance legibility and present information in a concise manner. Listing 9-11 is an example of using these tags to format text to look like Figure 9-6.

Listing 9-11   **HTML text and styling**

```
<mx:Style>
    @font-face
    {
    src: local("Myriad Pro");
    fontFamily: MyMyriad;
    fontWeight: regular;
    fontStyle:  normal;
    }

    @font-face
    {
    src: local("Myriad Pro");
    fontFamily: MyMyriad;
    fontWeight: bold;
    fontStyle:  normal;
    }
```

Listing 9-11   **Continued**

```
@font-face
{
src: local("Myriad Pro");
fontFamily: MyMyriad;
fontWeight: italic;
fontStyle:  normal;
}

</mx:Style>

<mx:Text
     x="210"
     y="166"
     fontFamily="MyMyriad"
     fontSize="14"
     color="#444444"
     leading="10"
     height="214"
     width="410"
     >
     <mx:htmlText><![CDATA[<font color="#FF8D22" size="24">Welcome to My
Application</font><br><textformat leading="6">To begin, click on the <font
color="#FF8D22">Begin</font> button to <b>Continue</b>.<br>If you have any
problems you can refer to the <font color="#095FB1"><u><a href="#">Help
section</a></u></font>.</textformat><br><br><b>For more information, you
can:</b><br><li>Call the toll-free number</li><li>Send us an email</li><li>Or
send us a letter</li>]]></mx:htmlText>
</mx:Text>
```

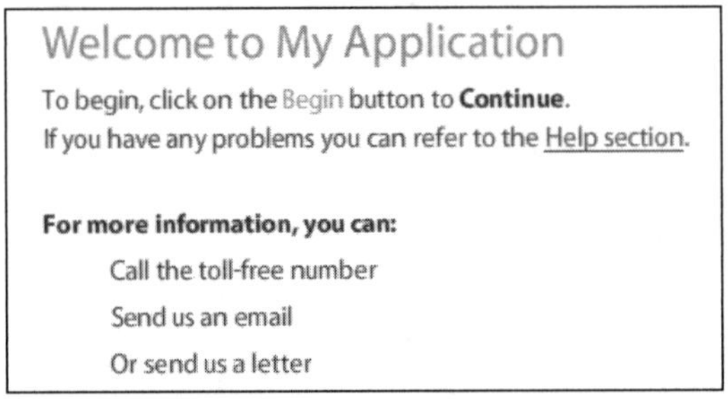

Figure 9-6   HTML text displayed in the application

Style Sheets for HTML Text

If you're familiar with working with HTML and CSS, you probably know that you can create styling for your text by specifying CSS properties for tags like h1, h2, body, and so on. You can use these tags in htmlText in Flex, but you can't use an external CSS file or

`<mx:Style>` block to style your HTML text. However, Exercise 9.3 shows how you can create a style sheet using ActionScript to set properties that are referenced by class selectors in your HTML text in order to apply styling. The style sheet you create can be assigned to a TextArea using the `styleSheet` property. Style sheets can also be switched at runtime to dynamically change the styling of your text. To learn more about creating a style sheet for HTML Text, you can follow Exercise 9.3 and walk through the process.

Summary

In this chapter, you learned about working with fonts and styling text within Flex. You have a lot of options, but legibility, application performance, and consideration of your audience are the most important when dealing with text. Taking the extra time to work with text can really add a polished look to your application, both aesthetically and from a usability standpoint. To put some of the methods discussed in this chapter into practice, refer to Exercises 9.1 through 9.3.

In the next chapter, you will learn about using filters and blends to add further detail to your Flex application. With filters and blends, you can achieve Photoshop-like effects like drop shadows, glows and blurs, and image blends like multiply, add, and more.

Filters and Blends

If you're working to achieve a sense of layering and depth within your Flex application, you may want to look at filters and blends. Filters—things like drop shadows, glows, bevels, blends, or blend modes—allow you to manipulate the way colors in objects interact with each other in different ways. Usually applications like Photoshop or Flash are used to make graphics with these types of filters and blends applied to them, and then those graphics are brought into Flex. However, you can apply some of these same filters and blends to objects within your application right inside of Flex.

Filters and blends are static, meaning that they must be re-rendered or applied in order to change their qualities. Both methods offer another method for creating rich user interfaces without having to rely on static graphics that must be altered in an external graphics program whenever a change is required. Be considerate of the number of instances that you create of a filter or blend. In some cases, too many can fragment the focus of a user or clutter the accessibility of the user's desired goal, and they can degrade performance. These filters and blends are not complicated features to work with in the Flex framework and can complement a solid user interface to achieve a sense of layering and depth.

In this chapter, you will learn about filters and blends, as well as gain an understanding of their capabilities. Additionally, you will see just how easy they can be to implement and how they can enhance your user interface.

Filters

Filters are static bitmap treatments that can be applied to objects within an application using MXML and ActionScript. Using filters, you can make things look raised, dimensional, or blurred, or completely alter pixels to achieve a heightened sense of depth and richness. Each filter has its own set of properties that can be changed in a multitude of ways to achieve a countless number of effects you can use throughout an application. Table 10-1 describes some of the basic filters available in Flex. Refer to Appendix B, "Filters Cheat Sheet," for more detail.

Table 10-1   **Available Basic Filters**

	Filter	Description
	Bevel	Creates the appearance of an inset or raised edge using a high-light and surface shadow.
	Blur	Blurs an object on an x and y axis.
	Drop Shadow	Applies an inner or outer shadow to a specified object. Properties (including `offset`, `color`, `strength`, `angle`, and `alpha`) can be adjusted.
	Glow	Applies an inner or outer glow to a specified object. Properties (including `distance`, `color`, `strength`, and `alpha`) can be adjusted.

Flex also has a series of additional filters including Gradient Bevel, Gradient Glow, Displacement Map, Convolution, and Color Matrix. Gradient Bevel and Gradient Glow allow you to add a more dimensional appearance on top of the basic Bevel and Glow filters. Using Color Matrix filter, you can manipulate the color of pixels to achieve things like making an image grayscale, sepia tone, and so on. The Convolution and Displacement Map filter allow for advanced bitmap manipulation as you might use in a 3D or image editing application. For more information on these advanced filters, refer to the Flex documentation.

> **Tip**
>
> There is a Filter Explorer that you can view online at http://www.merhl.com/flex2_samples/filterExplorer/ that shows several examples of filters (see Figure 10-1). You can adjust filter properties and see them update in real time. As you make adjustments, MXML code for the filter you create is written for you. This MXML can be used by copying and pasting it into an application.

Working with Filters

Each filter in Flex 3 has its own properties that can be adjusted to achieve a desired effect. Some filters are more advanced than others and require additional parameters that may be hard to visualize. However, for a filter to be visible, it must be applied to a visible object like a control or container within an application.

The boundaries of a filter are determined by the outermost edges of the object it is applied to. A filter also affects items within the object it is applied to wherever there is transparency. For example, if you apply a Drop Shadow filter to a transparent HBox that contains several components, a drop shadow would not only be visible around the HBox, but around the items it contains as well. Figure 10-2 shows the HBox without a filter; Figure 10-3 shows the same HBox with a transparent background.

Flex Filter Explorer ~2.0.1

FILTER CONTROLS

BevelFilter
BlurFilter
DropShadowFilter
GlowFilter

Canvas Background Color

Distance   4

Highlight Color

Angle   45

Highlight Alpha   0.5

Shadow Color

SANDBOX

MXML

```
<mx:HBox id='myHBox' left='10' top='30' right='10'
    backgroundColor='#b6ad87'
    borderStyle='solid' borderThickness='0' cornerRadius='8'
    paddingRight='5' paddingLeft='5'
    backgroundAlpha='1'
    height='80%' width='80%'>
<mx:filters>
    <flash.filters:BevelFilter id='bevelFilter' xmlns:flash.filters='flash.filters.*'
    angle='45'
    blurX='10' blurY='10'
```

Copyright (c) 2007 Adobe Systems, Inc. All Rights Reserved   Created by Adobe Consulting   Customized by Joe Johnston

Figure 10-1   Flex Filter Explorer

Note

Filters can go beyond the layout boundaries of a component to overlap other components. This is great for creating realistic looking visuals; however, it may take some strategic thinking on where to use a filter.

Figure 10-2   HBox with buttons and no filter applied

Figure 10-3   Filter example with transparent background

If you want an effect where each object has a drop shadow without the HBox shadow being visible inside, a separate shadow filter needs to be applied to each object. Also, a non-transparent background is required. Notice in Figure 10-4 that the HBox inner shadow is now gone.

Figure 10-4   Filter example with opaque background

> **Note**
>
> A lot of the default Flex skins use transparency, so you may need to make adjustments to components using styling or creating your own custom skins to remove the transparency. For example, in Figure 10-4, you can see the drop shadow showing through the button skin.

Filter Properties

With the capability to influence filter properties, you can produce countless unique visuals in your application. Some filters are more complex to work with than others, but the following information should help you gain an understanding of how to adjust each filter to achieve the look you want. Table 10-2 is a list and description of properties for the basic filters listed in Table 10-1; they are similar to properties you might expect in applications like Illustrator, Photoshop, Flash, and Fireworks. For a more in-depth breakdown of properties, refer to Appendix B.

> **Note**
>
> When working with filters, make sure you specify properties in the order they appear in code-hinting. In some cases, if the properties are not specified in the correct order, the filter will not render at all.

Table 10-2   **Filter Properties**

Property	Description
angle	Specifies the direction of the "light source" of the highlight and shadow.
blurX blurY	The amount of blur applied to a filter along the x and y axis.
distance	How far the highlight and shadow are from the edges of the object.
highlightAlpha highlightColor	The alpha of the highlight (specified with a percentage decimal) and highlight color (specified with a hex value).
knockout	If set to `true`, only the filter is visible.
quality	Determines smoothness of the highlight and shadow (higher quality equates to lower performance).

Table 10-2   **Continued**

Property	Description
shadowAlpha	The alpha of the shadow (specified with a percentage decimal) and shadow color shadowColor (specified with a hex value).
strength	Determines prominence of the highlight and shadow.
type	Inner: Applies the filter to the inner area of the targeted object. Outer: Applies the filter to the outer area of the targeted object. Full: Applies filter to both inner and outer areas of targeted object.
inner	If set to true, the filter is applied to the inner area of the targeted object.
hideObject	If set to true, the targeted object will be not be visible.

Using these properties, you can fine-tune the appearance of filters. Now that you have a basic understanding of filters and their properties, let's take a look at how they can be applied in Flex.

Applying Filters

Filters can be applied to containers or components in a few different ways using MXML or ActionScript. Before you apply a filter, it is best to visualize what you want to do. Based on the effect you are looking for, you may need to use one or more filters and experiment a little. You can always use a graphics application like Photoshop or Fireworks to mock up the effect you want and use the parameters set in those applications to get an idea of how to approach the effect in Flex.

Filters are applied to a component by specifying the **filters** property, which accepts an array of filter objects. Data-binding does not work with the filters property, which means that after it's applied, changes to the array, such as adding or removing filters, do not take effect unless it is reapplied. Similarly, updates to individual filters within the array have no effect without reapplying the array. MXML makes it easy to apply filters, but ActionScript is required if you want to dynamically add or remove filters from a target.

Using the Filters Tag

One way to apply a filter in MXML is to use the **<mx:filters>** tag. To apply a filter using this method, you need to do the following:

1. Import the filter or filters you want to apply using an **<mx:Script>** tag as in Listing 10-1 or add the namespace to your opening Application or Component tag as in Listing 10-2.

Listing 10-1   **Import filters**

```
<mx:Script>
    <![CDATA[
    import flash.filters.GlowFilter;
    ]]>
</mx:Script>
```

Listing 10-2   **Import filters using an XML namespace**

```
<mx:Application
    xmlns:mx="http://www.adobe.com/2006/mxml"
    layout="absolute"
    xmlns:flash.filters="flash.filters.*">
```

Note

You can import all filters by specifying an asterisk (*) instead of the filter name like this:
`import flash.filters.*;`.

2. After you've imported the filter classes or namespace, you can assign the filter to an object. To do this, add an <mx:filters> tag within the tags of the object you want to apply the filter to. You can specify the filter, or filters, you want to apply within the <mx:filters> tag. The MXML code snippet in Listing 10-3 shows a Drop Shadow and Bevel filter being applied to a VBox, which produces the visual results of Figure 10-5.

Listing 10-3   **Applying filters in MXML and the result**

```
<mx:VBox
    width="90"
    height="90"
    backgroundColor="#24A0CE"
    >
    <mx:filters>
      <mx:BevelFilter
          highlightAlpha=".5"
          shadowAlpha=".5"
          />
      <mx:DropShadowFilter alpha=".5"/>
    </mx:filters>
</mx:VBox>
```

Figure 10-5   Drop Shadow and Bevel filter

By combining filters, you can achieve similar results as you might get in Photoshop. However, the more filters and complexity you add can impact application performance.

Using the Filters Array

You can also create a filter inline using a filters array and specify the parameters of a filter within. Listing 10-4 shows a Glow filter applied to a button by defining the filter and then the desired parameters.

Listing 10-4   **Applying a Glow filter inline using a filters array**

```
<mx:Button  label="Glow Filters"
    fontSize="16"
    filters="{[new GlowFilter(0x62ABCD,.8,10,10)]}"/>
```

It is possible to create a filter outside of a visual component and then apply to several components, as shown in Listing 10-5.

Listing 10-5   **Applying filters to more than one component**

```
<mx:DropShadowFilter
    id="myDropShadowFilter"
    alpha="0.5"
    />

<mx:BevelFilter
    id="myBevelFilter"
    highlightAlpha="0.5"
    shadowAlpha="0.5"
    />

<mx:Button filters="{[myDropShadowFilter,myBevelFilter]}" />
<mx:ComboBox filters="{[myDropShadowFilter,myBevelFilter]}" />
```

Applying Filters Using ActionScript

You can also apply filters using ActionScript. The real value of using ActionScript is the capability to make conditional filters or affect your filters with variables. Listing 10-6 applies a Drop Shadow filter when a button is clicked.

Listing 10-6   **Applying a drop shadow using ActionScript**

```
<mx:Script>
    <![CDATA[

        public function applyFilter():void
        {
        myButton.filters =
            [
            new DropShadowFilter
            (
            5,                 // distance
            90,                // angle
            0x000000,          // color
            0.5                // alpha
            )
            ];
        }

    ]]>
</mx:Script>

<mx:Button
    id="myButton"
    label="Apply Filter"
    click="applyFilter()"/>
```

Filters can help you achieve some very rich visual treatments like drop shadows, glows, bevels, and blurs. Using filters, you can make components look more dimensional or completely alter their appearance pixel by pixel. In a broad sense, filters make things stand out. If you want to make colors of components blend together, Flex has a series of blend modes you can use.

Blends

Blends in Flex allow you to adjust the characteristics of how objects in Flex visually interact with each other as they overlap. Essentially, blends combine the colors of overlapping objects to create a new display that is visible onscreen. If you use Photoshop or Illustrator, some of these blend modes may be familiar to you.

Using blends, you can achieve similar visuals that you would otherwise be required to create using an external graphics application. Table 10-3 describes the available blend modes in Flex with a small visual example of what that filter looks like applied to the top object. The colors are used to illustrate the effect of each blend and are not part of the blend itself.

Table 10-3   **Blend Modes**

Visual	Blend mode	Description
	Normal	Used to override other blend modes to set the appearance back to normal. This is the default setting.
	add	Produces a dramatic lighting effect and transparency.
	alpha	The alpha of the foreground is applied to the background. Depending on the usage, certain objects may become invisible.
	darken	Combines the darkness of the foreground with the background.
	difference	Creates a reversed effect, in some cases producing more dramatic colors.
	erase	Knocks or cuts out background using the alpha of the foreground objects.
	hardlight	Creates an appearance of shading through transparency.
	invert	Inverts the colors and transparency of an object.

Table 10-3   **Continued**

Visual	Blend mode	Description
	`layer`	Forces the creation of a temporary buffer for precomposition for a particular display object.
	`lighten`	The lightest parts of the foreground object are emphasized.
	`multiply`	Produces a shading effect using alpha and darkness of a foreground object.
	`overlay`	Produces a shading effect using alpha and lightness of a foreground object.
	`screen`	Produces a highlight effect using the lightness of colors of the foreground object.
	`subtract`	Produces a dramatic shading effect and transparency.

Applying a Blend

Applying a blend takes no more than simply specifying one of the blend modes mentioned in Table 10-3 for the `blendMode` property of a component. Listing 10-7 shows the Multiply blend mode applied to a button; Figure 10-6 is the result.

Listing 10-7   **Applying a blend mode**

```
<mx:Button
    label="Button"
    blendMode="{BlendMode.MULTIPLY}"
    />
```

Button without a blend mode   Button with Multiply blend mode

Figure 10-6   Button with and without a multiply blend mode

> **Tip**
>
> To specify a blend mode, you need only to provide its name as a string—for example, "multiply", "lighten", and so on. However, it is recommended that you reference static properties defined in the BlendMode class as shown in Listing 10-7. This ensures that you don't misspell the name of the blend mode, and if you're using FlexBuilder, you'll get a list of available blend modes as you type. Other examples include `BlendMode.LIGHTEN`, `BlendMode.DARKEN`, and so on.

Blends also work great for getting images with extra white space to appear as "part of" the component or area they are overlaying. For example, Figure 10-6 is what an image with a large amount of white space looks like on a light gray background. However, you can make that same image blend into the background just by applying a blend mode of `multiply`. Be careful how you use this technique because it may affect images in unwanted ways. In Figure 10-7, the image does blend into the background, but this also affects the Fx letters, making them gray instead of white.

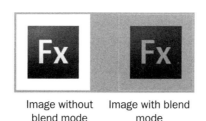

Image without   Image with blend
blend mode   mode

Figure 10-7   Filter example with transparent background

Summary

In this chapter, you learned about how to use filters and blends in Flex. Although filters and blends may be easy to implement and produce some interesting effects, they may not always be the best solution. If you're working with a designer, you may want to leverage his abilities to create graphics. In some cases, filters may be a bit more processor intensive to render versus using a graphic. You'll really just have to look at things on a case-by-case basis and weigh the cost versus benefits. As a reference for filters, you can use the Filters Cheat Sheet in Appendix B or refer to the Filter Explorer previously mentioned.

In the next chapter, you will learn about effects and transitions. Effects are similar to filters, but they are motion-based and offer many more variations. Transitions use effects to fluidly control dynamic layouts within Flex.

Effects and Transitions

Creating an application means more than just populating components with data. Flex as an application framework is unique because it utilizes the Flash Player. Within Flex, you can leverage this to create fluid interactions with visual animations, called effects. Flex 3 has numerous animated visual effects that can be applied to any component, or components, within an application. With effects, components can dynamically grow in size, glow on a rollover, slide to a new position, or do a number of other interesting things within an application.

Transitions use these same effects to control the changing views within your application. These views are called view states, and transitions can only be used in conjunction with them. Different views can occur application wide, as a portion of the application view, or within a component. Although it may be a hard task, some of the best applications are those that give the user the impression she is never really leaving the main view of an application. You will learn more about view states later in the chapter.

> **Note**
>
> If you are wondering about the difference between filters and effects: Filters are static, whereas effects are dynamic and can change over time. Filters are discussed at length in Chapter 10, "Filters and Blends."

Using Effects and Transitions

Effects and transitions can support usability by guiding a user, helping the user maintain context within a series of views, and add a level of interactivity to an application. Transitions and effects can be helpful for

- Smoothing out a change of a view within an application.
- Adding an object in a view
- Subtracting an object from a view
- Changing an object in a view

For example, if a user performs an operation that requires a display of information, a Resize effect can be used to open up an area to hold that information.

> **Tip**
>
> Consider using effects to smoothly show or hide content. To show content at a time only when it is needed is a great way to keep your application uncluttered and more approachable. It also keeps a user focused on the most important task at hand.

- Bringing emphasis to or centralizing an area within an application. For example, if there is a button that needs to be pressed in order to continue a process, a Glow effect can be used to make that button stand out.

- De-emphasizing an area within an application. For example, if a user performs an operation that requires other selections to be inactive or unnecessary, a Fade effect can be used to dim back that information so that its importance is less.

- Emphasizing an interaction. For example, a button can enlarge in size when a user rolls over it by using a Zoom effect. This type of implementation offers emotional and interactive value that can draw a user into an application.

Considerations

What does it mean to strategically use effects? Well, it would be very easy to not add any effects, or go overboard with them, but the ideal implementation needs to take into consideration the following things.

- What is the purpose? To call attention, smooth out the introduction to additional UI elements, enrich the experience, and so on? Think about the reason you may need an effect.

- What else is going on onscreen? Effects should complement your user experience, not deter from it. Be aware of what other motions are taking place on the screen before you decide to add more. As a rule, you may want to consider triggering large motions in a sequence versus all at the same time to prevent overwhelming the user and his computer's processor. As a sequence, each effect happens after the other, allowing the user to take things in bit by bit.

- How should you lay out your application? Effects and transitions are sometimes applied during the final stages of an application build. However, the sooner you can begin to think about where motion will be used in your application, the better you can prepare the layout of your application to be accommodating. This is especially true if you have effects that include movement and scaling because this may require the use of container components that react to such effects in the way you envision.

- How will the layout be affected? As you add effects, take into account how the effects may affect other elements of your application. For example, if you have a sliding drawer, will it go over content or push it to the side? If you have a resizing panel, will it cover other important elements of the user interface?

For more information on application layout, refer to Chapter 3, "Dynamic Layout."

Real-World Scenarios

To gain a better understanding of how to best use effects in an application, you need to look no further than other applications built in Flex. Figure 11-1 is an example of a pulsing Glow effect being used to call attention to the Next Step button on the form to help guide the user. This is helpful when there are similar elements on a page, or to let the user know that when the button is pushed something "different" or significant will happen.

Figure 11-1   Guiding with a Glow effect

Effects and transitions can also be used to display content as it is needed rather than cluttering the screen with a flurry of information. The Flex.org Showcase is an example of an expanding and contracting area that the user can toggle depending on what information she wants to see (see Figure 11-2). You can experience this application at http://www.flex.org/showcase.

Another example of using effects and transitions is animating a filtering action to dynamically rearrange items that fit specific criteria. The Flex Store sample application moves cell phones around the screen in response to the user's criteria; others that do not meet specified criteria are eliminated (see Figure 11-3). This creates a smooth effect as though the phones are sitting on a table right in front of the customer. As the customer gets closer to refining his selection, it's as though he is physically removing the phones from the table. You can experience this application at http://www.adobe.com/devnet/flex/samples/flex_store/.

To get inspiration, look around and see what others have done. Of course, what you find may not always be an example of the "right" thing to do. By taking those suggestions into account, you can begin to think about how effects might play a role in your application. Let's take a look at what options the Flex framework provides, starting with effects.

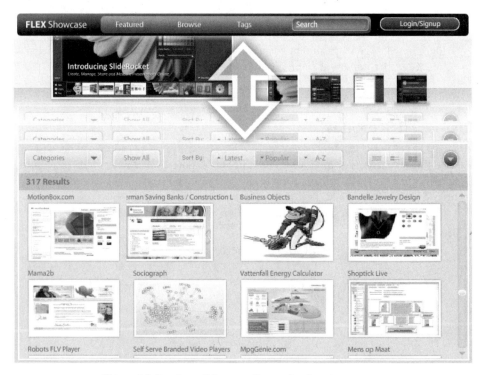

Figure 11-2   Smoothly expanding and collapsing an area

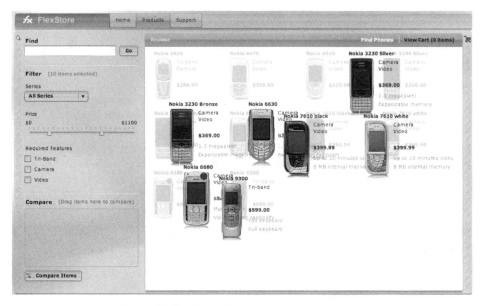

Figure 11-3   Dynamic rearrangement with motion

Effects

Motion is a way to grab attention or to smooth out visual changes in an application. Flex 3 has numerous animated visual effects that can be applied to any component, or components, within an application. Think of using effects as another layer to help guide a user, call attention, or enhance the experience. With effects, components can fluidly grow in size, emit a pulsing glow, or slide to a new position within an application.

Effects target components and can be triggered by functions or events fired within an application. Additionally, effects have events of their own that can trigger other functions. Table 11-1 provides a visual and description for each effect that is available in the Flex framework.

As you start to put your application together, try to visualize where these effects might work into the flow of the application. It's very easy to get drawn into using an abundance of different effects, but they should really be used strategically to enhance or complement the user experience.

> ### Note
>
> With Flex, you also have the ability to use your timeline animations and filters from Flash CS3. To learn more, refer to Chapter 12, "Flex and Flash Integration."

Table 11-1   Available Effects

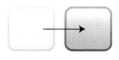	A Move effect moves a component's position along the shortest path.
	A Glow effect creates an inner or outer glow using properties like `color`, `alpha`, `distance`, and so on to create the desired look.
	The Resize effect changes the height and width of a component from its current dimensions to its target dimensions.
	Similar to the Resize effect, the Zoom effect changes the size of a component, but does so in a different manner. A Zoom effect changes the size of a component at a percentage of its initial width and height values. Note: The Zoom effect does not change the pixel dimensions of the object it's applied to. The effect "magnifies" the object.

Table 11-1   **Available Effects**

	An AnimateProperty effect allows you to animate any property of a component. For example, you could animate the x position, height, width, and so on. Additionally, you can also animate style properties like `fontSize`, `padding`, `cornerRadius`, and so on. Note: AnimateProperty effect adheres to layout constraints; other effects do not. Note: Animating a style uses the `setStyle()` method incrementally to create the effect, which can be an expensive process.
	A Wipe effect moves a mask over a targeted component in the direction specified: up, down, left, right. If a custom mask is not created, a vertical or horizontal wipe occurs.
	An Iris effect creates a growing/shrinking mask effect. If no custom mask is specified, a rectangular mask is applied.
	A Fade effect animates the alpha of a component.
	The Dissolve effect is similar to the Fade effect in that it animates the alpha of a component. However, you can also specify a color overlay for the Dissolve.
	The Rotate effect animates the rotation of a component based on a specified registration point or origin.
Pause	Pause is a nonvisual component that delays an effect for a specified period of time.

Applying Effects

Now that you have a basic understanding of the available effects in the Flex framework, we'll cover how you can work with these effects to achieve the motion and look you want. Like other components, effects have their own sets of properties that can be defined and fine-tuned to your liking. There are common properties and events for all effects, as well as effect-specific properties.

Targeting Components

To apply an effect to a component, you use the `target` or `targets` property of the effect, and specify the `id` of the component you'd like to target, as in Listing 11-1. If you want to target multiple components, you can use the `targets` property of the effect and specify an array of ids as in Listing 11-2.

Listing 11-1   Targeting a single component

```
<mx:Fade target="{myButton}"/>

<mx:Button id="myButton"/>
```

Listing 11-2   Targeting multiple components

```
<mx:Fade targets="{[myButton, myComboBox]}"/>

<mx:Button id="myButton"/>
<mx:ComboBox id="myComboBox"/>
```

Triggering an Effect

For an effect to play, it has to be triggered. You can trigger an effect by using events and functions within your application. For example, on a click of a button, you could play an effect. The MXML code snippet in Listing 11-3 is a simple example of a Fade effect being played when a button is clicked.

Listing 11-3   Triggering an effect

```
<mx:Fade id="myFade" target="{myButton}"/>

<mx:Button id="myButton" click="myFade.play();"/>
```

Being able to trigger an effect is great for controlling when you want that effect to play. However, if you want an effect to play every time a component is shown, hidden, and so on, there are default effects triggers for each component that do that. For example, you could specify an effect to play every time a component's `visible` property is set to `true` using the component's `showEffect` property, as shown in Listing 11-4.

Listing 11-4   Setting the showEffect

```
<mx:Fade id="myFade"/>

<mx:Button id="myButton" showEffect="{myFade}"/>
```

Each Flex component has a varying number of these event effects available to allow your own custom effects to be applied. However, you do not have to specify a custom effect as in Listing 11-4; you can also just specify a default effect like Fade, Dissolve, Resize, and so on, as in Listing 11-5. Other effect events include `hideEffect`, `rollOverEffect`, `creationCompleteEffect`, and more. Refer to the Flex documentation to see which of these event effects are available for each component.

Listing 11-5   Setting the showEffect using a default Fade effect

```
<mx:Button id="myButton" showEffect="Fade"/>
```

Using Start and End Events

You can use effects to set the stage for a view in your application, but what if you want something to happen before or after an effect plays? For each effect, there are events that can trigger other actions within an application. These events include `effectStart`, `effectEnd`, `tweenStart`, and `tweenEnd`.

These actions allow you to control the flow of your application. For example, let's say you had a Fade effect on a login window with a username text input, but you don't want a user to be able to type in that field until after the effect has finished playing. By using `effectEnd`, you could set the username text input to be active as soon as the effect has finished playing.

> **Tip**
>
> To create an endless looping effect, use the `effectEnd` event to trigger the effect to play again. Listing 11-6 shows two Glow effects that trigger each other to play at the end of their animation. The result is a button that emits a pulsing glow.

Listing 11-6   Repeating Glow effect creating a pulsing button glow

```
<?xml version="1.0" encoding="utf-8"?>
<mx:Application xmlns:mx="http://www.adobe.com/2006/mxml"
                initialize="glowUp.play();">

<mx:Glow id="glowUp"
        target="{sb}"
        alphaFrom="1" alphaTo=".8"
        blurXFrom="0" blurXTo="10"
        blurYFrom="0" blurYTo="10"
        color="#62ABCD"
        effectEnd="glowDown.play();"/>

<mx:Glow id="glowDown"
        target="{sb}"
        alphaFrom=".8" alphaTo="1"
```

Listing 11-6   **Continued**

```
        blurXFrom="10" blurXTo="0"
        blurYFrom="10" blurYTo="0" color="#62ABCD"
        effectEnd="glowUp.play();"/>

<mx:Button label="Submit" id="sb"/>

</mx:Application>
```

Customizing an Effect

Each effect has its own properties that can be adjusted to customize it. Getting an effect to react just the way you want may take some time as you adjust and test. Changing a few values can make all the difference. For example, a Glow effect has a number of different properties that affect the alpha, blur, color, and attributes of the glow. When you start working with effects, you can explore what these different properties do or refer to the Flex documentation for a full listing of properties for each effect.

> **Note**
>
> Any effect property that is time based expects values to be in milliseconds.

Controlling the Timing

Effects include motion over a period of time, which means you have the opportunity to dictate the timing, as well as how many times the effect plays. The following list represents properties you can use to set the timing of your effects:

- `duration`. The amount of time it takes to play an effect in milliseconds.
- `repeatCount`. The number of times to play an effect.

For example, in Listing 11-7, the Fade effect that targets `myButton` will play for a duration of 1 second and repeat 10 times when the button is clicked.

Listing 11-7   **Specifying a duration and repeat count**

```
<mx:Fade id="fade"
    target="{myButton}"
    duration="1000"
    repeatCount="10"/>

<mx:Button id="myButton"
    click="fade.play();"/>
```

Controlling the Play

Not only can you play effects, but you can also control them at any point during their play cycle. You can do things like pause, resume, reverse, stop, and end to detect whether an effect is playing. You can also create smooth motions that can react accordingly at any point during the effect being played. For example, if you have a Resize effect on an image that is triggered by a rollover, you could very smoothly reverse the transition any time the user rolls out of the image by checking if the effect is playing and then telling it to reverse. If you don't take that approach, the Resize effect just starts from the starting or ending values creating a stuttering effect. By using the following properties, you can gain fine-grained control of the effects in your application:

- `play()`. Tells the specified effect to play.
- `pause()`. Pauses an effect at any point while an effect plays.
- `resume()`. Resumes a paused effect.
- `reverse()`. Reverses an effect from any point of a playing effect.
- `end()`. Jumps an effect to the end.
- `stop()`. Stops an animation at any point while an effect plays.
- `isPlaying()`. Tells whether or not an effect is playing.

Compound Effects

Effects can be used together to create unique compound effects. You can group multiple single effects using Parallel and Sequence effects. A Parallel effect plays a group of effects at the same time. A Sequence effect causes combined effects to play sequentially. Compound effects can be used to create very interesting and customized effects.

Using these compound effects, you can add some dynamic motion to your user interface. It is important though to consider what kind of performance hits you might take on your application. The more effects you add or use at the same time, the slower it can make your application. Also, your users may not want to wait around for a long effect to complete. Table 11-2 provides a description of these compound effects.

Table 11-2   **Compound Effects**

	Parallel effects are composite effects made up of other effects. When triggered, a Parallel effect plays each effect within it at the same time. This is great for creating more interesting effects.
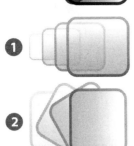	Sequence effects are composite effects made up of other effects. When triggered, a Sequence effect plays each effect one after the other in a type of domino execution. This is great for creating effects that create the appearance of something building or taking the user through a visual path or process.

The following MXML code snippet in Listing 11-8 produces an effect that fades, blurs, and moves all at the same time based on the properties you specify. In this case, no properties are specified.

Listing 11-8   **Compound effect**

```
<mx:Parallel
      id="myEffect"
      target="{myButton}">
      <mx:Fade/>
      <mx:Blur/>
      <mx:Move/>
</mx:Parallel>

<mx:Button
      id="myButton"
      rollOver="myEffect.play();"/>
```

You can make some advanced effects by grouping multiple effects into a composited series of effects. For example, the MXML in Listing 11-9 shows an advanced composite effect that uses two Parallel composite effects within a Sequence effect that is applied to two components.

Listing 11-9   **Advanced effect using multiple composite effects**

```
<mx:Sequence id="mySequenceEffect" target="{[myButton,myComboBox]}">
    <mx:Parallel target="{myButton}">
        <mx:Fade alphaFrom="0"
                 alphaTo="1"/>
        <mx:Zoom zoomXFrom=".5"
                 zoomXTo="1"
                 zoomYFrom=".5"
                 zoomYTo="1"/>
    </mx:Parallel>
    <mx:Parallel target="{myComboBox}">
        <mx:Move xBy="100"/>
        <mx:Rotate angleTo="30"/>
    </mx:Parallel>
</mx:Sequence>

<mx:Button id="myButton" click="mySequenceEffect.play();"/>
<mx:ComboBox id="myComboBox"/>
```

This Sequence effect would play the following in order:

1. The button with an `id` of `myButton` Fades from 0 to 1 while zooming from half its size to full size.

2. After the Parallel effect for `myButton` plays, the Parallel effect for `myComboBox` is triggered to play.

3. The Parallel effect for `myComboBox` moves the `ComboBox` along the `x` axis 100 pixels, while rotating it to an angle of 30 degrees.

4. Both `myButton` and `myComboBox` stop animating and are left in the final positions dictated by the effects.

Note

When working with a compound effect, like Parallel or Sequence, a duration value specifies the amount of time it will take to play all the effects within that compound effect.

Tip

When working with a Sequence, if you don't specify a duration, you can specify a duration for each of the individual effects within to fine-tune the timing.

For some examples of Flex effects in action, you can view the Component Explorer online at http://examples.adobe.com/flex3/componentexplorer/explorer.html. Navigate to the Effects folder to view the various effects.

Easing Functions

Effects and transitions represent change over time. The steps between the beginning value and the end value are calculated with an easing function, and different easing functions result in different types of motion. For example, when animating the `x` property of a component from 0 to 200 using the default linear easing function, the object moves horizontally 200 pixels at a constant speed—that is, it does not speed up or slow down as it moves. In contrast, using a different function such as `Quadratic.easeOut` causes the object to slow down as it reaches its destination (see Figure 11-4).

Other easing functions simulate more complex physical motion, like bouncing or elasticity. To see how different easing functions influence effects, check out "Easing Function Fun" at http://www.jamesward.org/easingFunctionFun/easingFunctionFun.html or an easing demo at http://www.robertpenner.com/easing/easing_demo.html.

To use easing functions, you must specify which variant you'd like to apply. Your choices are `easeIn`, `easeOut`, and `easeInOut`. Basically, these variants allow you to specify whether an animation speeds up or slows down (or both) over its duration. The `easeIn` variant begins slow and speeds up as it goes, whereas the `easeOut` variant does just the opposite. The `easeInOut` variant starts slow, speeds up, and then slows down again. The difference in variants is most noticeable on easing functions like `Back`, `Bounce`, and `Elastic`

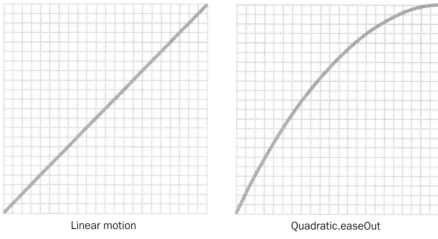

Linear motion   Quadratic.easeOut

Figure 11-4   Linear motion versus quadratic motion

because instead of just speeding up and slowing down, the object being animated actually changes direction. For example, applying the `easeOut` variant of the `Bounce` function when animating a component's `y` position from 0 to 100 causes the object being animated to bounce a few times at the end of its animation before settling at its final destination. We encourage you to explore all of the easing equations and variants. They're pretty cool.

Using an Easing Function

To use the easing functions, you must import the appropriate class in your MXML `<mx:Script>` tag. Listing 11-10 shows how you would import the `Bounce` easing function.

Listing 11-10   **Importing an easing function**

```
<mx:Script>
    <![CDATA[
    import mx.effects.easing.Bounce;
    ]]>
</mx:Script>
```

> **Note**
> You can import all easing functions by using an asterisk: `import mx.effects.easing.*;`.

The code snippet in Listing 11-11 shows how you can combine the imported `Bounce` easing function with an effect. In this example, the button moves to the right 100 pixels and appears to bounce as it ends at its final position.

Listing 11-11   **Using an easing function with an effect**

```xml
<?xml version="1.0" encoding="utf-8"?>
<mx:Application xmlns:mx="http://www.adobe.com/2006/mxml"
      layout="absolute">

    <mx:Script>
        <![CDATA[
        import mx.effects.easing.Bounce;
        ]]>
    </mx:Script>

    <mx:Move id="moveEffect"
        target="{myButton}"
        xBy="100"
        easingFunction="Bounce.easeOut"/>

    <mx:Button id="myButton"
        label="Move Me."
        click="moveEffect.play();"/>

</mx:Application>
```

These easing functions can add another level of animation to an effect, but should complement the importance of the content you want your users to access. Additional easing functions can distract what you want your users to interact with, so be considerate where you use them.

Creating a Custom Easing Function

If you want to create your own easing function and use it with an effect, you can do that too. A custom easing function is created using a function that follows the formula in Listing 11-12.

Listing 11-12   **Custom easing function formula**

```
public static function myCustomEase(time:Number,
                                    begin:Number,
                                    change:Number,
                                    duration:Number):Number
```

The variables of t, b, c, and d each specify different parameters of the custom ease function and return Number (see Listing 11-13). The descriptions of these parameters are described here:

- t. The amount of time it takes to complete the ease, specified with a number.
- b. The initial position of the targeted component, specified with a number.

- c. The total change of position of the targeted component, specified with a number.
- d. The duration of the custom ease.

> **Tip**
>
> You can find a custom easing explorer online at http://www.madeinflex.com/img/entries/200705/customeasingexplorer.html. The explorer lets you create your own custom easing function and provides the necessary function for you to copy and use in your Flex application.

Listing 11-13   **Example of custom easing function**

```
public function myCustomFunction(t:Number,
                                 b:Number,
                                 c:Number,
                                 d:Number):Number
{
    var ts:Number=(t/=d)*t;
    var tc:Number=ts*t;
    return b+c*(-3.4*tc*ts + 1.6*ts*ts + 9.5*tc + -9.2*ts + 2.5*t);
}
```

Using a Custom Easing Function

After using the preceding formula to create your easing function, you can use it just like any other easing function. However, specifying an `easeIn`, `easeOut`, or `easeInOut` parameter does not work for custom easing functions. Listing 11-14 is an example of a custom easing function used with a Move effect.

Listing 11-14   **Custom easing function used with a Move effect**

```
<mx:Script>
    <![CDATA[
    public function myCustomFunction(t:Number,
                                     b:Number,
                                     c:Number,
                                     d:Number):Number {
        var ts:Number=(t/=d)*t;
        var tc:Number=ts*t;
        return b+c*(-3.4*tc*ts+1.6*ts*ts+9.5*tc+-9.2*ts+2.5*t);
    }
    ]]>
</mx:Script>
<mx:Move id="myEffect"    xBy="100"
    easingFunction="myCustomFunction"/>
```

Listing 11-14   **Continued**

```
<mx:Button id="myButton"
     click="myEffect.play([myButton]);"
     x="60"
     y="60"
     label="Click Me"/>
```

Repurposing Effects

If you have an effect that you like and want to use on other components, you don't have to create a whole new duplicate effect for each instance that has different targets. You can specify parameters in the `play()` function to set an array of targets. For example, let's say you have a Glow effect that you'd like to play on two separate components when they are rolled over. The MXML code snippet in Listing 11-15 shows how you could accomplish that by specifying a `target` in the `play()` parameters.

Listing 11-15   **Repurposing an effect for separate targets**

```
<mx:Glow id="myGlow"/>

<mx:Button id="myButton"
     rollOver="myGlow.play([myButton]);"/>

<mx:ComboBox id="myComboBox"
     rollOver="myGlow.play([myComboBox]);"/>
```

Notice that a target was not specified in the properties for the Glow effect. This is because a target is being passed by the `play()` function when a component is rolled over. If you have to create a new Glow effect for every instance where you want to specify a different target, you end up with a lot of extra MXML. Consider using this method for repurposing effects whenever possible.

> **Tip**
>
> If you find yourself using the same effect repetitively, you can create an external MXML file for effects and repurpose them. For more information, refer to the Flex 3 documentation.

Data Effects

A new addition to Flex 3 is the capability to specify effects for the adding, removing, and changing of data items within a list-based component. Typically, if a data item is changed inside of a List component, it simply appears or disappears. With data effects, you can create a more dynamic interaction; items can fade in when they're added, slide out when they're deleted, change color when they're edited, or have any number of other effects performed on them.

To create a data effect, you can use any of the effects previously mentioned in this chapter, including `Sequence` and `Parallel`. However, there are default data effects for specific components.

The Component Explorer mentioned previously also has examples of data effects in action. View it online at http://examples.adobe.com/flex3/componentexplorer/explorer.html. Navigate to the Effects folder to view the various data effects.

Default Data Effects

Different list-based components have their own default data effects, which include `DefaultTileListEffect` and `DefaultListEffect`. These default data effects play anytime there is a change in the data items of a component that is assigned to use the effect. Each effect has properties you can use to control some default actions of the effect.

Default TileList Effect properties

`fadeOutDuration`. The amount of time it takes, in milliseconds, for a data item to fade out when changed.

`fadeInDuration`. The amount of time it takes, in milliseconds, for a data item to fade in when changed.

`moveDuration`. The amount of time it takes, in milliseconds, for a data item to move position when changed.

Default List Effect properties

`fadeOutDuration`. The amount of time it takes, in milliseconds, for a data item to fade out when changed.

`fadeInDuration`. The amount of time it takes, in milliseconds, for a data item to fade in when changed.

`growDuration`. The amount of time it takes, in milliseconds, for a data item to grow in size when it has been added or at the end of being moved.

`shrinkDuration`. The amount of time it takes, in milliseconds, for a data item to shrink in size when it has been removed or at the beginning of being moved.

`removedElementOffset`. The offset in time between effects of multiple items that are deleted at the same time.

Triggering a Data Effect

Just like other effects we've discussed, you must use a trigger to get a data effect to play. List-based components have a specific trigger for using data effects, called `itemsChangeEffect`. This trigger plays an effect any time the value of a data item is changed from its current value. This includes positioning or actual data values.

Using a Default Data Effect

Just by using these properties and triggers, you can achieve some very fluid effects that can smooth out the display of changing data within an application. The code snippet in Listing 11-16 is an example of a `DefaultListEffect` being applied to a `list`. An `itemRender` and `ArrayCollection` has been used to supply and display the data. In this example, an effect plays when a button is dragged to a new location. When the button is dropped, it shrinks and fades out, then it grows in size and fades in.

Listing 11-16   Applying a default data effect to a list

```
<?xml version="1.0" encoding="utf-8"?>
<mx:Application xmlns:mx="http://www.adobe.com/2006/mxml">

        <mx:DefaultListEffect id="myListEffect"
                fadeOutDuration="300"
                fadeInDuration="300"
                growDuration="300"
                removedElementOffset="20"
                shrinkDuration="300"/>

        <mx:ArrayCollection id="listData">
                <mx:source>
                        <mx:Object label="Item 1"/>
                        <mx:Object label="Item 2"/>
                        <mx:Object label="Item 3"/>
                        <mx:Object label="Item 4"/>
                        <mx:Object label="Item 5"/>
                        <mx:Object label="Item 6"/>
                </mx:source>
        </mx:ArrayCollection>

        <mx:List id="myList"
                itemsChangeEffect="{myListEffect}"
                dataProvider="{listData}"
                dragEnabled="true"
                dropEnabled="true"
                dragMoveEnabled="true"
                width="160"
                height="200">

                <mx:itemRenderer>
                        <mx:Component>
                                <mx:Button label="{data.label}"/>
                        </mx:Component>
                </mx:itemRenderer>
        </mx:List>

</mx:Application>
```

Custom Data Effects

If you want to go beyond the capabilities of a default data effect, you can make custom data effects using the same single or composite effects discussed at the beginning of this chapter.

When creating a custom data effect, you need to think about what you want to happen at the beginning, middle, and end of the addition, removal, or change of a data item. This means that you want to use a `Parallel` or `Sequence` effect to compose a series of effects to achieve something that's acceptable.

There are a number of events that take place as data items are manipulated, but you can control what effects get played for each event as well as control the layout of the data items as an effect is played. This is important to understand because if any effect is out of sync with the cycle of a data item being added, removed, changed, or moved, the effect won't look right. It's a similar way of thinking that you'll need to apply when working with transitions, as discussed in the next section.

Creating a Custom Data Effect

There are two important things to learn in building your own data effects: action effects and filter properties. Using action effects, you can control when items are added, removed, changed, or moved within the component. With filter properties, you can control which effects get applied to certain items, like an added, removed, replaced, or replacement item.

Action Effects

Action effects let you control the display and layout of data items within a list as an effect is being played. The following action effects are described here:

- `AddItemAction`. Specifies when an item is added to the data collection.
- `RemoveItemAction`. Specifies when an item is removed from the data collection.
- `UnconstrainItemAction`. An effect that allows items to move freely within a control without being constrained to layout.

Filter Properties

Using an effect filter property, you can designate which effects get applied to which type of item within a list as an effect is played. The available filter properties include

- `addItem`. Defines an effect to be used when an item is added to the data collection.
- `removeItem`. Defines an effect to be used when an item is removed from the data collection.
- `replaceItem`. Defines an effect to be used when an item replaces another.
- `replacementItem`. Defines an effect on an item that replaces another item.

As you compose your custom data effect, these action effects and filter properties are interspersed among the motion effects. It may be hard at first to translate a motion that you have envisioned in your head into a well-formulated block of code that does exactly what you want it to.

The MXML code snippet in Listing 11-17 is an example of a custom data effect for a List component with an `easingFunction` added as well. In this example, there are a series of buttons in a List component. When an item is dragged to a new location in the list, the item shrinks in size, other items move to make room for the moved item, and the moved item bounces into place.

Listing 11-17   **A custom data effect**

```
<?xml version="1.0" encoding="utf-8"?>
<mx:Application xmlns:mx="http://www.adobe.com/2006/mxml">

    <mx:Script>
        <![CDATA[
            import mx.effects.easing.Bounce;
        ]]>
    </mx:Script>

    <!- Custom Data Effect ->
    <mx:Sequence id="myCustomListEffect">
        <mx:Zoom
            zoomHeightTo="0" zoomWidthTo="0"
            duration="300"
            perElementOffset="150"
            filter="removeItem"/>
        <mx:SetPropertyAction
            name="visible" value="false"
            filter="removeItem"/>
        <mx:UnconstrainItemAction/>
        <mx:Parallel>
            <mx:Move
                duration="750"
                easingFunction="{Bounce.easeOut}"
               perElementOffset="20"/>
            <mx:RemoveItemAction
                startDelay="400"
                filter="removeItem"/>
            <mx:AddItemAction
                startDelay="400"
                filter="addItem"/>
        </mx:Parallel>
    </mx:Sequence>
    <!- Data Provider ->
    <mx:ArrayCollection id="listData">
        <mx:source>
            <mx:Object label="Item 1"/>
            <mx:Object label="Item 2"/>
```

Listing 11-17   **Continued**

```
                    <mx:Object label="Item 3"/>
                    <mx:Object label="Item 4"/>
                    <mx:Object label="Item 5"/>
                    <mx:Object label="Item 6"/>
            </mx:source>
        </mx:ArrayCollection>
            <mx:List
                id="myList"
                itemsChangeEffect="{myCustomListEffect}"
                dataProvider="{listData}"
                dragEnabled="true"
                dropEnabled="true"
                dragMoveEnabled="true"
                width="160"
                height="200">

                <mx:itemRenderer>
                    <mx:Component>
                        <mx:Button label="{data.label}"/>
                    </mx:Component>
                </mx:itemRenderer>
            </mx:List>

</mx:Application>
```

> **Note**
>
> Data items are affected in various ways depending on the effect that you use, whether it is a single or composite effect. For example, if you use a Resize effect, the data items surrounding the added item will shift their positions as the effect is played.

Other Tweening Options

In addition to the default Flex tween animations, there are several open-source community projects available for you to use in your Flex applications. There are a few options you might want to explore. Keep in mind that to use these projects well, they may require some ActionScript 3 knowledge.

Tweener

Tweener is a series of ActionScript 3 classes that allows you to create dynamic animations and transitions using only code. You can learn more about Tweener on Google Code at http://code.google.com/p/tweener/.

Boostworthy AS3 Animation System

The Boostworthy AS3 Animation System is an animation engine used through ActionScript 3 provides features like property animations, advanced color support, motion paths, and more. You can learn more about Boostworthy at http://www.boostworthy.com/blog/?p=170.

KitchenSync

KitchenSync is an ActionScript 3.0 library for sequencing animations and other time-based actions all through code. You can learn more about KitchenSync at http://code.google.com/p/kitchensynclib/wiki/KitchenSync.

In Summary then, with effects, you can achieve some very dynamic motion within a Flex application and use them in a multitude of ways to polish off the user experience. However, these effects can be used for more than animating specific instances. They can also be used to create fluid transitions for the changing views your user will encounter in your Flex application.

Transitions

Throughout a Flex application, there are many views that are presented to a user. By default, these views change very statically, as if they were static HTML pages. However, transitions in Flex allow you to choreograph those changes into smooth and flowing passages into other views. Through this choreography of state changes, you can control the way a user moves through your application.

The way your components move and interact with each other within an application is just as important as the way a button looks or the colors in a logo. Transitions can help create that additional spark or signature element that helps it stand out from other applications. Remember, the best applications are an entire package, from font selection to branding to color choices to motion.

Transitions are built upon view states, which are simply different views within an application. For example, a login panel component could have two view states. The base state could have login inputs, a register button, and a submit button. The second state could have text inputs for submitting registration information.

Initially, those states would change very statically. However, transitions employ effects to smooth out those state changes. For example, the login that was just discussed could use a Resize effect to smoothly change its height as the login inputs fade out to reveal the register inputs.

Transitions also give you the ability to control when a property, style, event, or component is added, subtracted, or changed from state to state. This gives you complete control over how the views of your application change as a user interacts with it.

View States

States are different views within an application or component that can vary in their complexity. Changes in view states can be changes in layout, adding or removing components, changing styles, or any number of things that may make one view state different from another.

As a simple example, Figure 11-5 shows a login panel component with two view states. The base state has login inputs, a register button, and a submit button. The second state has text inputs for submitting registration information.

Figure 11-5   View states example

With view states, you can also reveal content on an as-needed basis, showing only specific data or controls important for performing a focused task. For example, in the situation of a photo browsing application, images can be displayed without any additional clutter surrounding them, keeping the view nice and clean. However, options for displaying additional information, ordering a photo, and sharing a photo can be revealed as a user hovers her cursor over a particular image. Figure 11-6 shows a snapshot of what those two views might look like.

This technique is particularly helpful when working with item renderers. It enables you to keep the initial view very clean by showing important information when it is most relevant. Imagine what a TileList would look like if the available options for each item renderer were displayed. Very overwhelming!

Figure 11-6   View states in item renderers

Creating a View State

A view state is created by specifying a series of changes, also called overrides, to modify a base state to create a new one. With view states, you can define overrides that change properties or styles, or add and remove components. In addition, new states can be based on any other state. In DesignView, when a view state is based on another state, it appears as an icon branched off of the state it's based on.

All states, except for the base state, are defined within an **<mx:states>** tag. Each state is defined within an **<mx:State>** tag. It is important to assign each state an **id**. This is done by default when you name a state if you're working within the DesignView. You can create a new state using the States window (Window > States) and use that window to navigate between states.

The MXML code snippet in Listing 11-18 is a simple example of two states. The base state has one button and the second state, named **TwoButtons**, adds another button. Notice the **AddChild** defines the addition of the newly added button. **AddChild** is an override class that defines changes from state to state.

Listing 11-18   **MXML example of view states**

```
<mx:Application xmlns:mx="http://www.adobe.com/2006/mxml"
     layout="absolute">

    <mx:states>
        <mx:State name="TwoButtons">
            <mx:AddChild position="lastChild">
                <mx:Button x="276"
                    label="Button"
                    y="274"
                    click="currentState='';"/>
            </mx:AddChild>
        </mx:State>
    </mx:states>

    <mx:Button label="Button"
        verticalCenter="0"
        horizontalCenter="0"
        click="currentState='TwoButtons';"/>

</mx:Application>
```

Override Classes

To define the changes between your view states, you have several overriding classes that you can use. Each class affects different parts of your components. If you work in Design View, these classes will be added automatically as MXML tags as you create new states. The following list describes these available classes:

- **AddChild**. Adds a child in relation to a change in view state.

- **RemoveChild**. Removes a child in relation to a change in view state.

- **SetProperty**. Sets a component property in relation to a change in view state.

- **SetStyle**. Sets a style property in relation to change in view state.

- **SetEventHandler**. Adds, removes, or changes an event handler of a component in relation to a change in view state.

To switch between states, you can use an event to set the **currentState** property and define the name of the desired state you want to switch to. As you create multiple states and switch between them, you will notice that the transition between them is very static. As mentioned previously, Flex has mechanisms for creating very dynamic transitions between your view states.

Note
You can use states within an item renderer to show or hide additional content or controls.

Tip
Consider using multiple states for item renderers within data driven lists so you can show a loading animation on the base state and a "loaded" state for when the required content is finished loading. By showing a user something while processing background tasks like loading data, you give the user adequate feedback to let her know something is indeed going on, rather then giving the impression that the application has frozen.

Adding Transitions

To create a transition, you define effects that play as changes take place from state to state. The effects you use are no different than those covered in the preceding "Effects" section and will be interspersed with the overrides you defined. You can control the timing and behaviors of these changes, as well as define a transition between each starting and ending state.

There can be any number of changes taking place between each state, so you will need to formulate a plan of how you'd like to choreograph the transitions from state to state. You may find it helpful to write out what you'd like to see happen from state to state, similar to a script, or create storyboards to help you better visualize what you'd like to see happen. Figure 11-7 is a sample motion diagram of an envisioned transition.

In any case, it is best to have your transitions well thought out before getting into code, and it can save you a lot of time. At the same time, it is always fun just to experiment to see what sorts of animations you can create.

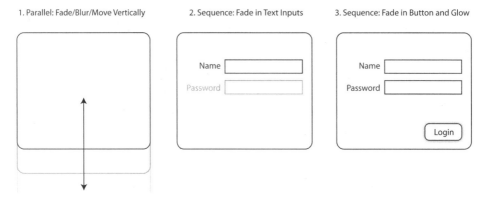

Figure 11-7   Motion diagram of an idea for a transition

> **Note**
>
> You can use transitions within any custom component that uses a container as its parent. This means you can also use transitions within an item renderer.

Creating a Transition

Transitions are constructed in a separate code block outside of your states, inside an `<mx:transitions>` tag. To specify when a transition is played, you specify the `id` of the starting state, `fromState`, and the ending state, `toState`, of the transition. For example, building upon the example in Listing 11-18, the code snippet in Listing 11-19 defines a transition to and from the base state to the `TwoButtons` state. By specifying an asterisk `"*"`, a transition will play from or to any state. If you are leery of leaving properties blank, you can also use an asterisk so that the `fromState` or `toState` properties are not left blank, like this `fromState="*"`.

Listing 11-19   **Simple transitions**

```
<?xml version="1.0" encoding="utf-8"?>
<mx:Application xmlns:mx="http://www.adobe.com/2006/mxml"
     layout="absolute">

    <mx:states>
        <mx:State name="TwoButtons">
            <mx:AddChild position="lastChild">
                <mx:Button id="addedButton"
                    label="Go Back to Base State"
                    y="67"
                    click="currentState='';"
                    left="34"/>
            </mx:AddChild>
```

Listing 11-19   **Continued**

```
                <mx:SetProperty target="{button1}"
                        name="label"
                        value="Two Buttons State"/>
            </mx:State>
    </mx:states>

    <mx:transitions>
        <mx:Transition fromState="*" toState="TwoButtons">
            <mx:Sequence target="{addedButton}">
                <mx:AddChildAction/>
                <mx:Parallel>
                    <mx:Fade alphaFrom="0" alphaTo="1"/>
                    <mx:Blur blurXFrom="20" blurXTo="0"
                            blurYFrom="20" blurYTo="0"/>
                </mx:Parallel>
            </mx:Sequence>
        </mx:Transition>
        <mx:Transition fromState="TwoButtons" toState="*">
            <mx:Sequence target="{addedButton}">
                <mx:Parallel>
                    <mx:Fade alphaFrom="1" alphaTo="0"/>
                    <mx:Blur blurXFrom="0" blurXTo="20"
                            blurYFrom="0" blurYTo="20"/>
                    </mx:Parallel>
            </mx:Sequence>
        </mx:Transition>
    </mx:transitions>

    <mx:Button id="button1"
                label="Go to Two Buttons State"
                click="currentState='TwoButtons';"
                left="34"
                y="37"/>
</mx:Application>
```

In Listing 11-19, when you click the Go to Two Buttons State, you go to the TwoButtons state. Rather than a static transition, the second button fades and blurs into the viewable area. Clicking the Back to Base State button should play a transition from the TwoButtons state to the base state. This transition causes the second button to blur and fade out.

However, you will notice that the fade/blur out of the button does not seem to be playing. This is because the button is removed before the effect can actually play. You can fix this by using one of the override actions that are available to control when that button is actually removed.

Override Actions

To control when an override is applied to objects from state to state, you can use override actions. These override actions say when an override you specified in a state actually gets applied.

In the case of the transition in Listing 11-19 where the button was disappearing before an effect could play, you could use a `RemoveChildAction` after the effects in the transition, as in Listing 11-20. This will tell the transition to remove the button *after* the effect has played.

Listing 11-20   **Using an override action**

```
<mx:Transition fromState="TwoButtons" toState="*">
    <mx:Sequence target="{addedButton}">
        <mx:Parallel>
                <mx:Fade alphaFrom="1" alphaTo="0"/>
                <mx:Blur blurXFrom="0" blurXTo="20"
                          blurYFrom="0" blurYTo="20"/>
        </mx:Parallel>
        <mx:RemoveChildAction/>
    </mx:Sequence>
</mx:Transition>
```

Using override actions is one of the keys to choreographing your transitions and effects throughout your application. Think of them as cue points of when you'd like changes imposed on components to actually be applied. The other override actions mirror the override classes that are available and are described as follows:

- `AddChildAction`. Defines a point when a child object should be added to the layout.

- `RemoveChildAction`. Defines a point when a child object should be removed from the layout.

- `AddItemAction`. Commonly used for Data Effects to define an effect when an item render is shown for an added item or replacing an existing item.

- `RemoveItemAction`. Commonly used for data effects to define an effect when an item render is hidden for a removed item or replacing with a new item.

- `SetPropertyAction`. Defines a point when a property should be changed, added, or removed for a specified object or objects. Specify a target, property name, values, and so on.

- `SetStyleAction`. Defines a point when a style should be changed, added, or removed for a specified object or objects. Specify a target, style name, values, and so on.

When working to create your transitions, you may need to experiment with different mixes of effects and override actions to achieve the look you're trying to achieve. The exercises for this chapter will expose you to a more advanced scenario of how you can use override actions and effects together.

Transitions and Layout

When you create transitions, you'll need to keep in mind how the various layout mechanisms in Flex affect the way your transitions react to the overrides. For example, if you have a component that you want to occupy a specific space within the application layout as it transitions from state to state, you may want to work with the `visible` and `includeInLayout` properties of that component to make sure that the layout stays intact. Otherwise, if you add the component from one state to another, other components may shift to make room for that newly added component.

Remember, as mentioned in Chapter 3, "Dynamic Layout," there are containers that allow for absolute positioning as well as constraint-based layouts. This is something you want to keep in mind if you plan on using effects that affect the positioning or size of a component. For example, if you were to use a Resize or Move effect in an HBox, the HBox would resize to accommodate the changing size/position of the animated component as in Figure 11-8.

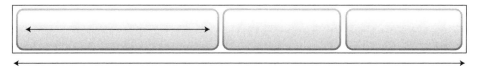

Figure 11-8   Transition within an HBox

Additionally, objects within that HBox would have to move in order to compensate for the changing component. You may want to consider using a Canvas in such cases to allow components to overlap and move without affecting the layout of the container or other container components as in Figure 11-9.

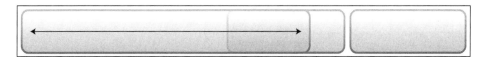

Figure 11-9   Transition within a Canvas

Summary

Effects and transitions can be used to add motion to your Flex application, from small instances to completely changing application views. They can be used to draw attention, move a user from one view to another, provide user feedback, and bring "life" into an application. In this chapter, you learned about different types of effects and how they can be used for different purposes. You also learned about transitions, which use effects. Transitions can fluidly animate changes between views of an application or within a component. To continue learning about effects and transitions, take a look at the exercises that support this chapter.

In the next chapter, you will learn about the integration features Flash has with Flex. Using the Flex Component Kit for Flash, you can use motion created in Flash in Flex, create custom components, and make rich animated skins for Flex.

Beyond Flex

Flex and Flash Integration

In Chapter 2, "Adobe Flex and AIR," you learned that Flex applications run in the Flash Player. This relationship allows you to capitalize on some of the tight integration between Flex and Flash CS3 to create stateful skins, smooth transitions, custom containers, and advanced motion. To implement these features in Flex, each has its own set of requirements that utilizes an extension called the Flex Component Kit, which was created by Adobe, or uses the Motion XML export function in Flash CS3. In this chapter, you will get an overview of some of the Flash and Flex integration features and how you can use them for your Flex projects.

Flex Component Kit

The Flex Component Kit is an extension for Flash that was created by Adobe to allow the capability to create custom Flex components using Flash. This gives you the ability to create animated skins, custom containers, and components. However, the Flex Component Kit can only be used with Flash CS3. If you don't have Flash CS3, you can download a free trial at http://www.adobe.com/downloads/ and download the Flex Component Kit at https://www.adobe.com/cfusion/entitlement/index.cfm?e=flex_skins.

Although there are many purposes for using the Flex Component Kit, each uses similar methods that you'll need to be aware of to take full advantage of the Flex Component Kit. These methods include understanding how the Flex Component Kit uses frame labels, naming conventions, defines bounds, and how to get your custom component working in Flex.

Working with Frame Labels

Working in Flash CS3, you have the ability to use the Timeline as a tool to define motion and transitions for the states of a Flex skin or custom component. Each of these states and transitions can be defined within a single Movie Clip symbol rather than across multiple symbols. This is different from other methods discussed in former chapters because they required completely separate pieces, whether symbols or layers, to be created for each state. For example, in Exercise 5.2, "Creating a Graphical Skin with Illustrator," you are required to make separate skin assets for the up, over, down, and disabled states. However, you implement the skin just like any other by using an `Embed` statement.

Using the Flex Component Kit, each of the states are defined on the Timeline using frame labels on different key frames and map directly to Flex component states. When skins or components are created using the Flex Component Kit and used in Flex, Flex recognizes these frame labels and acts accordingly to display the proper state.

One nice feature of the Flex Component Kit is the capability to create transitions between states—for example, a Button skin that fades between colors on a rollover. To create transitions, special frame labels are used to denote a transition start-point and end-point, in relation to a state. As an example, define a transition between a Button skin's up and over states, you would label one frame `up-over:start` and another `up-over:end` marking the first and last frames to be played in the transition.

It is also possible to define a reverse transition—for example, from over to up—though it is not required. If a reverse transition is not explicitly defined, the Flex Component Kit automatically reverses the forward transition that is defined. Consider the previous button example that transitions from up to over. When rolling off this button, it simply plays the same transition frames , but in reverse. Should you want to override this behavior, you can create frame labels named `over-up:start` and `over-up:end`.

If you'd like an animation to play between a view state and any other view state, you can use a wildcard symbol, an asterisk (`*`). For example, if you want a transition to play between up and any other view state, you could specify `up-*:start`. Conversely, if you want a transition to play from any view state to up, you could specify `*-up:start`. Figure 12-1 shows an example of the Flash Timeline using these frame labels. If you are new to Flash CS3, you can access the Timeline by selecting Window > Timeline.

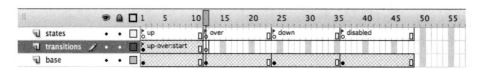

Figure 12-1   Timeline with frame labels

Table 12-1 shows several sample scenarios that illustrate how you may want to use frame labels to create a desired a transition.

Table 12-1   **Keyframe Labels for Transitions**

Frame label	Outcome
upState-downState	Defines transition between two specific view states
downState-upState	Reversed transition
*-downState	Transition from any state or reversed from any view state

Table 12-1   **Continued**

Frame label	Outcome
upState-*	Transition to any state or reversed to any view state
-	To/from any state forward/reversed

Specifying Bounds

One thing you want to be considerate of is the bounds of a custom asset created in Flash to be used in Flex. For example, a skin that changes vertical height as part of a transition may end up overlapping a component in Flex unless proper precautions are taken. In that case, you may want to create a transparent box that represents the total area that button will take up (see Figure 12-2). This prevents any odd behavior, like distortion or jumping in position, when the button skin is used in Flex. Of course, you need to think about how these types of situations affect your layout.

Figure 12-2   Setting common bounds

Note

Flex will adjust its layout to the actual width and height to any Flash object you bring into your application. With the Flex Component Kit, you can use a special Movie Clip called boundingBox to define the bounds of a custom Flex component created in Flash. You can learn more about the boundingBox feature by referring to the Flex 3 documentation at http://livedocs.adobe.com/flex/3/.

In a case where you are creating a custom container using the Flex Component Kit, you use a symbol provided by Adobe called FlexContentHolder that specifies the holding bounds of that container. These bounds tell Flex where components can be placed within the custom container. The process of using the FlexContentHolder Symbol is explained in more detail in Exercise 12.2.

Creating Full Custom Components

The Flex Component Kit can be used for more than skinning and creating custom containers; it is a very powerful tool that can be used to create advanced custom components with events, functions, and interactivity that can be accessed from Flex. We will not be going into great detail about creating custom components using the Flex Component Kit, but you can refer to the Flex 3 documentation to learn more about the topic.

We've already discussed using Flash CS3 to create custom skins and containers for your Flex components, but you can also use the custom timeline animations you create in Flash CS3 in your Flex projects. One feature that was added to Flash CS3 is the capability to export your timeline animations as an XML file. This is great because if you're familiar and more comfortable working with the Flash CS3 timeline and filters to create animations, you can bring them into a Flex application.

Motion XML

In Flash CS3, you can create custom tweened motions and apply filters to objects, which can then be exported as Motion XML and used in Flex. Although this may not be an appropriate solution for every case, it's always good to know what features you have available. You could probably achieve most of what you can do with Motion XML using the effects in Flex covered in Chapter 11, "Effects and Transitions." However, using Flash to create these motions provides a more visual workflow because you can see what's going on as you construct a custom motion.

To create a custom motion in Flash CS3, you use the Timeline and Filters properties palette. You can access the Filters (see Figure 12-3) by selecting Window > Properties > Filters in Flash CS3 and the Timeline (see Figure 12-4) by selecting Window > Timeline. If you're familiar with working with these panels, you should have no problem constructing a custom motion.

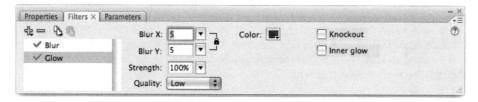

Figure 12-3   Filter properties in Flash CS3

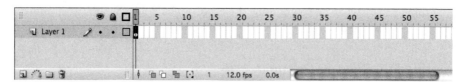

Figure 12-4   The Flash CS3 Timeline

To learn more about creating a simple motion that can be used in Flex, refer to Exercise 12.4. It's a simple example, but it exposes you to some of the primary aspects you can leverage in your Flex applications.

Summary

In this chapter, you learned different ways Flash integrates with Flex by using the Flex Component Kit. With the Flex Component Kit, you can create animated skins, export motion from Flash and use it in Flex, and repurpose Flash-created content in Flex.

Flash CS3 has a lot of interesting options to turn up the richness of your Flex applications. This will become even more apparent as you go through some of the exercises that support this chapter. You may end up using only one of these solutions, or all of them, depending on what you are trying to achieve. In some cases, you may find yourself combining these features. To be sure, there will be even more integration between Flash and Flex as the products evolve.

In the next chapter, you will learn how to customize some unique aspects of AIR applications. AIR stands for Adobe Integrated Runtime and allows developers to use Web technologies, including Flex, to create desktop applications. When working with AIR, you can use the same things discussed in previous chapters to carry the rich Internet experience to the desktop and customize desktop-specific attributes like application icons and window chrome.

13

Customizing AIR Applications

The Adobe Integrated Runtime (AIR) enables you to use Web technologies like Flex to create desktop applications. With AIR, you can extend a browser-based application to the desktop and have it run natively across multiple operating systems. Just like applications you create in the browser using Flex, you have an opportunity to create just as rich of an experience on the desktop. Most, if not all, of the methods discussed in this book can be used to customize an AIR application. In addition to what you already learned about customizing Flex applications, there are other ways you can customize your AIR application:

- Custom application icons. These icons show up in your OS X dock, Windows taskbar, desktop, and so on. Figure 13-1 shows a few examples of some icons for various AIR applications.

Figure 13-1   AIR application icons. (Adobe product screen shot(s) reprinted with permission from Adobe Systems Incorporated.)

- Skinning the window chrome, window buttons, and window resize gripper. Figure 13-2 is an example of some custom window chrome.

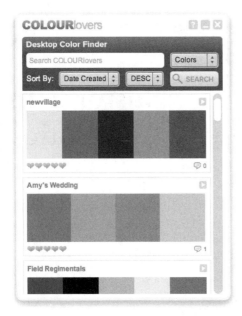 

Figure 13-2   AIR applications with custom window chrome.
(COLOURlovers.com Pownce: Pownce, Inc.)

- The ability to use transparency to customize the appearance and shape of your application's window chrome.

In this chapter, you will be guided through a series of examples so that you may gain an understanding of how you can make your AIR applications feel like custom and branded experiences. To customize and enable some of these nuances of an AIR application, you will be styling with CSS, skinning, and configuring your AIR application's settings XML file. When you do take advantage of customizing these areas, your AIR application will feel just as custom as the desktop applications you currently have running on your computer, if not more.

To learn more about the Adobe Integrated Runtime, or to see samples of some AIR applications, navigate to http://labs.adobe.com/technologies/air/.

Getting Started

The following examples require that you have an AIR application to work with. If you don't have an AIR application project already set up to use, you can create an AIR application very easily in Flex Builder. The following steps are only meant to provide a "dummy" application for testing the abilities to customize an AIR application.

1. To create an AIR application project, select File > New > Flex Project.

2. Name the project AIRSample and select Desktop Application (runs in Adobe AIR) as in Figure 13-3. Click Finish.

Figure 13-3   Creating a sample AIR project

3. You should see the newly created AIR Project structure in the Flex Navigator Panel (Window > Flex Navigator). Notice the app.xml file that was also created, in this case, AIRSample-app.xml. You will be working in this XML file to customize some of the visual aspects discussed at the beginning of this section.

By following those quick steps, you now have a sample AIR application to experiment with the techniques covered in this section. You can run this application, but it will only produce a blank windowed application. Let's see how you can change that.

Note

AIR applications use `WindowedApplication`, rather than `Application`, as the main application tag.

Working with Window Chrome

When working with the window chrome of your AIR application, there are style properties and parameters within the app.xml file that can be adjusted to help you achieve a desired look. By altering these parameters, you can create applications that break out of standard boxed windows into any shape you want, or appear to be unconstrained by any boundaries all together.

Customizing with Flex Chrome

A windowed application doesn't have to use the default system chrome. If you want to have more options to customize the window chrome, you can use the Flex window chrome. By default, the `useFlexChrome` property is set to `true`, but to see it you must alter the app.xml file. In the XML file, there is a place to specify parameters for `systemChrome`. By setting the parameters to `none`, shown in Listing 13-1, you disable the system chrome to allow the Flex chrome to be visible.

Listing 13-1   **Disabling the system chrome**

```
<systemChrome>none</systemChrome>
```

With `systemChrome` set to `none`, you see a difference shown in Figure 13-4. However, one thing you will notice is that the top-left and top-right corners show the gray-blue application background at the edges. To eliminate these blue-gray corners, set the `transparent` parameter in the app.xml file to `true`.

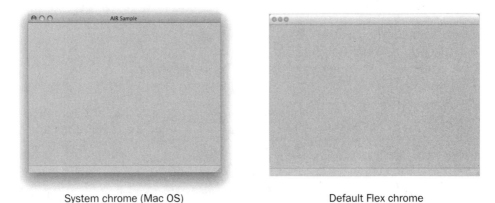

System chrome (Mac OS)   Default Flex chrome

Figure 13-4   System chrome versus Flex chrome

By using the Flex chrome, you have access to additional style properties that you can alter to customize the look of the window chrome. The following list describes each of these properties, some of which may not be as apparent, so you may need to experiment to get the exact appearance you're looking for. In many cases, you can assign custom skins for some of the parts to create a custom window. Some of these style properties act similarly to those discussed in the Chapter 4, "Styling," Chapter 5, "Graphical Skinning," and Chapter 6, "Programmatic Skinning."

- `buttonAlignment`. Positions the Minimize, Maximize, and Close button of the Flex chrome.

- `buttonPadding`. The amount of space in between each of the window buttons.

- `closeButtonSkin`. Specify a skin for the Close button of the window.

- `gripperPadding`. The gripper is the area of a window used to resize the size of the window, usually in the bottom-right corner. Gripper padding is the amount of space that the window resize gripper is inset from the window edges.

- `gripperStyleName`. Assign styling to the window resize gripper via a class selector.

- `maximizeButtonSkin`. Specify a skin for the Maximize button of the window.

- `minimizeButtonSkin`. Specify a skin for the Minimize button of the window.

- `restoreButtonSkin`. Specify a skin for the Restore button of a maximized window.

- `showFlexChrome`. If set to true, the default Flex chrome is used to house the application. However, you must change the `systemChrome` parameter in your app.xml file to `none`. Otherwise, you will have both the Flex chrome and system chrome showing.

- `statusBarBackgroundColor`. The color of the status bar at the bottom of the Flex chrome window.

- `statusBarBackgroundSkin`. The skin for the status bar at the bottom of the Flex chrome window.

- `statusTextStyleName`. The text style for text within the status bar, specified via a class selector.

- `titleAlignment`. Alignment of the application title.

- `titleBarBackgroundSkin`. The background skin of the application title bar.

- `titleBarButtonPadding`. The amount of space that the title bar buttons are placed away from the edge of the window.

- `titleBarColors`. The colors of the title bar, specified with an array of color values.

- `titleTextStyleName`. The text style name of the title bar text specified via a class selector.

Custom Window Chrome

You can bypass system chrome and Flex chrome altogether to make a completely custom window. To do this, you need to hide all the window chrome so your application appears that it is floating void of visible boundaries. This can be achieved using the following steps:

1. In the app.xml file, set `systemChrome` to none.

2. Also in the XML file, set `transparent` to `true`.

3. Lastly, for the `WindowedApplication` tag, set `showFlexChrome` to `false`.

> **Note**
> Be sure to uncomment the `systemChrome` and `transparent` parameters in the app.xml file or those parameters will not be properly applied.

Setting these parameters gives you a "blank" canvas for you to create a custom window chrome of any design you can think of, or an application that doesn't have any at all. Figure 13-5 shows some examples of AIR applications with custom window chrome.

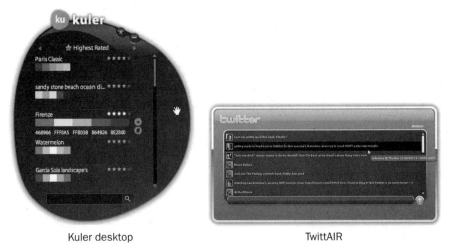

Kuler desktop   TwittAIR

Figure 13-5   AIR applications with custom window chrome. (Adobe product screen shot(s) reprinted with permission from Adobe Systems Incorporated.)

Because you've removed the default window chrome, the window functionality, like close, minimize, resize, and so on, has been removed as well. To apply that same functionality with your custom chrome, you need to assign functions to controls within your application. These functions could be called by any event, but more than likely you'll want to apply them to your custom close, minimize, and maximize buttons; or to a part of a window to allow for resizing and drag functionality. Refer to the Adobe Integrated Runtime section of the Adobe Developer Network at http://www.adobe.com/devnet/air/ for more information.

Custom Application Icons

AIR applications act just like a typical desktop application. As such, they can have their own custom application icons that will sit in the Mac OS dock or in the Windows Taskbar, just like any other desktop application. Giving your AIR application a custom icon isn't hard at all, and it adds that extra level of detail that says "custom."

Adding an application icon to your AIR project requires a graphic at 16 pixels, 32 pixels, 64 pixels, and 128 pixels in dimension square. Preferably, you should make this graphic a PNG to allow for transparency. After you have your icon graphic at those sizes, you specify those file names in the `icon` parameters in the `app.xml` file. Listing 13-2 shows different sizes of myIcon PNG being specified for the different icon sizes.

To see your application icon applied, you must export a release build of your AIR application and install it. After the application is installed, you should see your icon when you run the application. You can export a release build by selecting Project > Export Release Build.

Note

The images you use for your icons must match the exact dimensions called for in the XML. For example, an image you specify for a 32 by 32 icon must be exactly 32 by 32 pixels or you will get errors when you try to export a release build of your AIR application.

Listing 13-2 **Setting your application icons**

```
<icon>
     <image16x16>/icons/myIcon_16.png</image16x16>
     <image32x32>/icons/myIcon_32.png</image32x32>
     <image48x48>/icons/myIcon_64.png</image48x48>
     <image128x128>/icons/myIcon_128.png</image128x128>
</icon>
```

Note

You may need to uncomment areas within the `app.xml` file for the set parameters to take effect.

Summary

The Adobe Integrated Runtime allows you to bring applications out of the browser and onto the desktop. Because AIR applications can be built using Flex, you can repurpose the knowledge in this book to completely customize an AIR application. However, this chapter exposed you to customizing the window chrome and application icons of an AIR application.

There are a lot of resources available online and in books if you're interested in delving deeper into developing desktop applications using AIR. To learn more about the Adobe Integrated Runtime, navigate to http://labs.adobe.com/technologies/air/.

IV

Exercises

Loading a Style Sheet at Runtime

In Flex 3, you can compile a CSS file as a SWF (pronounced "swif") and load it at runtime. With this feature you could allow users to customize the look of an application with the click of a button or change the appearance of an application based on specific information, like login credentials. In this walkthrough, you will create two simple but different style sheets, compile them as SWFs, and then implement a way to switch between them at runtime.

1. Create a new MXML application called RuntimeStyling.mxml.

2. Create two new CSS files called red.css and blue.css (File > New > CSS file).

3. In both CSS files, you will be creating styling for a button. One will be red and the other blue. Open red.css and use a Button type selector to specify `fillColors`, `borderColor`, `fillAlphas`, and text `color` as shown in Listing 4.1-1. You also need to specify a blue color scheme for a button in blue.css (see Listing 4.1-2).

Listing 4.1-1 **Red button styling in red.css**

```
/* red.css*/

Button
{
    fillAlphas: 1.0, 1.0;
    fillColors: #FF0000, #870000;
    color: #FFFFFF;
    borderColor: #6A0000;
}
```

Listing 4.1-2   **Blue button styling in blue.css**

```
/* blue.css*/

Button
{
    fillAlphas: 1.0, 1.0;
    fillColors: #00B4FF, #005C87;
    color: #FFFFFF;
    borderColor: #000A6A;
}
```

4. With your two style sheets created, the next thing you need to do is compile them as SWFs. To do this, right-click on red.css and select Compile CSS to SWF (see Figure 4.1-1). When you compile a CSS file to a SWF it is placed into your bin folder. Do the same thing for blue.css.

Figure 4.1-1   Compile CSS to SWF

5. Now that your CSS files have been compiled as SWFs, you can easily load them at runtime using the StyleManager and the `loadStyleDeclarations` method. Create two functions called `loadRed()` and `loadBlue()`. Both of these functions will do pretty much the same thing, except one will load red.swf and the other will load blue.swf. Listing 4.1-3 shows how this can be achieved.

Listing 4.1-3   Using the StyleManager to load style declarations

```
...
<mx:Script>
      <![CDATA[
            import mx.styles.StyleManager;

            public function loadRed():void
            {
                  StyleManager.loadStyleDeclarations('red.swf');
            }

            public function loadBlue():void
            {
                  StyleManager.loadStyleDeclarations('blue.swf');
            }
      ]]>
</mx:Script>
...
```

6. To trigger these functions, add two buttons to your application. Label the first button "Go Red!" and the other "Go Blue!" Assign the `loadRed()` and `loadBlue()` functions shown in Listing 4.1-3 to each button, respectively (see Listing 4.1-4).

Listing 4.1-4   Adding functions to trigger the style change

```
...
<mx:Button
      x="100"
      y="100"
      label="Go Red!"
      click="loadRed()"/>

<mx:Button
      x="180"
      y="100"
      label="Go Blue!"
      click="loadBlue()"/>
...
```

7. Run your application. You should see the styling of the buttons change at runtime depending on which button you click. The final code should look similar to Listing 4.1-5.

Listing 4.1-5   **The final code for RuntimeStyling.mxml**

```
<!- RuntimeStyling.mxml ->

<?xml version="1.0" encoding="utf-8"?>
<mx:Application
      xmlns:mx="http://www.adobe.com/2006/mxml"
      layout="absolute">

      <mx:Script>
            <![CDATA[
                  import mx.styles.StyleManager;

                  public function loadRed():void
                  {
                        StyleManager.loadStyleDeclarations('red.swf');
                  }

                  public function loadBlue():void
                  {
                        StyleManager.loadStyleDeclarations('blue.swf');
                  }
            ]]>
      </mx:Script>

      <mx:Button
            x="100"
            y="100"
            label="Go Red!"
            click="loadRed()"/>

      <mx:Button
            x="180"
            y="100"
            label="Go Blue!"
            click="loadBlue()"/>

</mx:Application>
```

Summary

Runtime styling can be a very powerful feature depending on what you are trying to achieve. In this simple example, the styling of the application changed pretty quickly. However, the more styling you add, the longer the load time can be, especially if you're switching graphical assets. If you see the load time increase as you add more styling, consider using an indicator, such as a progress bar, to let the user know what's going on.

5.1

Creating a Graphical
Skin with Flash

Flash is an application that allows you to create graphics that can be animated to create highly interactive experiences. Creating skins for your Flex components is not a hard task. The method you use will depend on whether you have Flash CS3 or Flash 8. In both cases, you can use the Skin Import Wizard in Flex 3. This wizard helps automate an otherwise manual process of creating the required CSS rules and embed statements for your Flex component skins. For an overview of the Skin Import Wizard, refer to Chapter 5, "Graphical Skinning."

One method for creating skins for your Flex components involves using multiple symbols for each skin part. For example, a separate symbol would need to be created for the upSkin, overSkin, downSkin, disabledSkin, and so on of a button. It is with that basic understanding that you can create custom skins for Flex components. This exercise will cover how to use multiple symbols.

There are some pros and cons when working with Flash versus using Illustrator, Fireworks, or Photoshop. A primary benefit of using Flash is if you're already very familiar with the tool you'll be able to get going very quickly. Flash also supports animation, transparency for gradient colors, and live display of artwork that uses 9-slice scaling.

If you are working with Flash 8, you have to use this method. If you are using Flash CS3, you have the option to use this method; however, it is not advised. If you decide to use this method, you'll have to create your Flash file as an ActionScript 2/Flash Player 8 file.

The other option and preferred method for creating skins using Flash CS3 is to use the Flex Component Kit discussed in Chapter 12, "Flex and Flash Integration." There is one caveat though (runtime styling as described in Chapter 4, "Styling"): Styling will *not* work with skins created using the Flex Component Kit.

> **Note**
>
> You can also mix and match the Adobe CS3 tools to create your skins. For example, you can create skin artwork in Illustrator, then copy and paste that same artwork into Flash to make use of additional features Flash has to offer, like transparency on gradient colors. However, not everything will translate accurately to Flex, like filters and drop shadow effects. Many people generally use Flash as the tool to compile their skins together, whether they bring in artwork from Illustrator, Fireworks, or Photoshop.

Getting Started

To gain a full understanding on how to create skins using this method, you will exercise how to create skins for a `Button` component. For this example, you'll create some basic artwork (see Figure 5.1-1); however, you may have a mockup created by a designer, if you're not the designer yourself.

Figure 5.1-1   Button artwork

Before you get started, it is important to know what parts of a Button component can be skinned. By referring to Appendix A, "Skinning and Styling Diagrams," you will see that a `Button` has skins for its various states, including up, over, down, and disabled. These are the skins you will create.

> **Note**
>
> If you do not have Flash, you can download a free 30-day trial version at http://www.adobe.com/downloads/. Only Flash CS3 is available. For the optimal way to create skins using Flash CS3, skip ahead to Chapter 12 and follow the instructions starting there. To download the trial, you need to create a free Adobe ID if you don't have one already.

Creating the Artwork

Now that you have a basic understanding of a button's skinnable parts, you can start creating the vector-based skin artwork.

1. Open up Flash 8 or CS3 and create a new Flash File (ActionScript 2.0, Flash Player 8). You can use the default dimensions of 550 by 400 pixels and the default frame rate of 12 fps. Save this file as FlashButton.fla.

    Also, if you don't specify ActionScript 2.0 and Flash Player 8 for the file settings, you cannot import your skins using the Skin Import Wizard in Flex. Remember though, using the Flex Component Kit is the preferred method of skinning using Flash CS3. Refer to Chapter 12 for more information.

2. The first skin you will create for the button is the up skin. Using the Rectangle Tool, draw a rectangle that is 80 pixels wide by 22 pixels high. Fill this rectangle with white and give it a dark gray (#636363), 1-pixel border. Select the stroke and select Modify > Shape > Convert Lines to Fills. This changes the skin artwork to 81 pixels wide by 23 pixels high, which is okay. Group that rectangle's fill and stroke together.

Note

Converting lines to fills helps your skin artwork look better in Flex. This is because strokes in Flash are drawn half inside and half outside the bounds of the shape. Converting a line to a fill ensures that the entire stroke will be within the shape bounds. Figure 5.1-2 shows the difference.

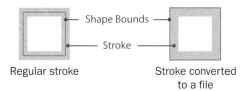

Regular stroke   Stroke converted
to a file

Figure 5.1-2   By default, strokes in Flash draw centered over the shape bounds. Converting the shape to a fill resolves this.

3. Draw another rectangle that is 78 pixels wide by 18 pixels high. Fill that rectangle with a vertical gradient of light blue (#26A7DF) on top and dark blue (#0375BF) on the bottom. Center this rectangle vertically and horizontally on top of the other rectangle. Your upSkin artwork should look like Figure 5.1-3.

Figure 5.1-3   Button upSkin

4. To create the over skin of the button, duplicate the artwork you created for the up skin (see Figure 5.1-3). Change the blue vertical gradient top fill color to lighter blue (#90D3F0) and leave the bottom fill color dark blue. This creates a highlight effect when a user rolls his cursor over the button. Your over skin should look similar to Figure 5.1-4.

Tip

When you're making skins for a series of states, as in this example, consider creating your artwork first and then convert each skin state to symbols after everything looks the way you want it to. This can speed up the production process and help ensure consistency across the states.

Figure 5.1-4   Button overSkin

5. Next, you need to create the button downSkin. Once again, duplicate the artwork you created for the button upSkin (see Figure 5.1-3). All you need to do for this skin is flip the vertical gradient as in Figure 5.1-5. This gives the impression that the button is inset when it is pressed.

Figure 5.1-5   Button downSkin

6. Finally, create the button disabledSkin by duplicating the upSkin artwork (see Figure 5.1-3). Change the blue gradient fill to a light gray (#A6A8AB) on top and a dark gray (#838588) on bottom. Your disabled skin should look like Figure 5.1-6.

Figure 5.1-6   Button disabledSkin

Converting Artwork to Symbols

To use the skin artwork you just created as skins in Flex, they have to be converted to symbols:

1. Select the artwork you created for the button upSkin (see Figure 5.1-3) and convert to a Symbol by selecting Modify > Convert to Symbol. Make the symbol a movie clip and name it Button_upSkin. Check the Export for ActionScript box. This action will also automatically check the Export in First Frame box as well. Also, check the Enable Guides for 9-Slice Scaling. The window should look like Figure 5.1-7.

> **Note**
> The reason you want to name symbols this way is because Flex Builder has a Skin Import feature that uses a naming convention to make it easy to assign skins to components. For more information on the naming convention, refer to Chapter 5.

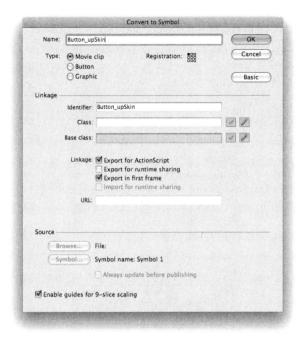

Figure 5.1-7   Converting artwork to a symbol

2. Convert the rest of the artwork for the other skin states using the same naming convention and name the other symbols Button_overSkin, Button_downSkin, and Button_disabledSkin, respectively. After doing so, your Library palette should look similar to Figure 5.1-8.

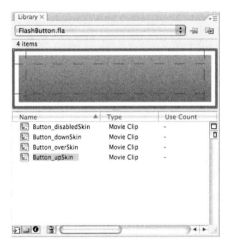

Figure 5.1-8   Library palette with symbols

Setting the 9-Slice Scale Grids

In Flex, components have the capability to scale according to the content they hold. To make sure that your skin artwork does not distort when a skinned component scales, you can set 9-slice grids. To learn more about 9-slice scaling, refer to Chapter 5.

1. To set the 9-slice scale grids on your button upSkin, double-click on the Button_upSkin symbol. Doing so should take you into the symbol, and you should see dashed grid lines as in Figure 5.1-9. You want to set these grids as in Figure 5.1-9 so that the artwork stretches correctly.

   Depending on your skin artwork, you may need to experiment with different scale grid placements. Sometimes setting the grid one pixel differently can produce different results. In some cases, like icons or other graphics that don't require scaling, you don't have to enable 9-slice scaling. A great way to test if you've set the 9-slice guides correctly is to scale your symbol right inside Flash and adjust the guides accordingly.

Figure 5.1-9   Setting the 9-slice grids

2. Set the 9-slice grids for the other symbols just as you did for the Button_upSkin.

Bringing Your Flash Artwork into Flex

Now that you walked through those steps, you're ready to take your custom skins into Flex. You should have four symbols created: Button_upSkin, Button_overSkin, Button_down_skin, and Button_disableSkin.

1. The first thing you need to do to get your Flash artwork into Flex is export it as a SWF (pronounced "swif"). Go to the Publish Settings, File > Publish Settings; on the first screen, deselect HTML under the Type column. You should only have the Flash selected, and you can specify the location of where you would like to publish the SWF file.

Note

In this scenario, you want to use a SWF, not a SWC. A SWC only needs to be specified when using the Flex Component Kit.

Also, click on the Flash tab and verify that Export for Flash 8 is specified. With those settings in place, click the Publish button. This publishes a SWF to the location you specified.

2. With the FlashButton.swf published, you can now shift over to Flex Builder 3. In Flex Builder, create a new Flex Project by selecting File > New > Flex Project, and name it FlashButton. You don't need to do anything more than name the project, so just click Finish.

3. In your Flex project, create a new folder (File > New > Folder) inside the src folder of your project and name it style. This is where all your skins and supporting CSS file will go. To learn more about the role the CSS file plays, refer to Chapters 4 or 5.

4. For this example, you also need to create a new CSS file. To do this, select File > New > CSS File. Name the file style.css and specify the style folder you created as the save location. When you have the proper information specified, click Finish.

Note

If you don't have a CSS file that you're already working with in a project, the wizard generates one for you. Rather than browsing for a file, just specify a file name in the Create Skin Style Rules In area.

5. With the Flex Project set up, you can now import the skins you created in Flash. Go to File > Import > Skin Artwork to bring up the Import Skin Artwork window. Specify SWC or SWF File and browse for the FlashButton.swf you published previously.

   For the Copy Artwork to Subfolder area, browse and specify the style folder you created previously. For the Create Skin Style Rules In area, browse and select the style.css file you created.

Note

You may see a warning at the top of the window that says, "The specified artwork folder already exists. Existing files might be overwritten." In this example, that's fine, but it's something to keep in mind when working on other projects.

6. After you have specified the information as in Figure 5.1-10, click Next.

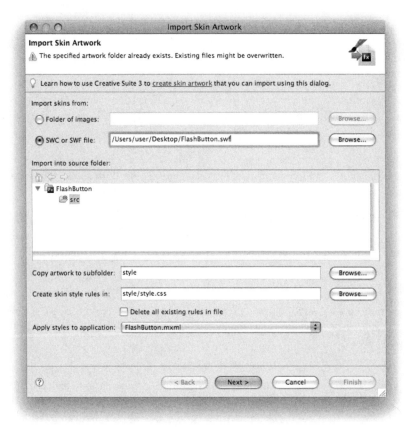

Figure 5.1-10   Selecting the skin assets and CSS file

7. On the next step of the Skin Import Wizard, you are presented with a list of skin parts. Notice that the Style Selector and Skin Part were properly assigned without any additional effort (see Figure 5.1-11). This is because of the naming convention you used when creating your Flash symbols. Leave all the items checked and click Finish.

Tip

You can change the Style Selector or Skin Part that an Image asset will be assigned to by clicking a name in either of the columns.

8. When you click Finish, the SWF you specified is added to your style folder and proper CSS code is written to the style.css file (see Listing 5.1-1). Also, the CSS file is specified in the application MXML in an `<mx:style>` tag.

Figure 5.1-11   Assigning the skin parts

Listing 5.1-1   **Generated CSS code**

```
Button
{
    disabledSkin: Embed(source="FlashButton.swf", symbol="Button_disabledSkin");
    downSkin: Embed(source="FlashButton.swf", symbol="Button_downSkin");
    overSkin: Embed(source="FlashButton.swf", symbol="Button_overSkin");
    upSkin: Embed(source="FlashButton.swf", symbol="Button_upSkin");
}
```

The Final Product

After you've gone through those steps, go ahead and run the application. You should see your **button** skins change as you interact with it (see Figure 5.1-12). You also see your newly skinned button in MXML Design View.

> **Note**
>
> To see how the disabled skin looks, set enabled="false" on the Button component and run the application.

Figure 5.1-12   The skinned button

> **Note**
>
> You can access the final Flex and Flash asset files in a folder called FlashButtonExample at http://www.cveflex.com.

Taking This Example Further

This example illustrates how you can take artwork from Flash and use it for skins in Flex. There are a number of ways you can take it further.

The skins you created were relatively simple. You could add shading, highlights, and shapes in addition to creating skins for the other parts of the button. It always helps to experiment with setting the 9-slice guides to different locations or changing the positions of the artwork within a symbol to see what the effects are to the skin.

> **Tip**
>
> You can add artwork for multiple components into one FLA file and reference them accordingly by using their symbol names. This is great for keeping all your skins in one place and makes it easy to refer to different skin parts to maintain consistency. Figure 5.1-13 is an example of this.

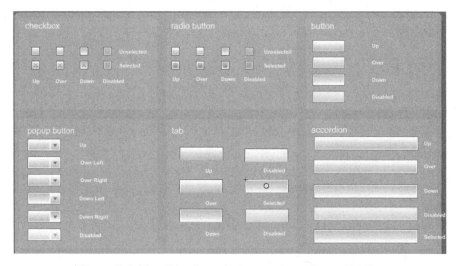

Figure 5.1-13   Skins for multiple components in one FLA file

Note

You can use multiple symbols when working with Flash CS3 by using the `Embed` statement in Flex that specifies the source and symbol. As mentioned, this method is not preferred, but that's for you to determine as there may be scenarios when you may feel it is appropriate to use this method.

Tip

When creating a skin set in Flash, consider placing a text label of each symbol name next to the corresponding symbol. This helps make figuring out the name of each skin part easy. You may also want to make the text labels selectable so any developer can pop open the published SWF or SWC to copy and paste symbol names wherever they may be needed. Text in Flash CS3 can be made selectable by selecting the text and checking the *selectable* toggle button in the Properties panel, as shown in Figure 5.1-14.

Selectable toggle button

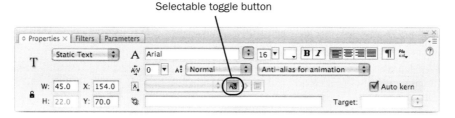

Figure 5.1-14   Setting text as selectable

Using this approach in Flash is not limited to just creating skins. You can also create icons, backgrounds, static graphics, and more using the same steps. The only difference may be in the way that you apply those graphics to your MXML layout.

Using Bitmap Assets in Flash

One of the nice things about Flash is that you can include bitmap graphics in movie clips. As mentioned, grouping your skin assets in one SWC or SWF file is a great way to keep your assets together. You can include graphics that you export as bitmaps from Photoshop, Fireworks, Illustrator, or another source in a skin file you might create in Flash.

If you're planning on using bitmap assets in Flash, there are a few things you need to be aware of.

- Currently, if you try to assign 9-slice grids to a bitmap asset in Flash, it will not work. This is something Adobe is working on, so it is advised that you check to see if this has been fixed.

- You can mix vector and bitmap assets into one movie clip; however, the 9-slice grids will not work on the bitmap portions as mentioned above.

Skin Templates for Flash

In Chapter 5, you read about the Skin Design Extensions and how they include skin templates for you to get started. However, with the changes from Flex 2 to Flex 3, the skin template was rendered obsolete. The new preferred method for creating skins does include a skin template and is discussed in Exercise 12.1.

If you need some kind of starting point, you can visit http://www.scalenine.com and download the altered skins to get you going. The majority of the skins there were created using Flash and targeted Flex 2.

Summary

In this exercise, you learned how to create skins using Flash, set 9-slice guides to prevent your graphics from distorting, and implemented a button skin in Flex. You can repeat this process as needed to skin additional components as your application evolves. There is another way to skin Flex components using the Flex Component Kit. Using the Flex Component Kit to create skins allows for transitions between states and additional motion. You can read more about using the Flex Component Kit in Chapter 12.

For more information and quick start examples of skins created in Flash, visit http://www.scalenine.com or check out Adobe's article on the topic at http://www.adobe.com/devnet/flex/articles/skins_styles.html.

Creating a Graphical Skin with Illustrator

Adobe Illustrator is a vector editing tool that allows you to export assets in a variety of formats. In Illustrator CS3, there is more integration with Flex and easier workflows to bring your final artwork into Flex. Similar to Flash, you can use symbols and export your skins as a SWF (pronounced "swif") to be used in Flex. In this exercise, you will learn how to create skins for Flex using Illustrator.

> **Note**
>
> Some of this may have changed with Adobe CS4 coming out for each of the tools mentioned— Illustrator, Flash, Fireworks, and Photoshop. For updates please go to http://www.cveflex.com/.

Using Illustrator, you can create skins for a Flex application using some of the same techniques and tools you would normally use to create vector artwork. Each skin-part of a component, cursor, background, icon, and so on must be a separate symbol before you can export it for use in Flex. For example, for a button, you would need to create separate symbols for the up, over, down, and disabled states.

There are some pros and cons when working with Illustrator versus using Flash, Fireworks, or Photoshop. A primary benefit of using Illustrator is if you're already familiar with the tool you'll be able to get going very quickly. Illustrator also has some precision tools, like a Pen tool, that is arguably better than other Adobe CS3 products. Some downsides include the inability to use transparency on gradient colors, lack of support for "live" display of artwork that uses 9-slice scaling, and the fact that each skin part must be a separate symbol.

> **Note**
>
> You can also mix and match the Adobe CS3 tools to create your skins. For example, you can create skin artwork in Illustrator, then copy and paste that same artwork into Flash to make use of additional features Flash has to offer, like transparency on gradient colors.

Getting Started

In this section, you will walk through the process of skinning a Button component using Illustrator CS3 to look like Figure 5.2-1. To help with the skin creation process in Illustrator, you also need to download the Flex Skin Design Extension for Illustrator. You can download the extension from http://www.adobe.com/cfusion/entitlement/index.cfm?e=flex_ skins. Install the extension after you download it. For instructions on how to install the necessary files, refer to the ReadMe.txt file included with the download.

Figure 5.2-1   The button skinned with
the artwork you'll create in Illustrator

Creating the Artwork

The first part of skinning a component, in this case a `button`, is understanding which parts of the component can be skinned. If you refer to Appendix A, "Skinning Styling Diagrams," you will see that a `button` can have skins for the up, over, down, and disabled states. In this example, you will create skins for each of those states.

1. In Illustrator, create a new Web Document that is 160 pixels wide by 200 pixels high. Make sure the document color mode is RGB. Save this file as IllustratorButton.ai.

2. The first thing you need to create is the `upSkin` for the button. Using the Rectangle Tool, draw a rectangle that is 80 pixels wide by 22 pixels high. Change the fill of the rectangle to white and the border stroke color to a dark gray (77,77,77).

3. Add another rectangle on top that is 76 pixels wide by 18 pixels high. Fill this rectangle with a vertical linear gradient with a light blue (41,171,226) on top and a dark blue (0,113,118) on bottom. You should have something similar to Figure 5.2-2.

> **Note**
>
> Transparency effects such as Multiply, Lighten, Overlay, and so on will not translate into Flex. If you need to use these types of effects, consider using Photoshop.

Figure 5.2-2   Button upSkin

4. For the `overSkin`, duplicate the artwork you created for your `upSkin` in Figure 5.2-2. Change the top gradient fill color to a lighter blue (148,213,241). That's all you need to do for the `overSkin`, which should look something like Figure 5.2-3.

Figure 5.2-3   Button overSkin

5. For the `downSkin`, duplicate the `upSkin` you made (see Figure 5.2-2). All that needs to be done for this skin is to reverse the gradient so the light blue color is at the bottom and the dark blue is at the top. This gives the impression that the button is being inset. You should now have artwork that looks something like Figure 5.2-4.

Figure 5.2-4   Button downSkin

6. Finally, for the `disabledSkin`, duplicate the `upSkin` and change the fill colors to a light gray (153,153,153) on top and a dark gray (102,102,102) on the bottom (see Figure 5.2-5).

Figure 5.2-5   Button disabledSkin

7. With the artwork for your `button` skins created, you must now convert them into symbols so they can be referenced in Flex. Make sure the Symbols window is open (Window > Symbols). Select the artwork that you created for the `upSkin` (see Figure 5.2-2). In the Symbols window, select New Symbol from the options dropdown. Name the Symbol Button_upSkin, select MovieClip, select Enable Guides for 9-Slice Scaling, and click OK (see Figure 5.2-6).

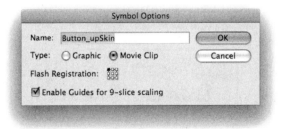

Figure 5.2-6   Creating a symbol

> **Note**
>
> The reason you name the symbols like this is to make the skin export and import process run smoothly. To learn more about this naming convention, refer to Chapter 5, "Graphical Skinning."

8. When you click OK, you should see the Button_upSkin added to your list of symbols. Repeat the same process for the Button_overSkin, Button_downSkin, and Button_disabledSkin. When you're finished, you'll have four symbols in your Symbol palette (see Figure 5.2-7).

Figure 5.2-7   Button skin artwork converted to symbols

9. The last step for preparing your artwork to be used in Flex is to set the 9-slice grids. If you double-click on a symbol on your artboard, you are shown the guides for the 9-slice grid. You should set these guides appropriately so the artwork does not distort when you scale your skin as in Figure 5.2-8.

> **Note**
>
> You may need to unlock your guides in Illustrator to move the 9-slice guides (View > Guides > Unlock Guides).

> **Note**
>
> Unlike Flash and Illustrator, any artwork that has 9-slice guides applied to it still distorts when working in Illustrator. The effect of 9-slice guides is not apparent until you take the skin into Flex.

Figure 5.2-8   Setting the 9-slice guides

By completing these steps, you've successfully created the skin artwork for a button and your Illustrator file should look similar to Figure 5.2-9. The next steps are to get the artwork you created into Flex.

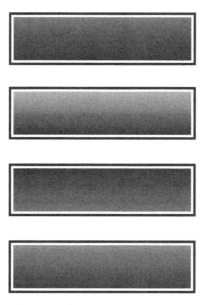

Figure 5.2-9   The final Illustrator file

Taking Your Skin Artwork into Flex

In these next steps, you'll apply the artwork you created as skins to a `Button` component.

1. Before you prepare your Illustrator artwork to be used as skins, you need to create a new project in Flex Builder 3. Open up Flex Builder, if you don't have it open already, and create a new Flex Project called IllustratorButton (File > New > Flex Project). After filling in the project name information, click Finish.

2. Inside of the src folder, create a new folder called style. Inside the style folder, create a new CSS file called style.css.

3. With a little prep work finished in Flex Builder, go back to Illustrator. Now you're ready to export your Illustrator artwork to be used in Flex.

    In Illustrator, select File > Scripts > Flex Skin > Export Flex Skin. Browse for the style folder you created in your IllustratorButton Flex Project. Name your export file IllustratorButton_Skins and click Save. Your skins are saved as a SWF.

4. Go back to Flex Builder to import your skins. Select File > Import > Skin Artwork to bring up the Skin Import Wizard.

5. On the first screen of the Skin Import Wizard, select SWC or SWF File for the Import Skins From option and browse for the IllustratorButton_Skins.swf file you saved in the style folder.

6. You will notice that the Copy Artwork to Subfolder option is grayed out. This is because the SWF file you specified is already in your Flex Project. If you had selected a SWF file outside of your Flex Project, you would be able to specify a location to copy those external assets to.

7. For the Create Skin Style Rules In option, browse for the style.css file you created earlier. You can leave everything else as it is, but make sure IllustratorButton.mxml is selected in the Attach Style Sheet to Application.

Note

You don't always have to create a CSS file before using the Skin Import Wizard. The wizard generates one for you if you specify a file name in the Create Skin Style Rules In area rather than browsing for a file.

8. With those details specified, similar to Figure 5.2-10, click Next.

Figure 5.2-10   Specifying assets in the Skin Import Wizard

9. On the next screen of the Skin Import Wizard, you'll see a data grid showing your skin artwork file names next to the component (Style Selector) and Skin Part they'll be applied to. Leave them all checked as in Figure 5.2-11 and click Finish.

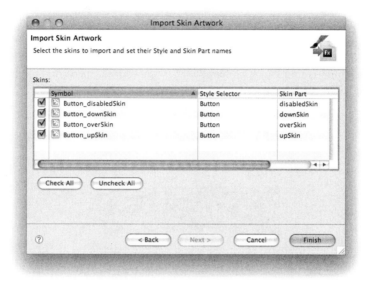

Figure 5.2-11   Selecting the skin assets

Tip

You can change the Style Selector or Skin Part that an Image asset will be assigned to by clicking a name in either of the columns.

10. When you click Finish, the Skin Import Wizard writes out the required CSS code to apply the graphic assets you created in Illustrator as skins for your `ComboBox` and attaches the CSS file to your application inside an `<mx:Style>` tag. If you open up your style.css file, you should see CSS code like Listing 5.2-1.

Listing 5.2-1   **Generated CSS code**

```
Button
{
    disabledSkin: Embed(source="IllustratorButton_Skins.swf",
                        symbol="Button_disabledSkin");
    downSkin: Embed(source="IllustratorButton_Skins.swf",
                        symbol="Button_downSkin");
    overSkin: Embed(source="IllustratorButton_Skins.swf",
                        symbol="Button_overSkin");
```

Listing 5.2-1   **Continued**

```
    upSkin: Embed(source="IllustratorButton_Skins.swf",
                  symbol="Button_upSkin");
}
```

11. With your graphic assets imported and CSS file created, you can now preview what your newly skinned button looks like. In your IllustratorButton.mxml file, add a Button component. Run your application to see your skinned combo box as in Figure 5.2-12.

Note

To see how the disabled skin looks, set `enabled="false"` on the Button component and run the application.

Figure 5.2-12   The skinned button

The Final Product

When you run your application, you should see the skins you created show up appropriately. As you interact with the button, you will see the different skin states you created. You can access the final Flex and Illustrator asset files in a folder called IllustratorButtonExample.

Taking This Example Further

This example illustrates how you can take artwork from Illustrator and use it for skins in Flex. There are a number of ways you can take it further. The skins you created were relatively simple. You could add shading, highlights, shapes, and create skins for the other parts of the `Button component`, like the selected states. It always helps to experiment with setting the 9-slice guides to different locations or changing the positions of the artwork to see what the effects are to the skin.

Creating Other Assets

Using this approach in Illustrator, you can create skins for other components; however, you can do more than create skins. You can also create icons, backgrounds, static graphics, and more using the same steps and referencing the relative properties like `upIcon`, `backgroundImage`, `borderSkin`, and so on. The only difference may be in the way that you apply those graphics to your MXML layout.

> **Tip**
>
> Symbols are also a great way to create design mockups quickly because you can easily drop in different component skins as you build the UI. Also, whenever you update a symbol, it will update throughout your document.

Using Skin Templates

Adobe has made available a set of Flex component skin templates that you can use as a starting point to create your own custom skins. These skin templates came with the Illustrator Skin Design Extension you installed in the "Getting Started" section in the beginning of this section.

With the extension installed, you can easily create a new skin for a single component or for all the Flex components. To access the skin templates in Illustrator, select File > Scripts > Flex Skin > Create Flex Skin. Upon doing so, you get a window (see Figure 5.2-13) that allows you to specify the Script to create skins for Multiple Flex Components or a Specific Component.

Figure 5.2-13   Creating a Flex Skin from a template

If you select Multiple Flex Components, you get an AI file with a template that has nearly all the Flex component skins there for you to customize. Selecting a skin for a Specific Component allows you to specify some additional options.

One option you have for a Specific Component is to create a skin to be applied to a Default Style of a component—for example, if you'd like the same look for all your buttons. If you choose this option and click OK, you are given a template that is set up to be used as a skin for all instances of the component you selected—that is, the symbols are named appropriately using a Type selector—for example, Button_upSkin, Button_overSkin, and so on.

The other option for a Specific Component is to create a skin to be applied to instances with a specified style name. For example, you could specify a style name of `blueButton` in the input. When you click OK, the Layers are named to reflect the style name you specified—for example, using `blueButton` as the style name, you would get Layer names of Button_blueButton_upSkin, Button_blueButton_overSkin, and so on.

After you customize the artwork in a template, you can export them to be used in Flex using the same techniques discussed in this section.

> **Note**
>
> Not all skinnable parts of a component are represented in these templates—for example, skins for Alert, drop-down, and other focus skins are not included. In some cases, you may need to create skins for those missing skins from scratch.

Summary

In this exercise, you learned how to create skins using Illustrator, set 9-slice guides to prevent your graphics from distorting, and implemented a button skin in Flex. You can repeat this process as needed to skin additional components as your application evolves or use the discussed skin templates as a starting point.

For more information on creating skins, check out Adobe's article at http://www.adobe.com/devnet/flex/articles/skins_styles.html.

5.3

Creating a Graphical
Skin with Fireworks

If you're familiar with Fireworks, you know it's an editor that exports bitmap graphics. Fireworks is different from other bitmap-based editors such as Photoshop because you can create artwork that can be manipulated like vector artwork, but becomes rasterized when exported for production usage. In this exercise, you will learn how to create skins for Flex using Fireworks.

Similar to Flash and Illustrator, you have the ability in Fireworks to create *symbols*. However, these *symbols* are used more for repurposing artwork and doing interface mockups than for exporting skin artwork.

To create skins for your Flex components in Fireworks, you export bitmap assets, such as a JPEG, GIF, or PNG, for each skinnable component part including states, icons, cursors, and so on. For example, skins for a button may include a separate PNG file for the up, over, down, and disable states.

Just like creating skins in other CS3 applications, there are a few standards that help you create skins in Fireworks. There are naming conventions, file organization methods, and tools at your disposal. As you go through this section, you'll be exposed to a number of these useful standards.

There are some pros and cons when working with Fireworks versus using Flash, Illustrator, or Photoshop. A primary benefit of using Fireworks is if you're already very familiar with the tool, you'll be able to get going very quickly. Fireworks allows use of bitmap filters, transparency on gradient colors, bitmap fills, vector-supported graphics, and "live" display of artwork that uses 9-slice scaling. Some downsides include the final export of assets as bitmaps and lack of support for carrying 9-slice values into Flex.

> **Note**
>
> You can also mix and match the Adobe CS3 tools to create your skins. For example, you can create skin artwork in Fireworks, then copy and paste that same artwork into Flash to make use of additional features Flash has to offer, like full vector support. However, you may need

to remove any filters you created in Fireworks when you paste that artwork in Flash. Pasted artwork from Fireworks into Flash may also require further refinement of the graphics to make sure they properly translate into Flex.

Getting Started

In this section, you will walk through the process of creating skins for a Button component using Fireworks CS3 to look like Figure 5.3-1. To help with the skin creation process in Fireworks, you also need to download the Flex Skin Design Extension for Fireworks. You can download the extension from http://www.adobe.com/cfusion/entitlement/index.cfm?e=flex_skins. Install the extension after you download it.

Figure 5.3-1   The button skinned with
the artwork you'll create in Fireworks

Creating the Artwork

As mentioned, you will be creating skins for a `button` from scratch. If you refer to Appendix A, "Skinning Styling Diagrams," you'll see that a button has skins for its states, including up, over, down, and disabled. In this exercise, you will be creating the `upSkin`, `overSkin`, `downSkin`, and `disabledSkin` for a button.

1. In Fireworks, create a new file at the default size (200 by 300 pixels) and resolution (72 dpi). Save this file as FireworksButton.png.

2. Before you start to create your skin artwork, you need to set up some additional file structure. Make sure the Layers window is open (Window > Layers) and create layers named Button_upSkin, Button_overSkin, Button_downSkin, and Button_disabledSkin. You Layers palette should look something like Figure 5.3-2.

> **Note**
>
> The reason you're creating these Layers and naming them like this is to make the skin export function runs smoothly. Basically, when the Export Flex Skin function is executed, it takes each folder that follows the naming convention mentioned in Chapter 5, "Graphical Skinning," flattens it, and saves it as a single PNG file. This is done for each folder.

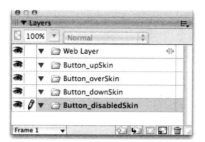

Figure 5.3-2   Layers palette with structure

3. The first thing you'll create is the upSkin for the button. On the Button_upSkin Layer, draw a rectangle that is 88 pixels wide by 22 pixels high using the Rectangle Tool. Change the fill color to white and add a 1-pixel stroke that is dark gray (#636363).

4. On top of that rectangle, draw a rectangle that is 76 pixels wide by 18 pixels high. Set a vertical linear gradient fill with light blue on top (#26A7DF) and dark blue (#0375BF) on bottom. Center this rectangle vertically and horizontally on top of the other rectangle as in Figure 5.3-3.

Figure 5.3-3   Button upSkin

Tip

When doing design mockups in Fireworks, consider using symbols for various UI elements. This speeds up the production process. You can access the Symbols palette by selecting Window > Common Library.

Note

Symbols in Fireworks are different than symbols in Flash or Illustrator in that they are not directly referenced when used in Flex.

5. Next, create the over skin by duplicating the upSkin artwork (see Figure 5.3-2) onto the Button_overSkin layer. Change the vertical blue gradient fill to use a lighter blue (#90D3F0) on top and keep the existing dark blue (#0375BF). Your overSkin artwork should look like Figure 5.3-4.

Figure 5.3-4   Button overSkin

6. For the downSkin, duplicate the upSkin artwork (see Figure 5.3-2) onto the Button_downSkin layer. To give the look that the button is inset when pressed, flip the vertical gradient as in Figure 5.3-5.

Tip

Consider creating styles in Fireworks to speed up the design process when creating application mockups (Window > Styles). This practice promotes consistency because styles are based on predefined rules, which translate to each object that has that style applied to it.

Figure 5.3-5   Button downSkin

7. Finally, create the disabledSkin by duplicating the upSkin artwork (see Figure 5.3-2) onto the Button_disabledSkin layer. Change the gradient colors to light gray (#A6A8AB) on top and dark gray (#838588) on bottom. You should have something like Figure 5.3-6 for your disabledSkin artwork.

Figure 5.3-6   Button disabledSkin

8. Your final Fireworks file may look something like Figure 5.3-7 and your Layers structure should look similar to Figure 5.3-8. With the skin artwork created, you can now take them into Flex.

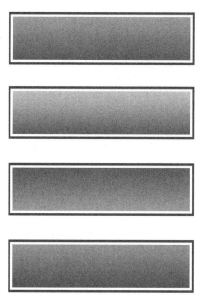

Figure 5.3-7   Created skin artwork

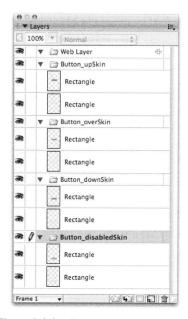

Figure 5.3-8   Final Layers structure

Bringing Your Skins into Flex

Now that you've successfully created the artwork for your custom skins, you can move on to preparing and exporting the assets to be used in Flex.

1. Open up Flex Builder 3 and create a new Flex Project called FireworksButton. After you name your project, click Finish.

2. In the src folder of your project, create a folder called style; in that folder, create a new CSS file called style.css (File > New > CSS file). Also in the style folder, create a folder called skins. This folder will hold your skin assets.

3. Go back to your FireworksButton.png file in Fireworks and select Commands > Flex Skinning > Export Flex Skin.

4. Browse to the location of the Flex Project folder you created called FireworksButton and select the skins folder. After you've selected that folder, click Choose.

   Success! Your graphical assets have now been exported and you can switch back to Flex Builder.

5. With your graphical assets prepared for Flex, you can now import them to be used in your project. To do this, select File > Import > Skin Artwork.

6. On the first screen, shown in Figure 5.3-9, select Folder of Bitmaps for the Import Skins From option, and browse for the skins folder in your project. For the Create Skin Style Rules In field, browse for the style.css file you created previously. Click Next.

> **Note**
>
> Notice that in this example the Copy Artwork to Subfolder option is grayed out. This is because the artwork you specified is already in your Flex Project. Had they been outside of the project, you could specify a separate location to copy the artwork into.
>
> You don't always have to create a CSS file before using the Skin Import Wizard. The wizard generates one for you if you specify a file name in the Create Skin Style Rules In area rather than browsing for a file.

7. On the next screen, shown in Figure 5.3-10, you'll see check boxes next to the different skins that will be applied to the `button`. Leave them all checked and click Finish.

> **Tip**
>
> You can change the Style Selector or Skin Part that an Image asset will be assigned to by clicking a name in either of the columns as in Figure 5.3-11.

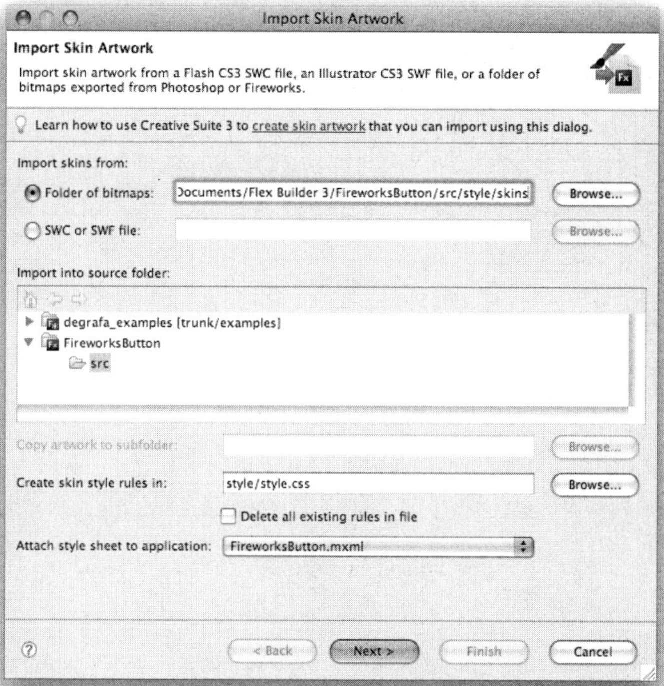

Figure 5.3-9   Skin Import Wizard

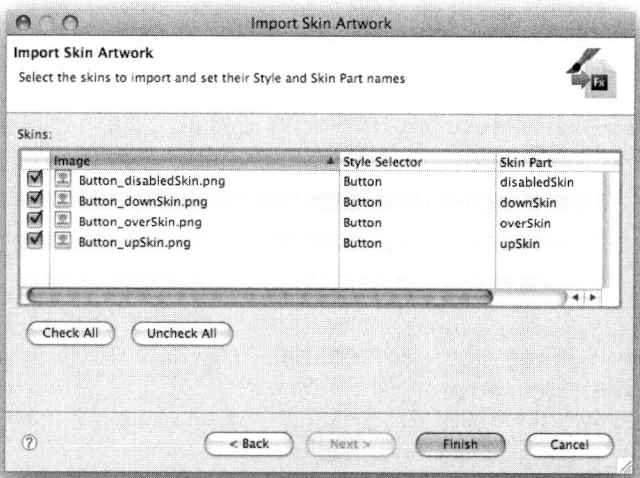

Figure 5.3-10   Skin Import Wizard

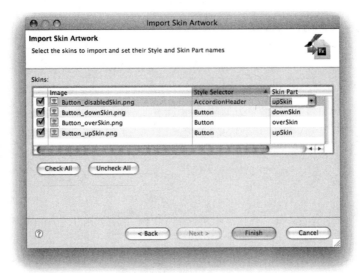

Figure 5.3-11   Editing the Style Selector and/or Skin Part

8. When you click Finish, the Skin Import Wizard writes out the required CSS code to apply the graphic assets you created in Fireworks as skins for your **button** and attaches the CSS file to your application inside an **<mx:Style>** tag. If you open up your style.css file, you should see CSS code like Listing 5.3-1.

Listing 5.3-1   **Generated CSS code**

```
Button
{
        disabledSkin:       Embed(source="skins/Button_disabledSkin.png");
        downSkin:           Embed(source="skins/Button_downSkin.png");
        overSkin:           Embed(source="skins/Button_overSkin.png");
        upSkin:             Embed(source="skins/Button_upSkin.png");
}
```

9. Next, you need to set the 9-slice grid values in the embed statement to make sure your Button will stretch without distorting when you have buttons of different sizes. With the style.css file open, click on the Design View button. You can now set the 9-slice grids on the **button** skins as in Figure 5.3-12.

Notice that when you change the positioning of a guide, that positioning changes on all the other skin states. For whatever reason, if you need to have different positioning of the

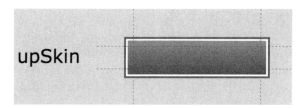

Figure 5.3-12   Setting the scale grid guides

9-slice grids on each skin, you can change the values that are generated in the CSS file (see Listing 5.3-2).

To learn more about working with the scale grid in CSS Design View, refer to Chapter 5.

Listing 5.3-2   **CSS and scale grid values**

```
Button
{
    disabledSkin: Embed(source="skins/Button_disabledSkin.png",
                        scaleGridLeft="5",
                        scaleGridTop="5",
                        scaleGridRight="75",
                        scaleGridBottom="17");
    downSkin: Embed(source="skins/Button_downSkin.png",
                        scaleGridLeft="5",
                        scaleGridTop="5",
                        scaleGridRight="75",
                        scaleGridBottom="17");
    overSkin: Embed(source="skins/Button_overSkin.png",
                        scaleGridLeft="5",
                        scaleGridTop="5",
                        scaleGridRight="75",
                        scaleGridBottom="17");
    upSkin: Embed(source="skins/Button_upSkin.png",
                        scaleGridLeft="5",
                        scaleGridTop="5",
                        scaleGridRight="75",
                        scaleGridBottom="17");
}
```

10. With your graphic assets imported and CSS file created, you can now preview what your newly skinned button looks like. In your FireworksButton.mxml file, add a Button component and run the application.

The Finished Product

If you run your application, you'll see your skins come alive. As you interact with the button in the application, you should see each skin for the different Button states (see Figure 5.3-13). You will also see your skinned button in the MXML Design View. You may need to refresh the view to display the newly skinned button. To see your disabled skin, set `enabled="false"` in your Button MXML.

> **Note**
>
> Skinned components only render in the main application file. To get a true sense of the look of a skinned component, you need to run/compile your application.

Figure 5.3-13   The skinned Button

> **Note**
>
> You can access the final Flex and Fireworks asset files in a folder called FireworksButtonExample.

Taking This Example Further

This example illustrates how you can take artwork from Fireworks and use it for skins in Flex. There are a number of ways you can take it further.

The skins you created were relatively simple. You could add shading, highlights, and shapes and create skins for the other parts of a `button`. It always helps to experiment with setting the 9-slice guides to different locations or changing the positions of the artwork to see what the effects are to the skin.

Creating Other Assets

Using this approach in Fireworks is not limited to just creating skins. You can also create icons, backgrounds, static graphics, and more using the same steps. The only difference may be in the way that you apply those graphics to your MXML layout. Refer to Appendix A, "Skinning and Styling Diagrams," to see where else you might like to implement skins.

If you're planning on using any bitmap assets in Flash, you may want to refer to Exercise 5.1 for more information.

Using Skin Templates

Included with the Flex Skin Design Extension for Fireworks are skin templates for Flex components. After the Skin Design Extension is installed, you can access these templates in Fireworks by selecting Commands > Flex Skinning > New Flex Skin (see Figure 5.3-14).

Figure 5.3-14   New Flex Skin window

When you select to make a new skin, you have the option to create a skin for a type of component, like Button, ComboBox, and so on, or create a skin for a variation of a component, like blueButton, orangeButton, and so on. For more information on Type selectors and Class selectors, refer to Chapter 4.

After making changes to a template, you can export the artwork using the preceding process, Commands > Flex Skinning > Export Flex Skin. After exporting the artwork, you can use the steps covered in this section to get your skin artwork working in Flex.

Note

Not all skinnable parts of a component are represented in these templates. For example, skins for Alert, drop-down, and other focus skins are not included. In some cases, you may need to create skins for those missing skins from scratch.

Tip

Consider making your own templates to be repurposed while working to customize your user interface.

Summary

In this exercise, you learned how to create skins using Fireworks, set 9–slice guides to prevent your graphics from distorting, and implemented a button skin in Flex. You can repeat this process as needed to skin additional components as your application evolves or use the discussed skin templates as a starting point.

For more information on creating skins, check out Adobe's article at http://www.adobe.com/devnet/flex/articles/skins_styles.html.

Creating a Graphical Skin with Photoshop

If you're familiar with Photoshop, you know it is a pixel-based editing tool. The artwork you create in Photoshop can be exported as a PNG, JPEG, or GIF to be used in Flex to customize your applications. Photoshop can be one of the more involved of the CS3 applications to create custom user interfaces for Flex, but if it's an application you're most comfortable with you shouldn't be deterred. In this exercise, you will learn how to create skins for Flex using Photoshop.

With Photoshop, you can use layers to create bitmap artwork to compose your Flex application design. You can use this artwork as exported PNGs, JPEGs, or GIFs for various UI elements like skins, cursors, backgrounds, icons, and more. Each skin part must be a separate graphic asset when using bitmaps.

Just like creating skins in other CS3 applications, there are a few standards that will help you create skins in Photoshop. There are naming conventions, file organization methods, and tools at your disposal. As you go through this section, you'll be exposed to a number of these useful standards.

There are some pros and cons when working with Photoshop versus using Flash, Illustrator, or Fireworks. A primary benefit of using Photoshop is that if you're already very familiar with the tool you'll be able to get going very quickly. Photoshop allows you to create very photorealistic visuals. Some downsides include the final export of assets as bitmaps, lack of any support for 9-slice guides, and a difficult workflow for skinning Flex applications.

Note

You can also mix and match the Adobe CS3 tools to create your skins. For example, you can create skin artwork in Photoshop, then copy and paste that same artwork into Flash.

Getting Started

In this section, you will walk through the process of creating skins for a Button component using Photoshop CS3 to look like Figure 5.4-1. To help with the skin creation process in Photoshop, you also need to download the Flex Skin Design Extension for Photoshop. You can download the extension from http://labs.adobe.com/cfusin/entitlement/ index.cfm?e=flex_skins. Install the extension after you download it. For instructions on how to install the necessary files, refer to the ReadMe.txt file included with the download.

Figure 5.4-1   The button skinned with
the artwork you'll create in Photoshop

Creating the Artwork

As mentioned, you will be creating skins for a Button component. If you refer to Appendix A, "Styling and Skinning Diagrams," you'll see that a button has skins for the up, over, down, and disabled states. In this example, you will be skinning each of these states to create a custom button skin.

1. In Photoshop, create a new file 160 pixels wide by 200 pixels high, make the background transparent, and the color space RGB. Change the name of Layer 1 to _HIDE and fill it with the color white. Save this file as PhotoshopButton.psd.

2. Before you start creating artwork, you need to set up a folder structure within the Layers palette. With the Layers palette open (Window > Layers), create Group Folders called Button_upSkin, Button_overSkin, Button_downSkin, and Button_disabledSkin. Your Layers palette should look like Figure 5.4-2.

Note

The reason you are creating these Group Folders and naming them like this is to make the skin export and import process run smoothly. When you get to the point of exporting your artwork, each folder that follows the naming convention mentioned in Chapter 5, "Graphical Skinning," gets flattened and saved as a single PNG file. This is done for each folder.

Tip

If you aren't familiar with Photoshop, Groups are great ways to keep your layers organized as you create more involved skin compositions.

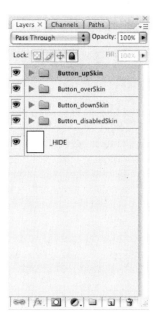

Figure 5.4-2   Layers palette structure

3. The first thing you need to create is the Button_upSkin. Create a new Layer inside of the folder you created called Button_upSkin and name the layer background.

4. On this new Layer, select the Rectangular Marquee Tool and create a selection that is 80 pixels wide by 22 pixels high. Fill that selection with white and add a Stroke effect that is 1 pixel wide, has 100% opacity, and a color of #636363.

Tip

Consider using Layer effects for creating rich, composite skin artwork. It makes it much easier to change the affected layers later.

5. Create a new layer above the background layer and name it gradient. Select the Rectangular Marquee Tool and create a selection that is 76 pixels wide by 18 pixels high. Using the Gradient Tool, fill this selection with a vertical linear gradient with light blue (#26A7DF) on top and dark blue (#0375BF) on the bottom. You should have an artwork that looks like Figure 5.4-3.

Figure 5.4-3 Button upSkin

Tip

When creating design mockups, you can use the Styles palette (Window > Styles) for creating stylized effects that can be easily repurposed with a simple selection. After you create a style, just select a layer and select a style to apply it. This helps maintain consistency as you're designing and can save time.

6. Create the overSkin by duplicating the Button_upSkin group and rename it Button_overSkin. In this renamed group, make a marquee selection of the gradient layer. Using the Gradient Tool, fill the selection with a vertical linear gradient with a lighter blue (#90D3F0) on top and the same dark blue (#0375BF) on the bottom. This artwork should look similar to Figure 5.4-4.

Figure 5.4-4 Button overSkin

7. For the button downSkin, duplicate the Button_upSkin group and name it Button_downSkin. All you need to do with this artwork is flip the gradient layer to give the impression that the button is inset when pressed.

To do this, you can either Transform the gradient layer (Edit > Free Transform) and Flip Vertical, or make a marquee selection of the gradient layer and fill it with a vertical linear gradient with dark blue (#0172BD) on top and light blue (#27A7E0) on the bottom. Using either method should give you something that looks like Figure 5.4-5.

Figure 5.4-5 Button downSkin

8. The last piece of artwork you need to create is the Button_disabledSkin. Again, duplicate the Button_upSkin and name it Button_disabledSkin. Make a marquee selection of the gradient layer and fill the selection with a vertical linear gradient with light gray (#A6A8AB) on top and dark gray (#838688) on the bottom. You should have artwork that looks like Figure 5.4-6.

Figure 5.4-6 Button disabledSkin

By completing these steps, you've successfully created the artwork for your button skin, and your Photoshop file should look similar to Figure 5.4-7. The next steps are to get the artwork you created into Flex.

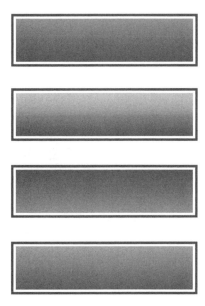

Figure 5.4-7 Final button skin artwork

Taking Your Skin Artwork into Flex

In these next steps, you'll apply the artwork you created in Photoshop to the `Button` component as skins.

1. Before you prepare your Photoshop artwork to be used as skins, you need to create a new project in Flex Builder 3. Open up Flex Builder if you don't have it open already and create a new Flex Project called PhotoshopButton (File > New > Flex Project). After filling in the project name information, click Finish.

2. Inside of the src folder, create a new folder called Style. Inside the Style folder, create a new CSS file called style.css.

3. With a little prep work finished in Flex Builder, go back to Photoshop. Now you're ready to export your Photoshop artwork to be used in Flex.

   Make sure the artwork in each group is not overlapping another group. Also, hide the layer called _HIDE.

4. Merge each group into a layer and make sure it maintains the folder names of Button_upSkin, Button_overSkin, and so on as in Figure 5.4-8. You can do this by selecting a group and select Layer > Merge Group.

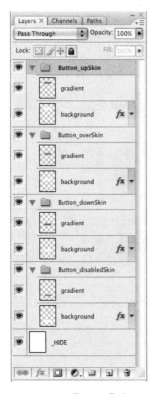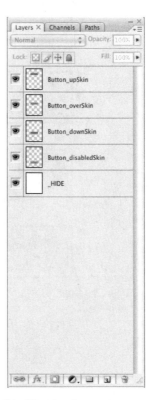

Figure 5.4-8 Flattening the skin artwork

> **Note**
>
> You don't have to use Group Folders. The most important thing is to make sure that your final merged Layers are named properly using the naming convention.

5. Save those changes, but if you ever need to close the file, make sure that you Undo to an unflattened version. Otherwise, you have to rebuild all the skin artwork to edit it.

6. Select File > Scripts > Export Flex Skin. Navigate to the style folder in your PhotoshopButton Flex Project folder and click Choose.

    When you click Choose, you'll see Photoshop create and save all your separate graphics out as PNGs in a folder called assets. This folder helps to keep all the individual PNG files together so they don't "overrun" your style folder.

7. Now that your skins have been exported from Photoshop, you can go back to Flex Builder to apply them to the Button component. To import your skin artwork, you can use the Skin Artwork Import Wizard. Select File > Import > Skin Artwork from the Flex Builder file menu.

8. On the first screen of the wizard, you are presented with some options. Select Folder of Bitmaps for the Import Skins From option and Browse for the skins folder where you export your Photoshop artwork to.

9. You will notice that the Copy Artwork to Subfolder option is grayed out. This is because the folder of assets you specified is already in your Flex Project. If you had selected a folder of assets outside of your Flex Project, you would be able to specify a location to copy those external assets to.

10. For the Create Skin Style Rules In option, browse for the style.css file you created earlier. You can leave everything else as it is, but make sure PhotoshopButton.mxml is selected in the Attach Style Sheet to Application.

11. With those details specified like Figure 5.4-9, click Next.

12. On the next screen of the Skin Import Wizard, you'll see a data grid showing your skin artwork file names next to the component (Style Selector) and Skin Part they'll be applied to. Leave them all checked as in Figure 5.4-10 and click Finish.

> **Note**
>
> You can uncheck an item if you don't want that asset to be assigned as a skin.

> **Note**
>
> You can change the Style Selector or Skin Part that an Image asset will be assigned to by clicking a name in either of the columns, as in Figure 5.4-11.

Figure 5.4-9   Specifying assets and CSS file

Figure 5.4-10   Assigning the skins

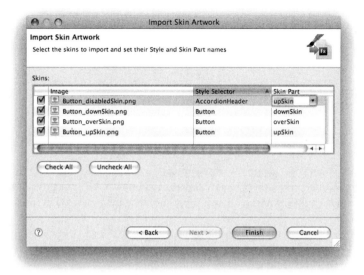

Figure 5.4-11   Editing the Style Selector and/or Skin Part

13. When you click Finish, the Skin Import Wizard writes out the required CSS code to apply the graphic assets you created in Photoshop as skins for your `button` and attaches the CSS file to your application inside an `<mx:Style>` tag. If you open up your style.css file, you should see CSS code like Listing 5.4-1.

Listing 5.4-1   **Generated CSS code**

```
Button
{
    disabledSkin: Embed(source="assets/Button_disabledSkin.png");
    downSkin: Embed(source="assets/Button_downSkin.png");
    overSkin: Embed(source="assets/Button_overSkin.png");
    upSkin: Embed(source="assets/Button_upSkin.png");
}
```

14. Set the 9-slice grid values in the embed statement to make sure your button will stretch without distorting when you have buttons of different sizes. With the style.css file open, click on the Design View button. You can now set the 9-slice grids on the `button` skins as in Figure 5.4-12.

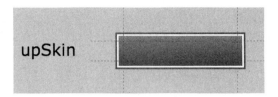

Figure 5.4-12   Setting the Scale Grid guides

Notice that when you change the positioning of a guide, that positioning changes on all the other skin states. For whatever reason, if you need to have different positioning of the 9-slice grids on each skin, you can change the values that are generated in the CSS file (see Listing 5.4-2).

To learn more about working with the scale grid in CSS Design View, refer to Chapter 5.

Listing 5.4-2   **CSS and scale grid values**

```
Button
{
        disabledSkin: Embed(source="assets/Button_disabledSkin.png",
                                scaleGridLeft="5",
                                scaleGridTop="5",
                                scaleGridRight="74",
                                scaleGridBottom="16");
        downSkin: Embed(source="assets/Button_downSkin.png",
                                scaleGridLeft="5",
                                scaleGridTop="5",
                                scaleGridRight="74",
                                scaleGridBottom="16");
        overSkin: Embed(source="assets/Button_overSkin.png",
                                scaleGridLeft="5",
                                scaleGridTop="5",
                                scaleGridRight="74",
                                scaleGridBottom="16");
        upSkin: Embed(source="assets/Button_upSkin.png",
                                scaleGridLeft="5",
                                scaleGridTop="5",
                                scaleGridRight="74",
                                scaleGridBottom="16");
}
```

15. With your graphic assets imported and CSS file created, you can now preview what your newly skinned button looks like. In your PhotoshopButton.mxml file, add a Button component and run the application.

The Final Product

After going through all those steps, when you run your application, you should see the skinned button as in Figure 5.4-13. You also see your skinned button in the MXML Design View. You may need to refresh the view to display the newly skinned button.

> **Note**
>
> Skinned components only render in the main application file. To get a true sense of the look of a skinned component, you need to run/compile your application.

As you interact with the button in the running application, the different state skins you created should appear. To preview the disabled skin, set `enabled="false"` in the button's MXML.

Figure 5.4-13   The skinned button

> **Note**
>
> You can access the final Flex and Photoshop asset files in a folder called PhotoshopButtonExample.

Taking This Example Further

This example illustrates how you can take artwork from Photoshop and use it for skins in Flex. There are a number of ways you can take it further.

The skins you created were relatively simple. You could add shading, highlights, and shapes, and create skins for the other parts of a button. It always helps to experiment with setting the 9-slice guides to different locations or changing the positions of the artwork to see what the effects are to the skin.

Creating Other Assets

Using this approach in Photoshop is not limited to just creating skins. You can also create icons, backgrounds, static graphics, and more using the same steps. The only difference may be in the way that you apply those graphics to your MXML layout. Refer to Appendix A, "Skinning and Styling Diagrams," to see where else you might like to implement skins.

> **Note**
>
> If you're planning on using any bitmap assets in Flash, you may want to refer to Exercise 5.1 for more information.

Using Skin Templates

Adobe has made available a set of Flex component skin templates that you can use as a starting point to create your own custom skins. These skin templates came with the Photoshop Skin Design Extension you installed in the "Getting Started" section in the beginning of this exercise.

With the extension installed, you can easily create a new skin for a single component, or for all the Flex components. To access the skin templates in Photoshop, select File > Scripts > New Flex Skin. Upon doing so, you get a window (see Figure 5.4-14) that allows you to specify the Script to create skins for Multiple Flex Components or a Specific Component.

Figure 5.4-14   New Flex Skin window

If you select Multiple Flex Components, you get a PSD file with a template that has nearly all of the Flex component skins there for you to customize. Selecting a skin for a Specific Component allows you to specify some additional options.

One option you have for a Specific Component is to create a skin to be applied to all instances of a component—for example, if you'd like the same look for all your buttons. If you select this option and click OK, you are given a template that is set up to be used as a skin for all instances of the component you selected. That is, the layers will be named appropriately using a type-selector—for example, `Button_upSkin`, `Button_overSkin`, and so on.

The other option for a Specific Component is to create a skin to be applied to instances with a specified style name. For example, if you want to create a style named `orangeButton`, you could specify that in the input. When you click OK, the symbols are named to reflect the style name you specified. For example, using `orangeButton` as the style name, you would get layer names of Button_ orangeButton_upSkin, Button_ orangeButton_overSkin, and so on.

After you customize the artwork in a template, you can export them to be used in Flex using the same techniques discussed in this section.

Note

Not all skinnable parts of a component are represented in these templates. For example, skins for Alert, drop-down, and other focus skins are not included. In some cases, you may need to create skins for those missing skins from scratch.

Tip

Consider making your own templates to be repurposed while working to customize your user interface.

Summary

In this exercise, you learned how to create skins using Photoshop, set 9-slice guides to prevent your graphics from distorting, and implemented a button skin in Flex. You can repeat this process as needed to skin additional components as your application evolves or use the discussed skin templates as a starting point.

For more information on creating skins, check out Adobe's article at http://www.adobe.com/devnet/flex/articles/skins_styles.html.

Creating a
Programmatic Skin

In this exercise, you'll create a skin similar to those you created in the exercises from Chapter 5, shown in Figure 6.1-1. However, rather than using a tool such as Photoshop or Flash to create the graphical assets, you'll draw them similar to those you created in Exercises 5.1–5.4. When you complete this exercise, you'll have created a single ActionScript class that will generate the visuals for the up, down, over, and disabled states of a button.

Because programmatic skins generate graphics dynamically, you can influence the skin created in this exercise with styles. You'll learn how to expose the background colors for this skin as a style, so that you can use it in a variety of different scenarios (see Figure 6.1-2).

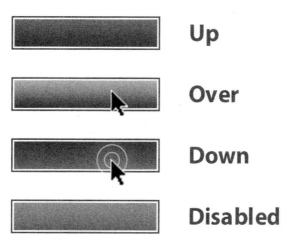

Figure 6.1-1   The button design for this exercise

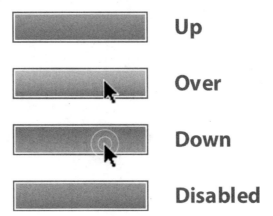

Figure 6.1-2   A variation of the button design
for this exercise will be accomplished using styling

Setting Up a Testing Harness

The first step of this exercise is to create a simple Flex application to test your button skin. You'll run this test several times throughout this exercise to verify that the ActionScript you write is drawing graphics as expected. Testing often is especially important when drawing complex graphics because you'll catch problems sooner, which will make them easier to fix.

1. In Flex Builder, create a new Flex Project by choosing File > New > Flex Project.
2. Name the project CVE_601_ProgrammaticSkinning and accept the rest of the default values in the New Flex Project dialog by clicking Finish.
3. If you're prompted to switch to the Flex Development perspective, go ahead and click Yes.
4. A file called CVE_601_ProgrammaticSkinning.mxml is automatically created with the new project. In this file, you'll create a couple of buttons, one enabled and one disabled, as shown in Listing 6.1-1.

Listing 6.1-1   **Testing harness with two buttons, one enabled and one disabled**

```xml
<?xml version="1.0" encoding="utf-8"?>
<mx:Application
    xmlns:mx="http://www.adobe.com/2006/mxml"
    layout="vertical" >

    <mx:Button enabled="true" label="Enabled" />
    <mx:Button enabled="false" label="Disabled" />

</mx:Application>
```

5. Run this application to make sure you have two buttons, one enabled and one disabled, as shown in Figure 6.1-3.

Figure 6.1-3   The testing harness before skinning

Creating the Skin Class

For this exercise, you'll extend the RectangularBorder base-class to create a custom button skin. By extending this class, all you have to do is extend the functionality of the `updateDisplayList` method to draw your artwork. Extending this class also gives you access to a utility method called `drawRoundRectangle`, which simplifies using the drawing API. For more information about extending base-classes and using the drawing API, see Chapter 6, "Programmatic Skinning."

1. Create a skins package in the source (src) folder of your application by creating a new folder (File > New > Folder) and naming it skins.

2. In Flex Builder, create a new ActionScript class called CustomButtonSkin that extends mx.skins.RectangularBorder by selecting File > New > ActionScript Class and completing the New ActionScript Class dialog, as shown in Figure 6.1-4.

Figure 6.1-4   Creating the CustomButtonSkin class

Applying the Skin to the Buttons

Now that you've created a skin class, you can apply it to the buttons in the testing harness. Because we've done nothing with the skin yet, running the test application after these steps causes the buttons to draw with no background at all, but that's okay. We just want to get the skin and button connected for now.

Open CVE_601_ProgrammaticSkinning.mxml and add an `<mx:Style>` block above the buttons. In the style block, create a Button type-selector that sets the `skin` property to your skin class using a ClassReference directive, as shown in Listing 6.1-2.

Listing 6.1-2   **Applying the skin to the buttons using ClassReference**

```
<!— CVE_601_ProgrammaticSkinning.mxml —>

<?xml version="1.0" encoding="utf-8"?>
<mx:Application
      xmlns:mx="http://www.adobe.com/2006/mxml"
      layout="vertical"
      >

      <mx:Style>

            Button
            {
                  skin: ClassReference('skins.CustomButtonSkin');
            }

      </mx:Style>

      <mx:Button enabled="true" width="100" label="Enabled" />
      <mx:Button enabled="false" width="100" label="Disabled" />

</mx:Application>
```

Note

If there are errors in your skin, they show up as soon as you apply the skin in the testing harness.

Tip

If you've ever needed a blank skin for a class, you could do what we've done so far in this exercise, but never draw anything in the skin. You could also set the skin property to null, but using an empty skin may play better with measurement and layout.

Drawing the Artwork

When a class is specified as the skin for a Button control (or any other control), an instance of the class is created and added as a child of that component. The skin is resized to match the button size, and its updateDisplayList method is called with width and height parameters. You override this method and draw your artwork utilizing the drawRoundedRect method.

Because of how strokes are drawn (described in the "Understanding How Strokes Are Drawn" section of Chapter 6), you create the artwork by creating a series of solid rectangles "nested" within each other.

Overriding updateDisplayList

Open CustomButtonSkin.as and add an override for `updateDisplayList` as shown in Listing 6.1-3. Make sure to call `super.updateDisplayList(w,h)` to keep any functionality defined by the base-class.

Listing 6.1-3   Overriding updateDisplayList in CustomButtonSkin

```
/* CustomButtonSkin.as */

package skins
{
import mx.skins.RectangularBorder;

public class CustomButtonSkin extends RectangularBorder
{

    public function CustomButtonSkin()
    {
        super();
    }

    override protected function updateDisplayList( w:Number,
                                                   h:Number):void
    {
        super.updateDisplayList(w,h);
    }

}
}
```

Drawing the Borders

The outer border (dark gray) and inner border (white) for this skin are the same no matter what state the button is in. You start by drawing them, and draw the state-dependent graphics later.

1. In the `updateDisplayList` method, below the call to `super.updateDisplayList`, create variables to store the colors of the borders, fetched using the getStyle method as shown in Listing 6.1-4.

Listing 6.1-4   Storing the colors for the borders in variables

```
// fetch the color for the outer border
var outerBorderColor:uint =
getStyle('outerBorderColor') || 0x636363; // dark gray
```

Listing 6.1-4   **Continued**

```
// fetch the color for the inner border
var innerBorderColor:uint =
getStyle('innerBorderColor') || 0xFFFFFF; // white
```

> **Tip**
>
> The double pipe syntax (| |) followed by a hexadecimal value allows you to specify a default color that is used if no style is specified. This is really handy for testing since you may not have specified these style properties yet.

2. Below the variables definitions, call **drawRoundRect** with the arguments described in Table 6.1-1 as shown in Listing 6.1-5. This draws the outer border at the full width and height specified for the skin, with the color stored in the previous step.

Table 6.1-1   **Arguments for Drawing the Outer Border**

x	0
y	0
width	w
height	h
cornerRadius	0
color	outerBorderColor
alpha	1

Listing 6.1-5   **Calling drawRoundRect to draw the outer border**

```
// draw the outer border at the full width and height
drawRoundRect(0,0,w,h,0,outerBorderColor,1);
```

> **Note**
>
> Don't forget to pass an alpha argument to the **drawRoundRect** method. If you do forget, the rectangle will be completely transparent.

3. Next, call **drawRoundRect** with the arguments described in Table 6.1-2 as shown in Listing 6.1-6 to draw the inner border. This rectangle is centered and smaller than the previous rectangle, creating a border effect with the dark gray.

Table 6.1-2   **Arguments for Drawing the Inner Border**

x	1
y	1
width	w-2
height	h-2
cornerRadius	0
color	innerBorderColor
alpha	1

Listing 6.1-6   **Calling drawRoundRect to draw the outer border**

```
// draw the inner border inset 1 pixel
drawRoundRect(1,1,w-2,h-2,0,innerBorderColor,1);
```

> **Note**
>
> The position of this rectangle is offset by 1 pixel on both the x and y axis, and the width and height is 2 pixels narrower than the previous rectangle. This is how you "nest" rectangles to make borders.

4. Verify that your CustomButtonSkin class matches Listing 6.1-7 and then run CVE_601_ProgrammaticSkinning.mxml. Your test harness application should now look like Figure 6.1-5. The inner "border" is just a solid white fill for now. It will resemble a border after you nest another rectangle inside to use for the fill.

Listing 6.1-7   **CustomButtonSkin.as with code for drawing**
                  inner and outer border rectangles

```
/* CustomButtonSkin.as */

package skins
{
import mx.skins.RectangularBorder;

public class CustomButtonSkin extends RectangularBorder
{
        public function CustomButtonSkin()
        {
              super();
        }

        override protected function updateDisplayList(w:Number,
                                                      h:Number):void
        {
```

Listing 6.1-7   **Continued**

```
        super.updateDisplayList(w,h);

        // fetch the color for the outer border
        var outerBorderColor:uint =
        getStyle('outerBorderColor') || 0x636363; // dark gray

        // fetch the color for the inner border
        var innerBorderColor:uint =
        getStyle('innerBorderColor') || 0xFFFFFF; // white

        // draw the outer border at the full width and height
        drawRoundRect(0,0,w,h,0,outerBorderColor,1);

        // draw the inner border inset 1 pixel
        drawRoundRect(1,1,w-2,h-2,0,innerBorderColor,1);

    }

}
}
```

Figure 6.1-5   The testing harness after drawing outer and inner borders

Drawing the Fills Based on Button State

When a skin is created and attached to a button, it is given a name based on the current state of the button, such as **"upSkin"** or **"overSkin"**. From within the skin, you can evaluate the **name** property and use it to determine the state that the skin should represent. For this exercise, you'll draw a gradient fill with colors based on the current state of the button.

1. In CustomButtonSkin.as, below the code from the previous section, create a variable to store the colors that will be used in the gradient fill, but do not set an initial value (see Listing 6.1-8).

Listing 6.1-8   Creating a variable to store the fill colors

```
// create a variable to store the fill colors
var fillColors:Array;
```

2. Next, set up an if-else block to dynamically fetch styles based on the current state of the button for which this skin is being drawn, as shown in Listing 6.1-9.

Listing 6.1-9   Setting the value of the fillColors variable based on the name of the skin

```
// populate the fill colors based on the name of the skin
if ( name == "upSkin" )
{
    fillColors = getStyle('upFillColors') || [0x26A7DF,0x0375BF];
}
else if ( name == "overSkin" )
{
    fillColors = getStyle('overFillColors') || [0x90D3F0,0x0375BF];
}
else if ( name == "downSkin" )
{
    fillColors = getStyle('downFillColors') || [0x90D3F0,0x0375BF];
}
else if ( name == "disabledSkin" )
{
    fillColors = getStyle('disabledFillColors') || [0x90D3F0,0x0375BF];
}
```

> **Note**
> We're using the double pipe (||), described in the previous section, to define an array of default colors. If you are making a programmatic skin that will not be customizable with styles, you can bypass using `getStyle` altogether and directly set `fillColors` to an array.

3. Now you have the colors defined for your gradient, but you must create a gradient matrix to specify the rotation, size, and position of the gradient. If you are not extending RectangularBorder, you have to do this manually, which can be a little painstaking. Fortunately, you can avoid the hassle by using either the

`horizontalGradientMatrix` or `verticalGradientMatrix` utility function defined in the base-class. For this exercise, you'll call the `verticalGradientMatrix` function, passing it the same x, y, width, and height parameters that you'll use when drawing the rectangle in the next step. (See Table 6.1-3 for the arguments to create a vertical gradient matrix.) Store the results of this function in a variable called matrix, as shown in Listing 6.1-10.

Table 6.1-3   **Arguments for Creating a Vertical Gradient Matrix**

x	2
y	2
width	w-4
height	w-4

Listing 6.1-10   **Using verticalGradientMatrix method to create a gradient matrix**

```
// define and store a vertical gradient matrix
var matrix:Matrix = verticalGradientMatrix(2,2,w-4,h-4);
```

Note

The position for the gradient is offset by 2 pixels on both the x and y axis, and the width and height are a total of 4 pixels less than the overall width of the skin. This is because the fill for which we're defining this gradient is inset within the skin to expose the inner and outer border created in the previous section.

4. With the gradient matrix defined, you can now call `drawRoundRect` with the values described in Table 6.1-4 to complete the gradient fill for this skin as shown in Listing 6.1-11.

Table 6.1-4   **Arguments for Creating a Vertical Gradient Matrix**

x	2
y	2
width	w-4
height	w-4
cornerRadius	0
alpha	1
gradientMatrix	matrix

Listing 6.1-11   **Drawing the inner fill**

```
// draw the inner fill with the fill colors and matrix
drawRoundRect(2, 2, w-4, h-4, 0, fillColors, 1, matrix);
```

5. Verify that the `updateDisplayList` method in your CustomButtonSkin class matches Listing 6.1-12 and then run CVE_601_ProgrammaticSkinning.mxml. Your test harness application should now look like Figure 6.1-6. When you roll over or press the Enabled button, you should see the button change as designed.

Listing 6.1-12   The final updateDisplayList method of CustomButtonSkin.as

```
override protected function updateDisplayList(w:Number, h:Number):void
{
    super.updateDisplayList(w,h);

    // fetch the color for the outer border
    var outerBorderColor:uint =
        getStyle('outerBorderColor') || 0x636363; // dark gray

    // fetch the color for the inner border
    var innerBorderColor:uint =
        getStyle('innerBorderColor') || 0xFFFFFF; // white

    // draw the outer border at the full width and height
    drawRoundRect(0,0,w,h,0,outerBorderColor,1);

    // draw the inner border inset 1 pixel
    drawRoundRect(1,1,w-2,h-2,0,innerBorderColor,1);

    // create a variable to store the fill colors
    var fillColors:Array;

    // populate the fill colors based on the name of the skin
    if ( name == "upSkin" )
    {
        fillColors = getStyle('upFillColors') || [0x26A7DF,0x0375BF];
    }
    else if ( name == "overSkin" )
    {
        fillColors = getStyle('overFillColors') || [0x90D3F0,0x0375BF];
    }
    else if ( name == "downSkin" )
    {
        fillColors = getStyle('downFillColors') || [0x0375BF,0x26A7DF];
    }
    else if ( name == "disabledSkin" )
    {
        fillColors = getStyle('disabledFillColors') ||
                        [0xA6A8AB,0x838588];
    }
```

Listing 6.1-12   **Continued**

```
    // define and store a vertical gradient matrix
    var matrix:Matrix = verticalGradientMatrix(3,3,w-6,h-6);

    // draw the inner fill with the fill colors and matrix
    drawRoundRect(3,3,w-6,h-6,0,fillColors,1,matrix);

}
```

Figure 6.1-6   The button skin with a default gradient fill

Applying Styles

One of the most compelling reasons to create a programmatic skin instead of using graphics is that programmatic skins can be customized with styles. Because no styles have yet been specified for the button, it has the default blue gradient fill as shown in Figure 6.1-6. In the following steps, you'll specify styles to create a green variation of the button skin.

1. Open CVE_601_ProgrammaticSkinning.mxml; in the Button type selector within the <mx:Style> block, specify an array of colors for the upFillColors, overFillColors, and downFillColors styles as shown in Listing 6.1-13. We won't be changing the disabledFillColors because the gray works well with the green variation, but we could.

Listing 6.1-13   **Applying styles to the Button type selector that
                   will be used by CustomButtonSkin**

```
<mx:Style>

Button
{
    skin: ClassReference('skins.CustomButtonSkin');
```

Listing 6.1-13   **Continued**

```
    upFillColors:   #69DE25, #55BF03;
    overFillColors: #BAF090, #55BF03;
    downFillColors: #55BF03, #69DE25;
}

</mx:Style>
```

2. Run CVE_601_ProgrammaticSkinning.mxml and verify that it looks like Figure 6.1-7. When you roll over or press the Enabled button, you should see the button change as designed, only green.

Figure 6.1-7   A green variation of the button skin defined with styles

The Final Product

You now have a single programmatic button skin that changes based on state and that can be customized using styles. Perhaps you want to emphasize a submit button by making it green or stylize a cancel button to be red. With this skin, you could do that while maintaining an overall consistent look and feel (see Figure 6.1-8).

Figure 6.1-8   The final product is a button skin with customizable fill colors

Taking This Example Further

This example demonstrates how to create a simple programmatic skin and expose some of the properties of the skin as styles. You could create a more complex skin and expose additional properties as styles, such as `cornerRadius` or the thickness of the inner and outer border. Also, you could use a color utility to dynamically calculate color variations as described in the following.

The problem with exposing the fill colors for each state of a programmatic skin is that it becomes rather tedious to change each color individually, especially if each state supports more than one color, as this examples does. Also, the button has been designed such that the over state appears highlighted and the down state appears sunken. If vastly different fill colors are specified for each state, these effects could be clobbered.

To maintain style, you could refactor your skin to support one "base" color, and then dynamically calculate the light and dark variations used for the gradients in the various states. Listing 6.1-14 shows fill colors being defined based on state, using dynamic colors.

Listing 6.1-14   Using verticalGradientMatrix method to create a gradient matrix

```
// fetch the a base color for all active fills
var baseFillColor:uint = getStyle('fillColor') || 0x26A7DF;

// fetch the a base color for the disabled fill
var disabledFillColor:uint = getStyle('disabledColor') || 0xA6A6A6

// create an empty array to store the fill colors
var fillColors:Array = [];

// populate the fill colors based on the name of the skin
if ( name == "upSkin" )
{
    fillColors[0] = baseFillColor;
    fillColors[1] = ColorUtil.adjustBrightness(baseFillColor, -50);
}
else if ( name == "overSkin" )
{
    fillColors[0] = ColorUtil.adjustBrightness(baseFillColor, 50);
    fillColors[1] = ColorUtil.adjustBrightness(baseFillColor, -50);
}
else if ( name == "downSkin" )
{
    fillColors[0] = ColorUtil.adjustBrightness(baseFillColor, -50);
    fillColors[1] = baseFillColor;
}
else if ( name == "disabledSkin" )
{
    fillColors[0] = disabledFillColor;
    fillColors[1] = ColorUtil.adjustBrightness(disabledFillColor, -50);
}
```

To test the dynamic colors, specify a `fillColor` style in CVE_601_ProgrammaticSkinning. mxml as shown in Listing 6.1-15 and run the application. You should have an orange variation of the button as shown in Figure 6.1-9.

Listing 6.1-15   **Specifying a fill color that will serve as the base color for gradient fills**

```
Button
{
    skin: ClassReference('skins.CustomButtonSkin');
    fillColor: #FF6600; /* orange */
}
```

Figure 6.1-9   An orange variation of the button, created with dynamic color calculation

Summary

In this exercise, you learned how to create programmatic skins in ActionScript. Although the skin created was fairly simple, a similar process can be applied to create more complex skins for a variety of components. It's often useful to look at the code used to create the Halo skin for the component that you want to enhance and use that as starting point for your custom skin.

Creating a Chat
Dialog Window Using a List

A List component relies on data and displays it in a vertical orientation. Typically, a List component may look something like Figure 7.1-1, but using styling, skinning, and an item renderer, you can create a much richer visualization of the same data while adding functionality.

Alabama
Alaska
Arizona
Arkansas
California
Colorado
Connecticut

Figure 7.1-1   A typical list

Getting Started

In this walkthrough, you will use an item renderer with a list to create a simple mockup of a chat dialog window, as seen in Figure 7.1-2. This example will expose you to some of the possibilities of what can be achieved using an item renderer as well as techniques discussed in previous chapters.

1. Create a new Flex Project called ChatList. You don't need to go further than the first screen of the setup wizard. After you've entered the project's name, click Finish.

2. Add a List component to the application. For this example, it doesn't matter where the list is placed; however, in a real-world scenario, you need to consider things like

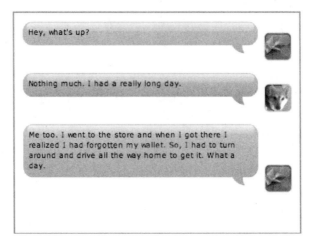

Figure 7.1-2   Chat dialog window mockup

layout and design requirements. For now, center the list within the application's viewable area and set its width to 400 pixels and height to 300 pixels, as shown in Listing 7.1-1.

Listing 7.1-1   Adding the List component to your application

```
<mx:List
        verticalCenter="0"
        horizontalCenter="0"
        width="400"
        height="300"/>
```

3. Use CSS styling to set the background color of the list to white and no border. You can apply the styling using a list type selector within an <mx:Style> tag added under the <mx:Application> tag shown in Listing 7.1-2.

Listing 7.1-2   Styling the List component using CSS

```
<mx:Style>
        List
        {
        backgroundColor: #FFFFFF;
        borderStyle: none;
        }
</mx:Style>
```

4. So far, you have a white list without anything showing up inside it. To populate the list with data, you use an external XML file that contains the data. The following XML contains data with nodes for an icon, background, and chatText. These bits of data create the content for the application chat dialogue.

5. Create a new XML file, call it ChatDataSource.xml, and give it the data structure shown in Listing 7.1-3.

Listing 7.1-3   **Creating an XML file to act as the data provider for the list**

```
<?xml version="1.0"?>
<chatItems>
    <chatItem>
        <icon>images/BuddyIcon_Pinwheel.jpg</icon>
<background>@Embed(source='images/GreenBalloon_backgroundImage.swf',
symbol='GreenBalloon_backgroundImage')</background>
        <chatText>Hey, what's up?</chatText>
    </chatItem>
    <chatItem>
        <icon>images/BuddyIcon_Dog.jpg</icon>
<background>@Embed(source='images/BlueBalloon_backgroundImage.swf',
symbol='BlueBalloon_backgroundImage')</background>
        <chatText>Nothing much. I had a really long day.</chatText>
    </chatItem>
    <chatItem>
        <icon>images/BuddyIcon_Pinwheel.jpg</icon>
<background>@Embed(source='images/GreenBalloon_backgroundImage.swf',
symbol='GreenBalloon_backgroundImage')</background>
        <chatText>Me too. I went to the store and when I got there I realized
I had forgotten my wallet. So, I had to turn around and drive all the way home to
get it. What a day.</chatText>
    </chatItem>
</chatItems>
```

6. The XML references various image assets that you can find at the book's Web site (http://www.cveflex.com/). Place those image assets in a folder called images that you create inside of your project's src folder, as shown in Figure 7.1-3.

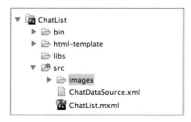

Figure 7.1-3   Adding an images folder to your project

7. With the XML data source created, hook it up to the list. In the main application's MXML file, add a Model tag beneath the closing `</Style>` tag as shown in Listing 7.1-4. Be sure to add the `id` of `ChatData`.

Listing 7.1-4   **Using a Model tag to create the data provider for the list**

```
<mx:Model
      id="ChatData"
      source="ChatDataSource.xml"/>
```

8. With the data source created, you can connect the data source and add a data provider specification to the list, as shown in Listing 7.1-5.

Listing 7.1-5   **Specify the model you created as the data provider for the list**

```
<mx:List
      dataProvider="{ChatData.chatItem}"
      verticalCenter="0"
      horizontalCenter="0"
      width="400"
      height="300"/>
```

Testing the Application

If you run your application, you see three lines of [`object Object`] within the list (see Figure 7.1-4). This means the list recognizes the three chatItem nodes in the XML file. However, it has no way of displaying the information. This is where using an item renderer comes into play.

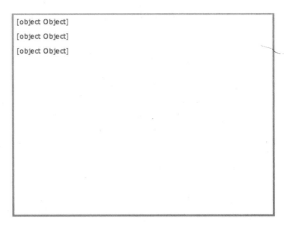

Figure 7.1-4   The list is populating with data,
but needs to be rendered properly

9. Now that you've got a list populated with data, the next step is to create the item renderer, which displays the chat information as shown earlier in Figure 7.1-2. For this, you create a new custom MXML component for the item renderer.

10. In Flex Builder, select File > New > MXML Component. Name the component ChatItemRenderer, select HBox as the base component, set the width to 100%, and delete the specifications for the height. When you click Finish, you should get an MXML file that looks like Listing 7.1-6.

Listing 7.1-6   **Using an HBox as the base for your item renderer**

```
<?xml version="1.0" encoding="utf-8"?>
<mx:HBox
     xmlns:mx="http://www.adobe.com/2006/mxml"
     width="100%">


</mx:HBox>
```

11. With the base MXML set, you need to add the parts for the item renderer. Add an Image component for the Buddy Icon, a Text component for the Chat Text, and a VBox component to help position the text (see Listing 7.1-7). These components are added in between the `<mx:HBox>` tags, as shown here. You'll also notice that some inline styling has been added to the HBox.

Listing 7.1-7   **Adding an Image, Text, and VBox component to make up the item renderer**

```
<mx:HBox
     xmlns:mx="http://www.adobe.com/2006/mxml"
     width="100%"
     verticalAlign="bottom"
     paddingLeft="10"
     paddingRight="10"
     paddingTop="10">
     <mx:VBox
          width="100%">
          <mx:Text
               width="300"/>
     </mx:VBox>
     <mx:Image/>
</mx:HBox>
```

12. Assign data values for the areas you want to populate the item renderer. For the image, the source needs to change; for the Text component, the text needs to change; and for the VBox, the backgroundImage needs to change.

Those data values can be tied from the XML file to the item renderer by assigning data variables using {data....}. Also, add some inline styling, as shown in Listing 7.1-8.

Listing 7.1-8   Adding inline styling and setting up components to update based on the data provider

```
<mx:VBox
      width="100%"
      backgroundImage="{data.background}"
      backgroundSize="100%"
      paddingBottom="30"
      paddingLeft="6"
      paddingRight="6"
      paddingTop="6">
      <mx:Text
            text="{data.chatText}"
            width="300"
            fontWeight="normal"
            color="#000000"/>
</mx:VBox>
<mx:Image
      source="{data.icon}"/>
```

13. Now that you've built the item renderer, implement it into your List component's MXML. You can specify ChatItemRenderer as the item renderer (see Listing 7.1-9).

Listing 7.1-9   Specifying the ChatItemRenderer as the item renderer for the list

```
<mx:List
      verticalCenter="0"
      horizontalCenter="0"
      width="400"
      height="300"
      dataProvider="{ChatData.chatItem}"
      itemRenderer="ChatItemRenderer"/>
```

14. If you run the application, you should see a working example of the application, as shown earlier in Figure 7.1-2. Except for one thing: The height of the VBox and text is larger than the viewable area of the list's item renderer, which causes a scrollbar to appear. This is because the height of the rows within the list defaults to the same height. To correct this behavior, set variableRowHeight to true in the list's properties as shown in Listing 7.1-10.

Listing 7.1-10   **Setting variableRowHeight to true allows rows with different**
                  amounts of content to influence the height of each row individually

```
<mx:List
    verticalCenter="0"
    horizontalCenter="0"
    width="400"
    height="300"
    dataProvider="{ChatData.chatItem}"
    itemRenderer="ChatItemRenderer"
    variableRowHeight="true"/>
```

15. Now when you run the application, you should get results shown in Figure 7.1-2.
    Your final ChatList.mxml file should look like Listing 7.1-11 and your ChatItem-
    Renderer.mxml file should look like Listing 7.1-12.

Listing 7.1-11   **The final MXML for the ChatList.mxml file**

```
<?xml version="1.0" encoding="utf-8"?>
<mx:Application
    xmlns:mx="http://www.adobe.com/2006/mxml"
    layout="absolute">

    <mx:Style>
        List
        {
            backgroundColor:   #FFFFFF;
            borderStyle:       none;
        }
    </mx:Style>

    <!- Chat data provider ->
    <mx:Model
        id="ChatData"
        source="ChatDataSource.xml"/>

    <!- Chat List ->
    <mx:List
        verticalCenter="0"
        horizontalCenter="0"
        width="400"
        height="300"
        dataProvider="{ChatData.chatItem}"
        itemRenderer="ChatItemRenderer"
        variableRowHeight="true"/>

</mx:Application>
```

Listing 7.1-12   **The final MXML for the ChatItemRenderer.mxml file**

```
<?xml version="1.0" encoding="utf-8"?>
<mx:HBox
      xmlns:mx="http://www.adobe.com/2006/mxml"
      width="100%"
      verticalAlign="bottom"
      paddingLeft="10"
      paddingRight="10"
      paddingTop="10">

      <!- Box for chat bubble background ->
      <mx:VBox
            width="100%"
            backgroundImage="{data.background}"
            backgroundSize="100%"
            paddingBottom="30"
            paddingLeft="6"
            paddingRight="6"
            paddingTop="6">

            <!- Chat text ->
            <mx:Text
                  text="{data.chatText}"
                  width="300"
                  fontWeight="normal"
                  color="#000000"/>
      </mx:VBox>

      <!- User icon ->
      <mx:Image
            source="{data.icon}"/>

</mx:HBox>
```

Note

Item renderers are recycled, which might cause problems when using one with a dynamic height. To avoid problems, try explicitly setting the height of each item renderer.

Tip

Layout Tip: If you want to adjust the space in between items within a list, you can set `paddingTop` and `paddingBottom` to negative values.

Summary

In this exercise, you learned how to use a list with an item renderer to create a chat dialog. This is just one example of what you can do to customize a list. Using these techniques, you can achieve many other things with a list or any other data-driven component that accepts item renderers. For example, you could add buttons that perform various functions, create an item renderer with different states, or incorporate visual effects. Flex 3 also includes the capability to add custom data effects to data-driven components. For more information, check out Chapter 11, "Effects and Transitions."

In Exercise 7.2, you will use some of the same techniques discussed in this exercise to create a Photo Gallery using a TileList. You will also add some controls that show and hide themselves as a user interacts with the images in the gallery.

Creating a Photo Gallery Using a TileList

A TileList component relies on a data source and displays items in a grid-like fashion. If you populate a tile list with data and not do anything else, it looks something like Figure 7.2-1.

Figure 7.2-1   Generic TileList component

However, with the use of item renderers, you can create a much richer visualization of the same data and add some functionality. For this example, you'll be walking through how a tile list can be used to mock up a photo gallery and display options for each photo when a user rolls over it (see Figure 7.2-2).

Tip

Design Tip: Only showing a user options when interacting with an item helps to keep his view uncluttered and brings focus to the content that is most important.

1. To get started, create a new Flex Project called PhotoGallery. The first thing is to apply some styling to your application background. You'll be using an external CSS file, so create a new CSS file and name it style.css. The CSS file can be attached to the application by using the `<Style>` tag and pointing the `source` to the CSS file as shown in Listing 7.2-1.

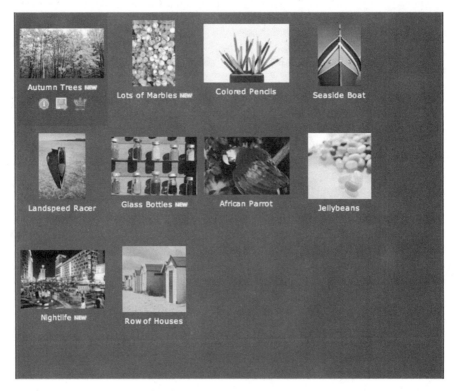

Figure 7.2-2   Custom Photo Gallery using item renderers and dynamically displayed controls

---

Listing 7.2-1   **Attaching an external CSS file using the Style tag**

```
<mx:Style source="style.css"/>
```

---

2. Make the application background a dark gray by adding the following to your CSS file that was just created (see Listing 7.2-2).

Listing 7.2-2   **Make the application background a dark gray**
               by specifying styles in the external CSS file

```
/* style.css*/
Application
{
        backgroundGradientAlphas:      1,1;
        backgroundGradientColors:      #333333, #333333;
}
```

3. Now that you have the base for the application set up, you can add a TileList to the layout. Set the height to 500, width to 600, center it within the Application view (see Listing 7.2-3), and add some styling to the CSS file (see Listing 7.2-4).

Listing 7.2-3   **Setting the width and height of the TileList and centering it vertically and horizontally in the application**

```
<!-- PhotoGallery.mxml -->
<mx:TileList
      width="600"
      height="500"
      verticalCenter="0"
      horizontalCenter="0">
</mx:TileList>
```

Listing 7.2-4   **Styling the TileList component in the external CSS file**

```
/* style.css*/
TileList
{
      backgroundColor: #444444;
      borderColor: #666666;
}
```

For this example, you'll be creating an external item renderer. Before you do that, let's take a look at the XML data so you can gain a better understanding of what you'll need to include in the item renderer. Listing 7.2-5 provides a sample block of data from the XML file you need to create. If you don't want to create the whole XML file yourself, you can get a finished XML file from the book's Web site.

Listing 7.2-5   **Sample block of XML to use as the data provider for the TileList component**

```
<galleryItem>
      <name>At the Park</name>
      <image>images/image_001.jpg</image>
      <new>true</new>
      <forSale>false</forSale>
</galleryItem>
```

4. Based on the data, you need a way to display the image, its name, whether it's new, and if it's for sale. The item renderer displays your items and offers some additional functionality when a user rolls his cursor over each item. Create a new MXML component and name it PhotoRenderer. Use VBox as the base component, set the height to 140, and the width to 120, as shown in Listing 7.2-6.

Listing 7.2-6   **Creating the PhotoRenderer.mxml file to act**
as the item renderer for the TileList

```
<!- PhotoRenderer.mxml ->
<?xml version="1.0" encoding="utf-8"?>
<mx:VBox
     xmlns:mx="http://www.adobe.com/2006/mxml"
     width="120"
     height="140">

</mx:VBox>
```

5. To make the view within the TileList less busy looking, set the `backgroundAlpha` of `PhotoRender` to 0 using the external CSS file (see Listing 7.2-7).

Listing 7.2-7   **Setting the PhotoRenderer backgroundAlpha to 0 in the external CSS file**

```
/* style.css*/
PhotoRenderer
{
     backgroundAlpha: 0;
}
```

6. Now you can start adding the necessary elements to the item renderer. You add an Image component to display your images, a Label for the image name, an Image for a New icon, and Buttons for Add to Cart, Information, and Share. The buttons are for mockup purposes only and do not have functionality tied to them. You use some HBoxes, alignment, and padding properties to get things positioned properly. In addition, you assign data items to their relevant components and assign some ids. Listing 7.2-8 shows the MXML required to do this.

Listing 7.2-8   **Setting up the PhotoRenderer.mxml file to support required functionality**

```
<!- PhotoRenderer.mxml ->
<?xml version="1.0" encoding="utf-8"?>
<mx:VBox
     xmlns:mx="http://www.adobe.com/2006/mxml"
     width="130"
     height="150">

     <mx:Image
          source="{data.image}"/>
     <mx:HBox
          width="100%"
          horizontalGap="0"
          horizontalAlign="center">
```

Listing 7.2-8   **Continued**

```
            <mx:Label
                text="{data.name}"
                color="#FFFFFF"/>
            <mx:Image
                width="18"
                height="18"
                includeInLayout="{data.new}"
                visible="{data.new}"
                source="images/new.png"/>
    </mx:HBox>
    <mx:HBox
            id="optionsBox"
            height="18">
        <mx:Button
                width="18"
                height="18"
                styleName="infoButton"/>
        <mx:Button
                width="18"
                height="18"
                styleName="shareButton"/>
        <mx:Button
                width="18"
                height="18"
                styleName="cartButton"
                enabled="{data.forSale}"/>
    </mx:HBox>
</mx:VBox>
```

7. You also need to update the style.css file with more styling for the PhotoRenderer and skins for the buttons within (see Listing 7.2-9). You can find the image assets used in the CSS file on the Web site for this book.

Listing 7.2-9   **Adding styling to the style.css file for the PhotoRenderer**

```
/* style.css*/
PhotoRenderer
{
    backgroundColor: #444444;
    backgroundAlpha: 0;
    horizontalAlign: center;
    verticalAlign: bottom;
    verticalGap: 4;
    paddingTop: 4;
    paddingRight: 4;
```

Listing 7.2-9   **Continued**

```
        paddingBottom: 4;
        paddingLeft: 4;
}

Button.infoButton
{
        upSkin: Embed(source='images/information.png');
        overSkin: Embed(source='images/information.png');
        downSkin: Embed(source='images/information.png');
        disabledSkin: Embed(source='images/information.png');
}

Button.shareButton
{
        upSkin: Embed(source='images/picture_go.png');
        overSkin: Embed(source='images/picture_go.png');
        downSkin: Embed(source='images/picture_go.png');
        disabledSkin: Embed(source='images/picture_go.png');
}

Button.cartButton
{
        upSkin: Embed(source='images/cart_put.png');
        overSkin: Embed(source='images/cart_put.png');
        downSkin: Embed(source='images/cart_put.png');
        disabledSkin: Embed(source='images/cart_put_disabled.png');
}
```

Note

The reason `backgroundColor` is specified with a `backgroundAlpha` of 0 is because `backgroundColor` is required to create the "hit area" for the item renderer, but is made not visible so that it doesn't cover up the `TileList` rollOver and selection colors.

8. With your item renderer set up, you can go back to the PhotoGallery.mxml file to define a data source, assign the data to the TileList component, and specify the item renderer as shown in Listing 7.2-10.

Listing 7.2-10   **Defining a data source and item renderer for the TileList component**

```
<!-- PhotoRenderer.mxml -->
<mx:Model id="galleryData" source="galleryDataSource.xml"/>

<mx:TileList
        width="600"
        height="500"
```

Listing 7.2-10   Continued

```
verticalCenter="0"
horizontalCenter="0"
dataProvider="{galleryData.galleryItem}"
itemRenderer="PhotoRenderer"/>
```

9. If you run the application, you should see the data you specified populate the TileList using the item renderer you built. There's still a couple things left to do.

10. You want to make the view less busy by only showing the Information, Share, and Add to Cart buttons when a user rolls his cursor over the item renderer area. To do this, you change the `visible` property of `optionsBox` based on a `mouseOver` and `mouseOut` event on the main VBox of `PhotoRenderer`. To make sure `optionsBox` is not visible when the item render is first drawn, you set the `visible` property of it to `false`. This is shown in Listing 7.2-11.

Listing 7.2-11   Setting the photo options to display on mouseOver and hide on mouseOut

```
<!-- PhotoRenderer.mxml -->
<mx:VBox
        xmlns:mx="http://www.adobe.com/2006/mxml"
        width="130"
        height="150"
        mouseOver="optionsBox.visible=true"
        mouseOut="optionsBox.visible=false">

   ...

<mx:HBox
        id="optionsBox"
        height="18"
        visible="false">

   ...
```

11. You also want to change the `rollOverColor` and `selectionColor` of the TileList from the default blue to a gray blue. In the TileList styling in the style.css file, add rollOverColor (#618BA0) and selectionColor (#6AA3C1) to change the colors (see Listing 7.2-12).

Listing 7.2-12   Styling the TileList component's rollOver and selection colors in style.css

```
/* style.css*/
TileList
{
```

Listing 7.2-12   **Continued**

```
        backgroundColor:        #444444;
        borderColor:            #666666;
        rollOverColor:          #343C40;
        selectionColor:         #5A7E90;
}
```

12. With those changes made, you can run the application and check what you have done. Notice that the buttons are no longer visible until you roll over an item. Also, the colors for rollOverColor and selectionColor are muted blues.

Note

Because item renderers are their own components, you can add to what was just created. Consider adding effects and transitions (Chapter 11) or more interactive skins as discussed in Chapter 12, "Flex and Flash Integration."

---

13. When working with a TileList component, there are a number of ways to fine-tune the positioning of items within. TileList is made of rows and columns that can be changed to adjust spacing and layout.

    Using columnWidth and rowHeight, you can adjust the size of the rows and/or columns. You can change how many rows and columns are used to lay out the items within the TileList by setting the columnCount and rowCount. Also, the direction items layout inside of a TileList can be adjusted by setting the direction to vertical or horizontal.

14. Adjust `paddingTop`, `paddingRight`, `paddingBottom`, and `paddingLeft` with positive and negative values to get items within a TileList closer or further apart. Figure 7.2-3 is a diagram of how these properties influence a TileList visually.

Summary

In this exercise, you learned how to create a Photo Gallery with dynamic controls for each image. This is one example of what you can do to customize a TileList. You used an XML file, but you could adapt this example to use a dynamic data provider as well. You could also add some data effects to this example. For more information, check out Chapter 11, "Effects and Transitions."

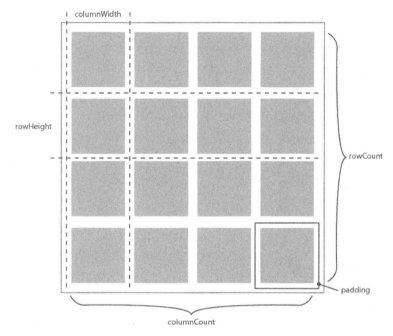

Figure 7.2-3   How different properties affect the layout of items in a TileList

Embedding a Font in a SWF File Using Flash

In this exercise, you will be using Flash to embed a font in a SWF (pronounced "swif") to be used in Flex. Packaging a font into a SWF using Flash can be done in a few simple steps, but you'll need Flash CS3. You can download a trial from Adobe's site if you don't have it already.

1. Open Flash CS3 and create a new Flash file at the default size. Save this file as MyFont.fla.

2. Add a Text area to your stage and set it to Dynamic Text in the Properties panel (Window > Properties > Properties). Select the font for the area, in this case Verdana. Type the name of the font into the text area as shown in Figure 9.1-1. You can type whatever you want into that text area; it is just for reference and gives you a visible reference on the stage.

Note

Depending on your computer and operating system, your fonts may be located in a variety of places. Your best bet is to do a search for TTF or OTF files.

Figure 9.1-1   Assigning a font to a Dynamic Text area

3. Click the Embed button in the Properties panel, shown in Figure 9.1-2, and specify the characters you'd like to embed.

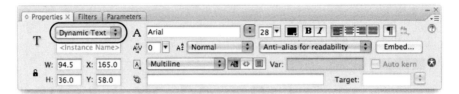

Figure 9.1-2   Embedding specific characters using the Properties panel

4. Publish the FLA file as an SWF to your Flex Project.

5. In Flex, use an `@font-face` declaration within an `<mx:Style>` tag or external CSS in your Flex Project. Example 9.1-1 shows an example of the font `Verdana` being embedded.

Example 9.1-1   **Embedding a SWF packaged font**

```
@font-face
{
    src:        url("assets/fonts/MyFonts.swf");
    fontFamily: Verdana;
    fontStyle:  normal;
    fontWeight: normal;
}
```

6. That's it! With the font embedded, you can assign the `fontFamily` to a component or style.

Summary

This exercise showed how to use Flash to embed a font in a SWF and use it in Flex. Exercise 9.2 will walk through how you can use Flex to generate a font SWF using CSS and compile it as a SWF.

9.2

Packaging a CSS File with a Font as a SWF

In this exercise, you will learn another way to compile and embed fonts as a SWF (pronounced "swif") in your Flex application by using the Compile CSS to SWF feature in Flex. The nice thing is that you don't need to have Flash. This is the same method discussed in Chapter 4, "Styling," for compiling a CSS file of component styles into a SWF. However, this method does not require you to use Flash and is done entirely within Flex Builder.

1. In Flex Builder, create a new CSS file called fonts.css and a folder called fonts. Drop an OTF or TTF font into the fonts folder. The OTF font Myriad Pro Bold will be used in this example.

2. In the fonts.css file, create a new `@font-face` declaration and specify the necessary parameters like `src`, `fontWeight`, `fontFamily`, and so on, as shown in Listing 9.2-1.

3. Depending on the font you're embedding, the values you specify for `fontFamily` and `fontWeight` may be different. Sometimes it can be tricky getting the right combination.

Listing 9.2-1   **Specifying the font to embed**

```
/* fonts.css*/

@font-face
{
    src: url("fonts/MyriadPro-Bold.otf");
    fontFamily: "Myriad Pro Bold";
    fontWeight: Bold;
}
```

4. Now that you have the font specified in your CSS file, you can compile it to a SWF. In the Flex Navigator view, right-click on the fonts.css file and select Compile CSS to SWF, as shown in Figure 9.2-1.

Note

As mentioned previously, be conscious of the number of characters you embed when you use this method. Refer to the section on specifying character ranges in Chapter 9, "Fonts and Text."

Figure 9.2-1   Compiling CSS to SWF

5. Look in your bin folder and you should now see a fonts.swf. This is your compiled CSS file that can be used in a few different ways. You could use this SWF file the same way outlined in Exercise 9.1, by copying the fonts.swf file to the fonts folder and referencing it from a new CSS file called styles.css, shown in Listing 9.2-2.

Listing 9.2-2   **Referencing the compiled fonts.swf**

```
/* styles.css */

@font-face
{
    src: url("fonts/fonts.swf");
    fontFamily: "Myriad Pro Bold";
    fontWeight: Bold;
}
```

6. You can also use this compiled SWF to load different fonts at runtime. This makes the initial load time and size of your application SWF smaller. To do this, you use the StyleManager similar to the way you loaded a CSS file outlined in Chapter 4. Listing 9.2-3 shows a basic function that loads the fonts.swf file you compiled previously and makes it available in your application.

   Because you are loading an asset at runtime, you need to make sure that asset is available in the final published location of your application.

Listing 9.2-3   **Using StyleManager to load fonts at runtime**

```
<mx:Script>
    <![CDATA[
        import mx.styles.StyleManager;

        public function loadFonts():void {
        StyleManager.loadStyleDeclarations("fonts/fonts.swf")
    }
    ]]>
</mx:Script>
```

Summary

In this exercise, you learned how to compile fonts specified in a CSS file into a SWF. Doing this enables you to load fonts at runtime rather than loading all your fonts up front when a user first opens your application. You'll find this may come in handy when you work to optimize the size of your compiled application.

9.3

Creating a Style
Sheet for HTML Text

If you want to create text styling for your HTML, you need to use ActionScript to create the style sheet and assign it to a TextArea using the `styleSheet` property. In this exercise, you will create three styles and apply them to a TextArea. Additionally, you will create a second style sheet that gets applied when you click a button. The final result will look like Figure 9.3-1 and allow you to toggle between style sheets.

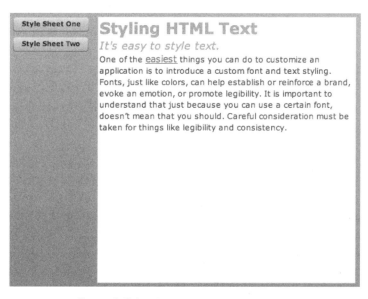

Figure 9.3-1   Style sheet in HTML example

1. Create a new Flex application and name it TextStyleSheet.mxml.

2. Add a TextArea to your application and give it an `id` of `myText`. This is where you add the text that will be styled with the style sheet you create. Set the TextArea to 400 pixels wide, 400 pixels high, `verticalCenter` of 0, and `horizontalCenter` of 0 (see Listing 9.3-1).

Listing 9.3-1   **Adding the TextArea**

```
<!- TextStyleSheet.mxml ->
...
<mx:TextArea
      id="myText"
      verticalCenter="0"
      horizontalCenter="0"
      width="400"
      height="400">
</mx:TextArea>
...
```

3. To create the first style sheet using ActionScript, you need to create a new function called `setStyleSheetOne()` with in an `<mx:Script>` block. The style classes you need to make are `h1`, `subtitle`, and `p`. The `h1` and `p` styles are type selectors assigned to tags within the htmlText, whereas the subtitle style is a class selector assigned to a span tag. The ActionScript in Listing 9.3-2 shows the required function to create your style sheet by setting the properties of the text styling and applies that style sheet to myText.

Listing 9.3-2   **Creating the style sheet**

```
<!- TextStyleSheet.mxml ->
...
<mx:Script>
      <![CDATA[
            public function setStyleSheetOne():void
            {
            var styleOne:StyleSheet = new StyleSheet();

            var h1:Object = new Object();
            h1.fontWeight = "bold";
            h1.color = "#62ABCD";
            h1.fontSize = 24;

            var subtitle:Object = new Object();
            subtitle.fontStyle = "italic";
            subtitle.color = "#999999";
            subtitle.fontSize = 16;
```

Listing 9.3-2   **Continued**

```
                var p:Object = new Object();
                p.color = "#444444";
                p.fontSize = 12;

                styleOne.setStyle("h1", h1);
                styleOne.setStyle(".subtitle", subtitle);
                styleOne.setStyle("p", p);

                myText.styleSheet = styleOne;
        }
        ]]>
</mx:Script>
...
```

4. Now that you have your style sheet created, you need to add some text to the text area to be styled. The text you specify needs to be in htmlText and use references to the styling you created in your style sheet: h1, subtitle, and p. The code snippet in Listing 9.3-3 shows htmlText block to add.

Listing 9.3-3   **Adding the htmlText**

```
<!-- TextStyleSheet.mxml -->
...
<mx:htmlText>
        <![CDATA[<h1>Styling HTML Text</h1><span class='subtitle'>It's easy to style
text.</span><br><p>One of the easiest things you can do to customize an applica-
tion is to introduce a custom font and text styling. Fonts, just like colors, can
help establish or reinforce a brand, evoke an emotion, or promote legibility. It
is important to understand that just because you can use a certain font, doesn't
mean that you should. Careful consideration must be taken for things like legibil-
ity and consistency.</p>]]>
</mx:htmlText>
...
```

5. For this exercise, you'll be using a button to fire the setStyleSheetOne() function and apply the style sheet to your TextArea. However, if you want to apply the text styling immediately, you could use initialize or creationComplete on your Application tag.

   Add a button to your application, give it a label of "Style Sheet One" and set the setStyleSheetOne() function for the button's click event (see Listing 9.3-4).

Listing 9.3-4   Adding a button to set the style sheet

```
<!- TextStyleSheet.mxml ->
...
<mx:Button
      x="40"
      y="40"
      label="Style Sheet One"
      click="setStyleSheetOne()"/>
...
```

6. If you run the application, you should see text without any styling in the TextArea. Click the Style Sheet One button and you should see the text get styled with the properties you specified in the style sheet you created.

7. What if you want to change the styling of your text at runtime? In this case, you can copy the **setStyleSheetOne()** function, give the function a new name of **setStyleSheetTwo()**, and change the style properties (see Listing 9.3-5).

Listing 9.3-5   Creating a second style sheet

```
...
public function setStyleSheetTwo():void
{
      var styleTwo:StyleSheet = new StyleSheet();

      var h1:Object = new Object();
      h1.fontWeight = "italic";
      h1.color = "#CC5500";
      h1.fontSize = 18;

      var subtitle:Object = new Object();
      subtitle.fontStyle = "bold";
      subtitle.color = "#62ABCD";
      subtitle.fontSize = 14;

      var p:Object = new Object();
      p.fontStyle = "bold";
      p.color = "#999999";
      p.fontSize = 12;
      styleTwo.setStyle("h1", h1);
      styleTwo.setStyle(".subtitle", subtitle);
      styleTwo.setStyle("p", p);
      myText.styleSheet = styleTwo;
}
...
```

8. To trigger the style sheet to change, create a new button, give it a label of "Style Sheet Two" and set the click event to `setStyleSheetTwo()`, as shown in Listing 9.3-6.

Listing 9.3-6   **Adding a second button to set the second style sheet**

```
<mx:Button
      x="40"
      y="70"
      label="Style Sheet Two"
      click="setStyleSheetTwo()"/>
```

9. With this new button and style sheet, run your application; you can now toggle between style sheets.

Summary

In this exercise, you learned how to create a style sheet that can be applied to HTML text. This can be helpful for styling dynamic text or formatting text generated by Flex's Rich Text Editor.

Applying a Custom Effect

Effects can be very useful for providing user feedback. As a user is interacting with various parts of your application, you can use effects to send meaningful messages just by using motion. In this exercise, you'll reproduce an effect that is common in the Mac OSX operating system. On a Mac OSX login screen, if you enter incorrect login information the window shakes as if to say "No, that's incorrect!" This is quite easy to reproduce in Flex using a Sequence and Move effect. You'll be making a panel shake when a button is clicked, as shown in Figure 11.1-1.

Figure 11.1-1   Panel with a shake motion

1. Create a new MXML file and name it WindowShake.mxml.
2. Add a Panel component with a **verticalCenter** and **horizontalCenter** of 0. Give the panel an **id** of **myPanel** and add a button to the panel as in Listing 11.1-1.

Listing 11.1-1   **Adding the panel and button to your application**

```
<mx:Panel
     id="myPanel"
     width="250"
     height="200"
```

Listing 11.1-1   **Continued**

```
        layout="absolute"
        verticalCenter="0"
        horizontalCenter="0"
        title="Panel">
        <mx:Button
            x="80"
            y="60"
            label="Shake!"/>
</mx:Panel>
```

3. To make the window shake, you can use a series of Move effects within a sequence. Create a Sequence effect and give it an id of `windowShake`.

    Inside the sequence, create two Move effects. Set the `xBy` property for the first Move effect to 20 pixels and the second Move effect to –20 pixels (see Listing 11.1-2). This creates the back and forth motion, but you need to repeat that motion multiple times in order to make the window shake. Add a `repeatCount` value of 5 to repeat the Sequence effect five times and set the target to `myPanel`.

Listing 11.1-2   **Creating the Sequence effect**

```
<mx:Sequence
        id="windowShake"
        target="{myPanel}"
        duration="50"
        repeatCount="5">
        <mx:Move
            xBy="20"/>
        <mx:Move
            xBy="-20"/>
</mx:Sequence>
```

4. Now, you just need to trigger the Sequence effect (see Listing 11.1-3). On the button inside the panel, specify `windowShake.play()` for the click event.

Listing 11.1-3   **Triggering the Sequence effect**

```
<mx:Button
        x="80"
        y="60"
        label="Shake!"
        click="windowShake.play()"/>
```

5. Run your application and watch the window shake when you click the button. To change how quickly the effect plays, you can adjust the duration on the Sequence

effect. This is a simple implementation of this effect, but you could tie it to form validation. Listing 11.1-4 is the entire MXML for this exercise.

Listing 11.1-4   **WindowShake.mxml**

```
<?xml version="1.0" encoding="utf-8"?>
<mx:Application
      xmlns:mx="http://www.adobe.com/2006/mxml"
      layout="absolute">
      <mx:Panel
            id="myPanel"
            width="250"
            height="200"
            layout="absolute"
            verticalCenter="0"
            horizontalCenter="0"
            title="Panel">
            <mx:Button
                  x="80"
                  y="60"
                  label="Shake!"
                  click="windowShake.play()"/>
      </mx:Panel>

      <mx:Sequence
            id="windowShake"
            target="{myPanel}"
            duration="100"
            repeatCount="5">
            <mx:Move
                  xBy="20"/>
            <mx:Move
                  xBy="-20"/>
      </mx:Sequence>

</mx:Application>
```

Summary

In this exercise, you learned how to use effects to make a panel shake based on a user interaction. With this base knowledge, you can begin to explore other ways effects might be
used in your application. Try extending this example by adding more effects or interactions
that trigger other effects.

Creating a Transition between View States

At the beginning of the "Transitions" section in Chapter 11, "Effects and Transitions," Figure 11-5 was an example of a panel that expands to show additional fields required for the user to "Sign Up." Rather than having to go to a completely different area to access these fields, it all happens in the same area. This helps the user maintain context and can be a welcome experience. In this exercise, you will create a panel that has two states and a transition between them as shown in Figure 11.2-1. The base state will have two text inputs: the first state is user login and the second state adds text inputs for a new user to sign up.

Figure 11.2-1   Revealing panel

1. Create a new Flex application and call it RevealingPanel.mxml.
2. Add a panel to your application that is 290 pixels wide by 170 pixels high and give it a title of "Login" (see Listing 11.2-1).

Listing 11.2-1   **Adding the panel**

```
<?xml version="1.0" encoding="utf-8"?>
<mx:Application
      xmlns:mx="http://www.adobe.com/2006/mxml"
      layout="absolute">
      <mx:Panel
            width="290"
            height="170"
            title="Login">
      </mx:Panel>

</mx:Application>
```

3. Inside the panel, add a form with a width of 100%, a bottom style property value of 40 pixels, and a top style property value of 0. Give the form an id of myForm (see Listing 11.2-2).

Listing 11.2-2   **Adding the form**

```
<?xml version="1.0" encoding="utf-8"?>
<mx:Application
      xmlns:mx="http://www.adobe.com/2006/mxml"
      layout="absolute">
      <mx:Panel
            x="270"
            y="160"
            width="290"
            height="170"
            layout="absolute"
            title="Login">
            <mx:Form
                  id="myForm"
                  x="0"
                  width="100%"
                  bottom="40"
                  top="0">
            </mx:Form>
      </mx:Panel>

</mx:Application>
```

4. Inside the form, add two text inputs with labels of "Name" and "Password" (see Listing 11.2-3).

Listing 11.2-3 **Adding text inputs to the form**

```
<mx:Form
      id="myForm"
      x="0"
      width="100%"
      bottom="40"
      top="0">
      <mx:FormItem
            label="Name">
            <mx:TextInput/>
      </mx:FormItem>
      <mx:FormItem
            label="Password">
         <mx:TextInput/>
      </mx:FormItem>
</mx:Form>
```

5. At the bottom-left of the panel, add a button with a `bottom` property value of 10, `left` property value of 10, and a label of `"Sign Up"`. Also, add a button in the bottom-right area of the panel with a `bottom` property value of 10, `left` property value of 10, and label of `"Login"` (see Listing 11.2-4).

Listing 11.2-4 **Adding buttons to the bottom of the panel area**

```
<mx:Button
      label="Login"
      right="10"
      bottom="10"/>
<mx:Button
      label="Sign Up"
      left="10"
      bottom="10"/>
```

At this point, your MXML should look something like Listing 11.2-5 and the layout of your panel should look something like Figure 11.2-2.

Listing 11.2-5 **Panel in the base state**

```
<?xml version="1.0" encoding="utf-8"?>
<mx:Application
      xmlns:mx="http://www.adobe.com/2006/mxml"
      layout="absolute">
      <mx:Panel
            x="270"
            y="160"
            width="290"
```

Listing 11.2-5   **Continued**

```
                    height="170"
                    layout="absolute"
                    title="Login">
                    <mx:Form
                            id="myForm"
                            x="0"
                            width="100%"
                            bottom="40"
                            top="0">
                            <mx:FormItem
                                    label="Name">
                                    <mx:TextInput/>
                            </mx:FormItem>
                            <mx:FormItem
                                    label="Password">
                                    <mx:TextInput/>
                            </mx:FormItem>
                    </mx:Form>
                    <mx:Button
                            label="Login"
                            right="10"
                            bottom="10"/>
                    <mx:Button
                            label="Sign Up"
                            left="10"
                            bottom="10"/>
            </mx:Panel>

    </mx:Application>
```

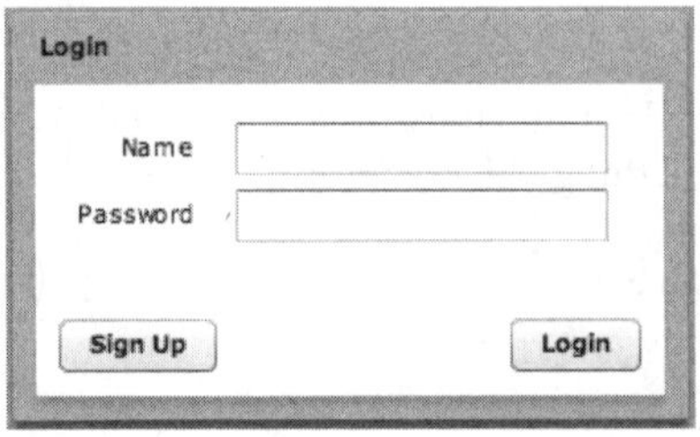

Figure 11.2-2   Panel in first state

6. With the base state defined, you can move on to the second state. In this state, you'll change the labels of the text inputs, title of the panel, and add some text inputs for the extra information that is required for a new user to sign up.

Create a new View State called SignUpView. You can do this in MXML Design View, in the States window (Window > States) as shown in Figure 11.2-3. You can also add this new state in MXML using the `<mx:states>` tag within your Application tag (see Listing 11.2-6).

Figure 11.2-3   Adding the SignUpView state using the States window

Listing 11.2-6   The SignUpView state added in MXML

```
<?xml version="1.0" encoding="utf-8"?>
<mx:Application
     xmlns:mx="http://www.adobe.com/2006/mxml"
     layout="absolute">

     <mx:states>
          <mx:State
               name="SignUpView">
               <!— State changes will go here. —>
          </mx:State>
     </mx:states>

</mx:Application>
```

7. In the new SignUpView state, the first thing you need to do is change the title of the panel to "`Sign Up`". Also, change the label of the Sign Up button to "`Cancel`", make the label of the first Text Input "`First Name`", the label of the second text input "`Last Name`", and change the label on the Login button to "`Submit`". If you're working in Design View, you'll see that when you switch to MXML Source View, your MXML is being updated accordingly.

After making those changes, your MXML should look something like Listing 11.2-7. You'll notice that ids were automatically assigned to the items you changed. Now, by switching back and forth between states in the States panel, you can see what your different states look like.

Listing 11.2-7   **Changes for the SignUpView state**

```
<mx:states>
    <mx:State
        name="SignUpView">
        <mx:SetProperty
            target="{panel1}"
            name="title"
            value="Sign Up"/>
        <mx:SetProperty
            target="{formitem1}"
            name="label"
            value="First Name"/>
        <mx:SetProperty
            target="{formitem2}"
            name="label"
            value="Last Name"/>
        <mx:SetProperty
            target="{button1}"
            name="label"
            value="Cancel"/>
    </mx:State>
</mx:states>
```

8. To add the text inputs needed for a user to sign up, you need to make the panel taller in the SignUpViewState. Change the height of the panel to 220 pixels.

    Add two more TextInputs under the newly labeled Last Name TextInput. The third text input needs a label of `"Email"` and the fourth text input needs a label of `"Password"`. There's your second state! The MXML you add to accomplish the addition of the text inputs should look something like Listing 11.2-8 and in Design View should look like Figure 11.2-4.

Listing 11.2-8   **Adding the text inputs**

```
<mx:AddChild
    relativeTo="{myForm}"
    position="lastChild">
    <mx:FormItem
        label="Email">
        <mx:TextInput/>
    </mx:FormItem>
</mx:AddChild>
<mx:AddChild
    relativeTo="{myForm}"
    position="lastChild">
    <mx:FormItem
        label="Password">
```

Listing 11.2-8   **Continued**

```
            <mx:TextInput/>
        </mx:FormItem>
</mx:AddChild>
<mx:SetProperty
        target="{button2}"
        name="label"
        value="Submit"/>
```

Figure 11.2-4   Panel in second state

9. Now that you have your states created, you can tackle making the transition. For the transition, you want the panel to grow in height to reveal the additional text inputs in the SignUpView state by fading them in. Add the MXML for the transitions shown in Listing 11.2-9. Be sure that the form you added at the beginning of the exercise has an `id` of `myForm`. Also, to speed up the transition, set the duration for the Parallel effects to 300.

Listing 11.2-9   **Adding the transitions**

```
<mx:transitions>
    <mx:Transition
        fromState="*"
        toState="SignUpView">
        <mx:Parallel
            duration="300">
            <mx:Resize
                target="{panel1}"/>
            <mx:Fade
                target="{form1}"
                alphaFrom="0"
                alphaTo="1"/>
        </mx:Parallel>
```

Listing 11.2-9   **Continued**

```
        </mx:Transition>
        <mx:Transition
                fromState="SignUpView"
                toState="*">
                <mx:Parallel
                        duration="300">
                        <mx:Resize
                                target="{panel1}"/>
                        <mx:Fade
                                target="{form1}"
                                alphaFrom="0"
                                alphaTo="1"/>
                </mx:Parallel>
        </mx:Transition>
</mx:transitions>
```

10. The transitions specified in Listing 11.2-9 use a Parallel effect for both transitions. In fact, they are the same for each transition except for the `toState` and `fromState` values.

> **Tip**
>
> Because both transitions are the same, you could change the MXML for this example to be one transition, but specify an asterisk (*) for both the `toState` and `fromState` values, as in Listing 11.2-10. Doing that would produce the same effect as the MXML in Listing 11.2-9; but for the purposes of this exercise, we'll make two transitions in case you want to experiment later.

Listing 11.2-10   **Using one common transition**

```
<mx:transitions>
        <mx:Transition
                fromState="*"
                toState="*">
                <mx:Parallel
                        duration="300">
                        <mx:Resize
                                target="{panel1}"/>
                        <mx:Fade
                                target="{form1}"
                                alphaFrom="0"
                                alphaTo="1"/>
                </mx:Parallel>
        </mx:Transition>
</mx:transitions>
```

11. Everything is now in place for you to test your transition. The last thing you need to do is set some functions to switch between states. When you click the Sign Up button on the base state, it should go to the SignUpView, and when you click the Cancel button in SignUpView, it should go back to the base state.

On your base state, add the function in Listing 11.2-11 to the click event on the Sign Up button.

Listing 11.2-11   Adding a function to the click event of the Sign Up button

```
click="currentState='SignUpView'"
```

Now, clicking the Sign Up button sends you to the SignUpView state, but to get back to the base state, you need to specify a SetEventHandler override to change the function to one that sends you back to the base state. Add the SetEventHandler override shown in Listing 11.2-12 into the MXML of the SignUpView state.

Listing 11.2-12   Adding the SetEventHandler override for the button

```
<mx:SetEventHandler
      target="{button1}"
      name="click"
      handler="currentState=''"/>
```

12. Run your application. You should see the states of the Login panel change states when you click the Sign Up or Cancel button. Listing 11.2-13 is the entire MXML for this exercise.

Listing 11.2-13   RevealingPanel.mxml

```
<?xml version="1.0" encoding="utf-8"?>
<mx:Application
      xmlns:mx="http://www.adobe.com/2006/mxml"
      layout="absolute">
      <mx:states>
          <mx:State
              name="SignUpView">
              <mx:SetProperty
                  target="{panel1}"
                  name="title"
                  value="Sign Up"/>
              <mx:SetProperty
                  target="{formitem1}"
                  name="label"
                  value="First Name"/>
              <mx:SetProperty
                  target="{formitem2}"
                  name="label"
```

Listing 11.2-13   **Continued**

```
                                value="Last Name"/>
                        <mx:SetProperty
                                target="{button1}"
                                name="label"
                                value="Cancel"/>
                        <mx:SetProperty
                                target="{panel1}"
                                name="height"
                                value="220"/>
                        <mx:AddChild
                                relativeTo="{form1}"
                                position="lastChild">
                                <mx:FormItem
                                        label="Email">
                                        <mx:TextInput/>
                                </mx:FormItem>
                        </mx:AddChild>
                        <mx:AddChild
                                relativeTo="{form1}"
                           position="lastChild">
                                <mx:FormItem
                                        label="Password">
                                        <mx:TextInput/>
                                </mx:FormItem>
                        </mx:AddChild>
                        <mx:SetProperty
                                target="{button2}"
                                name="label"
                                value="Submit"/>
                        <mx:SetEventHandler
                                target="{button1}"
                                name="click"
                                handler="currentState=''"/>
                </mx:State>
        </mx:states>

<mx:transitions>
        <mx:Transition
                fromState="*"
                toState="*">
                <mx:Parallel
                        duration="300">
                        <mx:Resize
                                target="{panel1}"/>
                        <mx:Fade
                                target="{form1}"
```

Listing 11.2-13   **Continued**

```
                            alphaFrom="0"
                            alphaTo="1"/>
                </mx:Parallel>
        </mx:Transition>
</mx:transitions>

        <mx:Panel
                x="270"
                y="160"
                width="290"
                height="170"
                layout="absolute"
                title="Login"
                id="panel1">
                <mx:Form
                        x="0"
                        width="100%"
                        bottom="40"
                        top="0"
                        id="form1">
                        <mx:FormItem
                                label="Name"
                                id="formitem1">
                                <mx:TextInput/>
                        </mx:FormItem>
                        <mx:FormItem
                                label="Password"
                            id="formitem2">
                                <mx:TextInput/>
                        </mx:FormItem>
                </mx:Form>
                <mx:Button
                        label="Login"
                        right="10"
                        bottom="10"
                        id="button2"/>
                <mx:Button
                        label="Sign Up"
                        left="10"
                        bottom="10"
                        id="button1"
                        click="currentState='SignUpView'"/>
        </mx:Panel>

</mx:Application>
```

Summary

In this exercise, you learned how to use states, effects, and transitions to make a panel fluidly change views based on a user interaction. This is only a small example of what you can accomplish with transitions. To extend this exercise, you could add an easing function to the Resize effect of the panel, add more choreographed motion using compound effects, or create more states.

Creating a Graphical Skin Using the Flex Component Kit

The preferred method of creating skins in Flash involves using the Flex Component Kit and Flash CS3. This is because when using the Flex Component Kit you can add interactivity and animations. With the Flex Component Kit, there are naming conventions, techniques, and shortcuts that you should be aware of to make sure your pixel precise artwork translates into Flex 3.

In this exercise, you'll be guided step-by-step through the process of creating, from scratch, a skin for a `Button` component using Flash CS3 and the Flex Component Kit. To get started, you need to install the Flex Component Kit extension, which can be downloaded from https://www.adobe.com/cfusion/entitlement/index.cfm?e=flex_skins. After you have the Flex Component Kit installed, you may have to restart Flash. While you are there, you may also want to download the Skin Design Extension for Flash CS3, which provides templates for Flex skins.

If you'd like to start with a set of skin templates, refer to Exercise 12.2, "Using Flash Skin Templates." Using skin templates can cut down on production time, but it's always helpful to understand just what goes into putting them together so you can troubleshoot any issues you might have. Additionally, you can create skins that may not fit the mold of the skin templates.

Creating the Skin Structure

Because you'll be creating skins for a `button`, it is important to know what parts of the component you can skin. By referring to Appendix A, "Skinning and Styling Diagrams," you will see that a `button` has skins for the up, over, down, and disabled states.

Those are the states you will create in this exercise, as well as transitions.

Note

Currently, if you set filters like a Drop Shadow, Outer Glow, and so forth on artwork you create in Flash, it will not transfer to Flex. If you want to create those same effects, you may need to work with bitmap artwork or apply the filters in Flex. To learn more about using filters in Flex, refer to Chapter 10, "Filters and Blends."

1. Open up Flash CS3 and create a new Flash file (ActionScript 3.0). You can use the default dimensions of 550 pixels by 400 pixels, but set the frame rate to 24 frames per second (fps). Save this new file wherever you like and name it FlashFCKButton.fla.

Note

The reason you want to set the frame rate to 24 is because that is the default frame rate at which Flex SWFs play. If you don't set the frame rate to 24, you will have an opportunity to change it later.

2. Before you begin to create artwork for the `button` skin, you need to create the structure for the symbol. From the application menu, select Create New Symbol and make your new symbol a Movie Clip. Name the symbol Button_skin, check Export for ActionScript, and check Enable Guides for 9-Slice Scaling, as in Figure 12.1-1. You may need to toggle the New Symbol dialog from Basic to Advanced mode in order to see the 9-slice scaling check box. With those options specified, click OK.

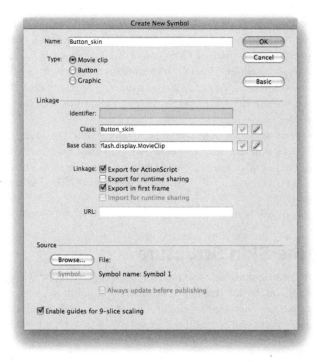

Figure 12.1-1   Setting the symbol properties

Note
You may get a warning prompt that looks like Figure 12.1-2. Click OK.

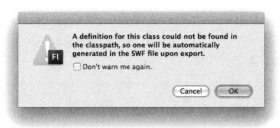

Figure 12.1-2   Warning prompt

Notice the name you specified follows the naming conventions discussed in Chapter 5, "Graphical Skinning." You also specified _skin for the skinnable part of the button instead of upSkin, overSkin, and so on. This is because with Flex 3, you can create a symbol in Flash that contains all the states of a component skin inside of it. You can reference this symbol by specifying the skin property and have it work in Flex 3.

Using the Flex Component Kit allows you to create one symbol with different skin states in it because the Flex Component Kit will turn your symbol into a custom component that the Flex framework will recognize; it will then act appropriately to display your skins correctly.

Note
You can learn more about the naming convention for sub-component styles in Chapter 5.

3. After creating the symbol, you should be taken into the new symbol you've created. If the Timeline is not visible, turn it on (Window > Timeline). This is where you'll create the structure to make the symbol work within Flex.

Note
You may notice dashed grid lines on the stage area. Don't worry. We'll get to those later in the "Setting the 9-Slice Grid" section.

4. On the Timeline, create three layers and name them "states," "transitions," and "base." The "states" layer has frame labels for the various states of your skin. The "transitions" layer has frame labels and artwork for animated transitions. The "base" layer contains any other artwork. This should look similar to Figure 12.1-3.

Note
You don't have to set up your Timeline and layers like this, but for this example it helps to keep things organized.

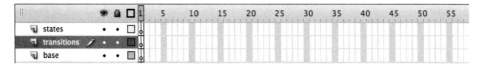

Figure 12.1-3   Setting up the layer names

For this `button` skin, you'll be focusing on the `up`, `over`, `down`, and `disabled` states. As mentioned in the previous paragraph, you'll be adding frame labels to identify the various states of your skin.

5. The first state for the button is the `up` state. Select frame 1 on the states layer and name the frame label `up` in the Properties Inspector.

6. Go to frame 12 and add `over` as the frame label on the same states layer. Move another 12 frames over to frame 24 and label it `down`.

7. Finally, move to frame 36 and label it `disabled`. In this example, you're using 12 frames between each state, but you can add as few or as many frames between states as you'd like. You'll want to have some space though for transitions. Your Timeline should now look similar to Figure 12.1-4.

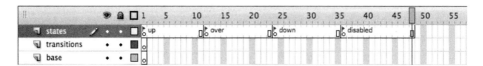

Figure 12.1-4   State frame labels

> **Note**
>
> Because the default frame rate in Flex 3 is 24, each state transition will end up being one half-second long. If you'd like to learn more about changing the default frame rate of your Flex 3 project, refer to the Flex documentation.
>
> You can add the other states for a button to the Timeline as needed. For example, you could add `selectedUp`, `selectedOver`, and so on.

Creating the Skin Artwork

Now that you have an idea of where the artwork for each state needs to go, you can start creating some artwork for each skin state.

1. Move to the base layer and create a key frame at the same frame position as the frame in the states layer labeled `up`. Create key frames for the other states as well as in Figure 12.1-5. Whatever artwork you create on these frames will appear for the states of your button in Flex.

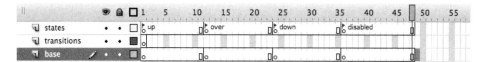

Figure 12.1-5   Added base layer key frames

2. For the upSkin, create a rectangle on the base layer, at the same position as the **up** frame label. Make this rectangle 80 pixels wide by 22 pixels high. Set the rectangle to a white fill and a 1-pixel stroke that is dark gray (#636363). Make sure that the upper-left corner of the artwork you create is positioned at 0,0.

   Also, select the stroke and select Modify > Shape > Convert Lines to Fills. This changes the skin artwork to 81 pixels wide by 23 pixels high, which is okay. Group that rectangle's fill and stroke together. Your artwork should look like Figure 12.1-6.

> **Note**
>
> The default height of a `button` is 22 pixels, but feel free to experiment with a different height.

Figure 12.1-6   Button upSkin

> **Note**
>
> Converting lines to fills helps your skin artwork look better in Flex. This is because strokes in Flash are drawn half inside and half outside the bounds of the shape. Converting a line to a fill ensures that the entire stroke will be within the shape bounds. Figure 12.1-7 shows the difference.

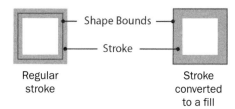

Figure 12.1-7   Stroke variances

3. For the rest of the frames on the base layer, duplicate the artwork you created for the upSkin and place the artwork on each one of the frames as in Figure 12.1-8.

Now comes the fun part. Using the Flex Component Kit, you can create transitions to animate between skin states. You'll create these next.

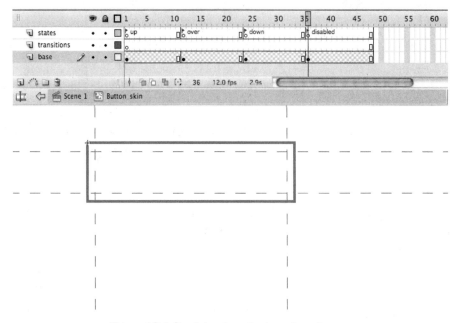

Figure 12.1-8   Artwork on the base layer frames

Creating Transitions

Creating transitions between your skin states is easy as long as you follow the frame label naming conventions mentioned previously. Transitions in your skins can add another level of detail and richness to your application. You will be creating transitions between the up and over states, and then between the over and down states.

1. On frame 1 on the transitions layer, draw a rectangle that is 76 pixels wide by 18 pixels high. Fill this rectangle with a vertical linear gradient with a light blue (#26A7DF) on top and a dark blue (#0375BF) on bottom. Group this rectangle and position it on top of the rectangle on the base layer below, vertically and horizontally centered. This rectangle should look like Figure 12.1-9 as it is overlaying the artwork on the base layer below it.

Figure 12.1-9   Transition layer and base layer artwork overlayed

2. Add a blank key frame at frame 12 on the transitions layer. Name frame 1 on the transitions layer `up-over:start` as in Figure 12.1-10. This tells Flex where the up to over transition starts.

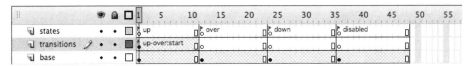

Figure 12.1-10   Setting the up-over transition start

3. Add blank key frames on frames 13 and 24. These will hold more artwork and frame labels.
4. Create the artwork for the over transition state by duplicating the rectangle you created on frame 1 of the transitions layer and placing it on frame 12. Change the blue gradient to a lighter blue (#90D3F0) and leave the bottom fill color dark blue. This creates a "highlight" effect when a user rolls his cursor over the button. This artwork should look like Figure 12.1-11 as it's overlaying the artwork on the base layer below.

Figure 12.1-11   Over transition layer and base layer artwork overlayed

5. If you scrub between frames 1 and 12, you should see the blue gradients change, but not very smoothly. Click on a frame on the transitions layer between frames 1 and 12; in the Properties Inspector, select `Shape` from the `Tween` combo box. Now when you scrub through frames 1 through 12, you should see a nice, smooth animation. This will be what a user sees when she rolls over your button.

   However, you need to tell the transition when to end. On frame 12, on the states layer, label the keyframe `up-over:end`. This tells Flex when the transition ends.

6. Create the transition for the over to down states. Create a blank key frame on frame 13 on the transitions layer. Duplicate the artwork on frame 12 and place it at the same position on frame 13. Name frame 13 `over-down:start` to set the transition start.

7. For the end of the over to down transition, go to frame 24 and label it `over-down:end`. Duplicate the artwork from frame 1 on the transitions layer and place it at the same position on frame 24. Change the blue gradient by flipping it vertically. The artwork for this state should look like Figure 12.1-12 as it is overlaying artwork on the base layer.

Figure 12.1-12   Down transition layer and base layer artwork overlayed

8. Finally, add artwork for the disabled transition state by creating a blank key frame at frame 36 on the transitions layer. Duplicate the artwork from frame 1 on the same layer and place it in the same position on frame 36. Change the gradient colors to light gray (#A6A8AB) on top and dark gray (#838588) on the bottom. This artwork should look like Figure 12.1-13.

Note

For this example, you aren't creating a transition between the down and disabled states. This is because you may rarely see this transition take place. However, if your application design requires it, feel free to create it.

As you scrub through the Timeline, you should see the various transitions animate between states.

Figure 12.1-13   Disabled transition layer and base layer artwork overlayed

Setting the 9-Slice Grid

When you initially created the Movie Clip symbol for the Flash skin, you probably noticed dashed guides. These guides are used to set the 9-slice grid. (Refer to Chapter 5 for more information on 9-slice grids.)

Now that you have your skin artwork created, you can set the 9-slice grid. All you have to do is drag these guides so that your skin scales without getting distorted. Figure 12.1-14 shows an example of a 9-slice grid.

> **Note**
>
> Depending on your skin artwork, you may need to experiment with different scale grid placements. Sometimes setting a grid a difference of a pixel can produce different results.

Figure 12.1-14   Setting the 9-slice grids

Bringing the Flash Skin into Flex

To get the frame labels and how they relate to the artwork to be recognized in Flex, you need to convert the Button_skin symbol to a Flex component. You need to have the Flex Component Kit installed to do this, as mentioned at the beginning of this section.

1. Open up the Publish Settings and make a few adjustments. You don't want to publish an HTML file, so uncheck the HTML check box. Additionally, you'll be publishing a SWC, so click on the Flash tab and check the Publish SWC check box. That's all you need to do there, so click OK.

2. Select the symbol you made named Button_skin in the Library panel (Window > Library). To convert the symbol to a Flex Component, select Convert Symbol to Flex Component from the Commands menu (see Figure 12.1-15).

Figure 12.1-15   Commands menu

Also, you will notice that a component named FlexComponentBase has been added to your Library (see Figure 12.1-16).

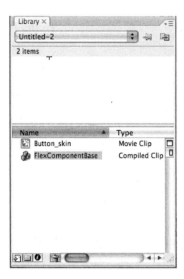

Figure 12.1-16   Library with FlexComponentBase

3. Publish the FLA file containing your skins as a SWC (File > Publish). You can publish the SWC to any location; just remember where you publish it. If you did not set the frame rate of your FLA file to 24, you get a window asking if you'd like to convert the frame rate to 24. You can click OK.

Note

If you're working with a frame rate other than 24 and then convert the frame rate to 24, you might have timing or other issues in Flex. It is advised that whenever working with Flash to create components for Flex you always set the frame rate of your Flash assets to the same frame rate as your Flex application.

4. When you publish your Flash file, you'll notice a SWC and SWF will be produced (see Figure 12.1-17). You only need to be concerned about the SWC.

FlashFCKButton.swc   FlashFCKButton.swf

Figure 12.1-17   Export SWF and SWC

5. Now that you've published the SWC, switch over to Flex Builder 3.

6. Create a new Flex project by selecting File > New > Flex Project and name it Flash-FCKButton.

7. In your Flex project, create a new folder (File > New > Folder) inside the src folder of your project and name it style. This is where all your skins and supporting CSS file go. To learn more about the role the CSS file plays, refer to Chapter 4, "Styling" or Chapter 5.

8. For this example, you also need to create a new CSS file. To do this, select File > New > CSS File. Name the file style.css and specify the style folder you created as the save location. When you have the proper information specified, click Finish.

Note

You don't always have to create a CSS file before using the Skin Import Wizard. The wizard generates one for you if you specify a file name in the Create Skin Style Rules In area rather than browsing for a file.

9. To bring in the FlashFCKButton skin, you can use the Skin Import Wizard in Flex Builder 3; select File > Import > Skin Artwork from the Flex Builder application menu.

10. In the first screen of the Skin Import Wizard, you have a few options. At the top, select the SWC or SWF File radio button and then browse for the SWC that was published. Make sure you select the file with the .swc extension, not the one with the .swf extension.

11. In the Copy Artwork to Subfolder field, browse for the skins folder you created in the style folder. In the Create Skin Style Rules In field, specify style/style.css. Leave the default selection for the Attach Style Sheet to Application option. Figure 12.1-18 shows what these specified settings look like.

Figure 12.1-18   Specifying the skin and CSS assets

12. Click the Next button and you are presented with a list of check box items for the Style Selector and Skin Part for your skin (see Figure 12.1-19). Leave Button_skin checked and click Finish.

> **Tip**
>
> You can change the Style Selector or Skin Part that an image asset will be assigned to by clicking a name in either one of the columns.

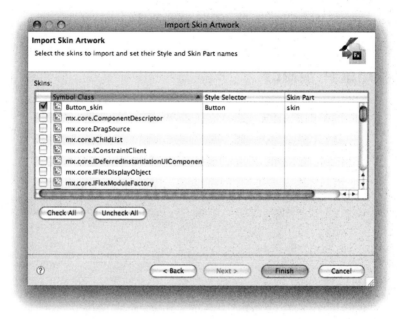

Figure 12.1-19   Verifying the skin parts

13. When you click Finish, the style.css file is created and the skin parts are assigned to the Accordion by embedding a skin class via CSS. If you look at the style.css that was created, you will see the appropriate CSS code as in Listing 12.1-1.

Listing 12.1-1   **Generated CSS**

```
/* style.css*/
Button
{
    skin: Embed(skinClass='Button_skin');
}
```

> **Note**
>
> If you run into issues with a skinClass name not being recognized, check the Linkage Class name of the symbol in Symbol Properties. Sometimes, when creating a skin using Convert Symbol to Flex Component, special characters, like a dollar sign ($), can get stripped from the

> Linkage Class name. If this occurs, add the special characters that got removed back in and click OK.
>
> When working with a set of skins compiled as a SWC, sometimes you might get an error that reads, "Can't resolve source...." This might be because the SWC is not in the same folder as your CSS file. Try moving the CSS file and the SWC into the same folder.

The Final Product

You have successfully created skins for a `Button` component. Now all that's left is to add a `button` to the application layout so you can see the results. After you've added a `button` to the application layout, run the application. You should see the `button` transition between the skin states as you interact with it.

> **Note**
>
> You can access the final Flex and Flash asset files in a folder called FlashFCKButtonExample.

> **Tip**
>
> When creating a skin set in Flash, consider placing a text label of each symbol name next to the corresponding symbol. This helps make figuring out the name of each skin part really easy. You may also want to make the text labels selectable so any developer can pop open the published SWF or SWC to copy and paste symbol names wherever they may be needed. Text in Flash CS3 can be made selectable by selecting the text and checking the *selectable* toggle button in the Properties panel, as shown in Figure 12.1-20.

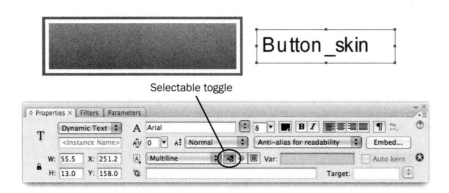

Figure 12.1-20   Setting text as selectable

Creating Other Assets

The Flex Component Kit is a powerful tool. This example was for just for the `button`, but these same processes can be repeated to create skins for any other Flex component. In addition, this approach in Flash is not limited to creating skins. You can also create icons, backgrounds, static graphics, and more using the same steps. The only difference may be in the way that you apply those graphics to your MXML layout.

> **Note**
>
> If you are using a graphic as a static element, like a background or static icon, you do not have to convert the symbol to a Flex component.

Summary

The Flex Component Kit allows you to extend content created in Flash into Flex. In this exercise, you learned how to use Flash and the Flex Component Kit to create a Button skin. The Button skin you created had a relatively simple transition, but you could use the Flex Component Kit to create skins that animate in a variety of ways to add another level of richness to your application.

Using Flash Skin Templates

Want more of a starting point for creating skins in Flash? Adobe has a set of skin templates that comes packaged with the Flash Skin Design Extensions. This extension provides individual templates for components as well as a single template that has all the required symbols for your Flex components. Each of the templates can be modified to meet your needs and is perfect for creating individual skin variations. In turn, because you aren't starting from scratch, the templates can help speed up the process of creating skins, and the majority of the required symbols for the component skins have been created for you. The extension can be downloaded from https://www.adobe.com/cfusion/entitlement/index.cfm?e=flex_skins. In these short steps, you will walk through the process of getting set up with the Flash Skin Design Extension.

1. Download and install the Flash Design Extension from the preceding URL. You may need to restart Flash after the install.

2. After you have the Flash Skin Design Extension installed for Flash, you can easily access the skin templates. You can access the templates by creating a New Flash file and clicking on the Templates tab at the top of the New Document dialog, next to General (see Figure 12.2-1). Simply select the template you want to work with and click OK.

   Additionally, you can access the Templates dialog from the Create from Template column in Flash's Getting Started window (see Figure 12.2-2).

3. After you've edited the skin template to your liking, you can follow the steps in the Exercise 12.1, "Creating a Graphical Skin Using the Flex Component," to use your skins in Flex.

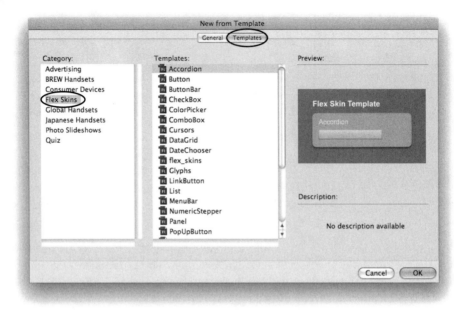

Figure 12.2-1   Flash skin templates

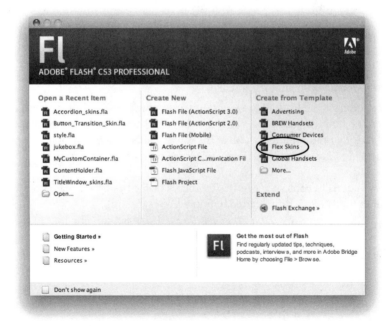

Figure 12.2-2   Flash's Getting Started window

Summary

In this exercise, you learned how to use the Flash skin templates that are part of the Skin Design Extensions. These templates are a great way to get a head start on skinning your Flex application. Keep in mind that you aren't limited to what these templates provide, and you may find it useful to extend this template to include additional components that your project requires.

Creating a Custom Container Using the Flex Component Kit

As mentioned in the Chapter 3, "Dynamic Layout," you can use container components within Flex to define the layout of your application. Using the Flex Component Kit, you can create your own custom container components in Flash and use them in Flex.

Just like any other container within Flex, your custom container can have other controls or containers added and arranged as you see fit. When creating a custom container within Flash, you control its appearance and the way it positions items within its boundaries.

Creating a Basic Container in Flash

Creating a container using the Flex Component Kit in Flash is similar to creating a skin. Your custom container will be a Movie Clip symbol that will be converted to a Flex component and imported into your Flex application. The following steps will guide you through the creation of a basic Flex container.

There are a few steps you need to take to create your custom container.

1. In Flash, create a new FLA file (ActionScript 3.0) called MyCustomContainer. You can leave the default dimensions and frame rate.

2. Select the Rectangle Tool and, in the Properties Inspector, change the corner radius to 10 for all corners. Set the fill color to #444444 and no border color.

   On the stage, draw a rectangle roughly 200 pixels by 200 pixels (see Figure 12.3-1).

Figure 12.3-1   Container artwork

3. Select the rectangle you just created and convert it to a Movie Clip symbol (Modify > Convert to Symbol). Name this symbol RoundedRectangle.

4. In your Library, you should see the newly created RoundedRectangle symbol. Select the symbol in the Library and select Commands > Convert Symbol to Flex Container from the application menu.

   When you convert the symbol to a container, you get a notice stating that the default frame rate of Flex is 24 and the frame rate of your symbol will be converted to that. You can click OK.

   Now you should see a component called FlexComponentBase and a symbol called FlexContentHolder in your Library. The FlexContentHolder defines the boundaries for the Flex components that will be added to it.

5. Open up your RoundedRectangle symbol by double-clicking on it in your Library or on the stage.

6. Now that you're within the RoundedRectangle symbol, drag the FlexContentHolder symbol within the defined area of the RoundedRectangle artwork.

7. Change the dimensions and positioning of the FlexContentHolder symbol to define the area that components can be added when in Flex (see Figure 12.3-2).

Figure 12.3-2   Placing the FlexContentHolder

8. You're ready to publish your custom container to be used in Flex. Select File > Publish Settings and uncheck HTML. Verify that under the Flash settings Publish SWC is checked.

9. After those settings have been verified and set, click Publish. Remember the publish location.

   Now that you've created your custom container in Flash, you're ready to bring it into Flex. To do that, you'll need to create a new Flex Project.

Bringing Your Custom Container into Flex

To use your newly created container, you'll need to go through a few steps, starting with creating a new Flex Project.

1. In Flex Builder, create a new Flex Project called ContainerExample (File > New > Flex Project). You don't need to do more than specify the name of the project, so click Finish.

2. To use the custom container in the Flex Project, it needs to be added to the project's Library Path. Select ContainerExample project and open its properties (Project > Properties).

3. Select Flex Build Path from the list on the left and click on Library Path in the area to the right (see Figure 12.3-3).

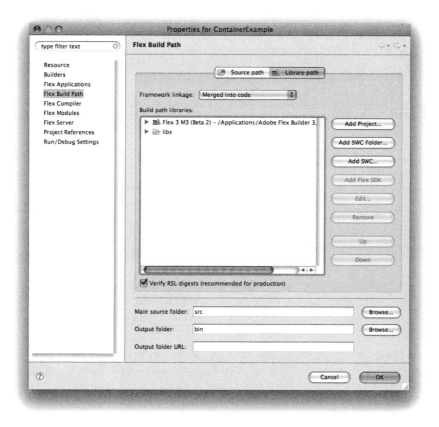

Figure 12.3-3   Adding the component to the library path

4. Click the Add SWC button and in the add SWC window browse for the
   MyCustomContainer.swc you published (see Figure 12.3-4). After selecting it,
   click OK.

Figure 12.3-4   Adding the SWC

5. You'll see the MyCustomContainer.swc file added to the Build Path Libraries list.
   Click OK.

6. Now you can add the custom container to the application layout. To access the
   RoundedRectangle container inside the MyCustomContainer component, you
   must first add the MyComps name space to your Application tag as represented in
   Listing 12.3-1.

Listing 12.3-1   Adding the MXML

```
<!- ContainerExample.mxml ->
<?xml version="1.0" encoding="utf-8"?>
<mx:Application xmlns:mx="http://www.adobe.com/2006/mxml"
                layout="absolute"
                xmlns:myComps="*">

</mx:Application>
```

7. In between your Application tags, open a new tag and start typing `RoundedRectangle`.
   You will notice that as you type the RoundedRectangle component shows up using
   the myComps namespace. Select it and close out the tag to create an area to drop in
   some other components.

8. Inside the tags for the RoundedRectangle component, add a VBox with a background color of white and add a few buttons inside the VBox as in Listing 12.3-2.

Listing 12.3-2   Adding styling and buttons

```
<!- ContainerExample.mxml ->
<?xml version="1.0" encoding="utf-8"?>
<mx:Application xmlns:mx="http://www.adobe.com/2006/mxml" layout="absolute"
xmlns:myComps="*">
```

Listing 12.3-2   **Adding styling and buttons**

```
<myComps:RoundedRectangle>
        <mx:VBox backgroundColor="#FFFFFF">
                <mx:Button/>
                <mx:Button/>
                <mx:Button/>
        </mx:VBox>
</myComps:RoundedRectangle>


</mx:Application>
```

9. If you run your Application, you'll see the VBox and Button groups inside of the RoundedRectangle container you created.

   However, you will notice that the VBox placed inside the RoundedRectangle container has been sized to 100% in width and height. In addition, if you were to change the dimensions of the RoundedRectangle component, it and the objects inside would stretch or compress. You will probably want to create any custom containers for Flex at 100% scale in Flash to prevent any kind of distortion.

> **Note**
> You can access the final files for this exercise in a folder called BasicCustomContainer.

Summary

In this exercise, you learned how to create a custom container using Flash and the Flex Component Kit. This exercise covered the basics, but custom containers can be extended to include additional functionality. For more information, refer to the Flex documentation.

Using Motion XML

This exercise will guide you through the process of creating and using Motion XML from Flash in Flex. The first thing you'll do is create a simple motion, then bring it into Flex and apply it to a component. To create these motions for Flex, you must have Flash CS3 installed. If you don't have Flash CS3, you can download a free trial from http://www.adobe.com/downloads/.

The first step to importing and using Motion XML exported from Flash CS3 is, of course, to create the motion. To keep things easy, you'll create a simple horizontal motion with a Blur filter applied.

1. In Flash CS3, create a new file (ActionScript 3.0) and leave the default dimensions of 550 pixels by 400 pixels. Set the frame rate to 24 frames per second (fps) to match the default frame rate in Flex.

2. To create the motion, you need to create something to animate. Select the Rectangle Tool and draw a box roughly 60 pixels square. The fill and stroke of the square do not matter. Place the square close to the left edge of the stage as in Figure 12.4-1.

Note

If you have a certain component in mind that you will be animating in Flex, it may help to draw a shape with similar dimensions to get a better idea of what it will look like in Flex.

3. Convert the square you just created into a Movie Clip symbol by selecting Modify > Convert to Symbol. In the Convert to Symbol window, name the symbol square and make sure Movie Clip is selected for the Type. You don't have to worry about the linkage in this case. With the name filled in, as in Figure 12.4-2, click OK.

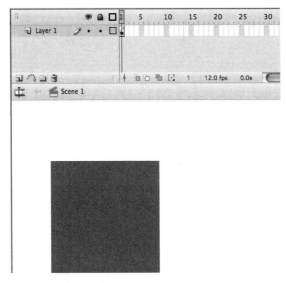

Figure 12.4-1   Creating a square

Figure 12.4-2   Creating a Movie Clip symbol

4. Create an animation using the Timeline. Select frame 48 on the Timeline and convert it to a keyframe (Modify > Timeline > Convert to Keyframes). On the keyframe you created on frame 48, move the square close to the right edge.

5. Create your tween animation by selecting a frame in between the first and last keyframes and selecting Insert > Timeline > Create Motion Tween. If you scrub through the Timeline, you should see the square move left to right. Your workspace should look something similar to Figure 12.4-3.

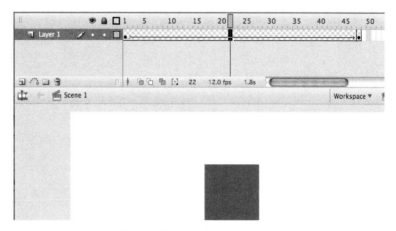

Figure 12.4-3   Tweened square

6. You've got an animating square. Now to add the blur: On frame 1, select the square and click on the Filters tab in the Properties Inspector (Window > Properties > Filters). Click the + button to add a filter and select Blur. To make the square look like a horizontal motion blur, set the Blur X to 20 and the Blur Y to 5. You may need to unlock the constrained values by clicking on the lock icon. Your Filters panel should look similar to Figure 12.4-4.

Figure 12.4-4   Setting the Blur filter

7. Now when you scrub through the Timeline, your square not only moves horizontally, but animates from blurry to sharp. You now have an animation that you can export and use in Flex.

> **Tip**
>
> If you want to finesse your tweened animation, you can use the Custom Ease In / Ease Out panel shown in Figure 12.4-5. This panel allows you to change the qualities of the tween by manipulating a global curve for each property or by manipulating a separate curve for each property you animate in your tween. Using this panel, you can create tweens similar to those discussed in Chapter 11, "Effects and Transitions."

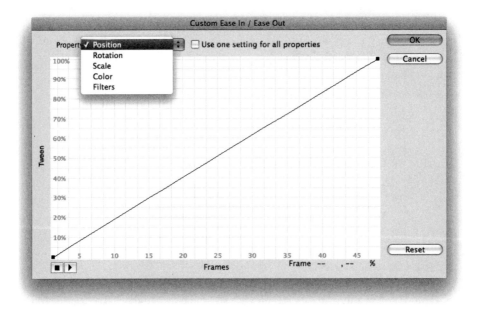

Figure 12.4-5   The Custom Ease In / Out panel

You can access this panel by clicking on a frame that is part of a tweened animation and clicking the Edit button in the Properties panel shown in Figure 12.4-6.

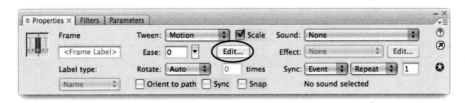

Figure 12.4-6   Properties panel

8. To use this tween animation in Flex, you must export it as Motion XML. Select Commands > Export Motion XML. Browse for a location and save the XML as myMotion.xml.

Now it's time to jump into Flex.

Preparing Flex

To use your exported Motion XML file in Flex, you need to import some classes from your Flash CS3 application folder.

1. In Flex Builder, create a new MXML application called MotionXMLExample. Select the project and select Project > Properties.
2. Click on the Flex Build Path option in the left column and select the Source Path tab.
3. Click Add Folder and navigate to your Flash CS3 application folder. Find the Classes folder (Configuration/ActionScript 3.0/Classes) and click OK.
4. After clicking OK, you should see a folder appear in the list of Source Path folders as in Figure 12.4-7. Click OK to exit the project properties.

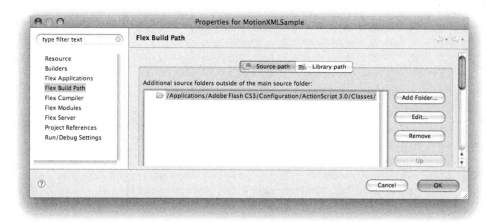

Figure 12.4-7   Adding the Flash CS3 Classes folder

You can now access the necessary classes to work with a Motion XML file by importing the class you want to use. The code snippet in Listing 12.4-1 is an example of the Animator class being imported.

Listing 12.4-1   Importing a class from fl.motion

```
...
<mx:Script>
    <![CDATA[
        import fl.motion.Animator;
    ]]>
</mx:Script>
...
```

5. You'll be using the myMotion.xml file you created in previous steps as an animation in Flex. However, you need something to animate. Add a Button component, with a label of Click Me and an id of motionButton to your application layout.

6. To access the myMotion.xml file, copy it into your Flex project src folder into a new folder called xml. Use an HTTPService and specify the location of your myMotion.xml file for the url property, e4x for the resultFormat, and an id of motionService. The code snippet in Listing 12.4-2 shows what your MXML should look like.

Listing 12.4-2   Specifying an HTTPService to access the myMotion.xml file

```
...
<mx:HTTPService    id="motionService"
                   url="xml/myMotion.xml"
                   resultFormat="e4x"/>
...
```

7. To animate the button when you click on it, you need to add the following bit of ActionScript into your Script block as shown in Listing 12.4-3.

Listing 12.4-3   Setting up the appropriate functions and variables

```
...
public var myMotion:Animator = null;
        private function playMotion():void {
            if (myMotion) myMotion.rewind();
                myMotion = new
Animator(XML(motionService.lastResult),motionButton);
                myMotion.play();
        }
...
```

8. The final thing you need to do is call the playMotion() function and a send method on motionService when you click the button. Add this to your Button MXML as shown in Listing 12.4-4.

Listing 12.4-4   **Calling the Motion XML to play in the Button MXML**

```
...
<mx:Button
      id="motionButton"
      label="Click Me."
      click="playMotion();
      motionService.send();"/>
...
```

9. Compile your application and click on the Click Me button. You should see the button animate across the screen mirroring the same motion you created in Flash CS3 using the Timeline and Filters Panel. Pretty cool, huh? The full code for this exercise is shown in Listing 12.4-5.

   Depending on what type of container the animated object is inside, the layout surrounding that object may be severely affected as the object animates. Refer to Chapter 3, "Dynamic Layout," for more information.

Listing 12.4-5   **MotionXMLExample.mxml**

```
motionService


<mx:Application
      xmlns:mx="http://www.adobe.com/2006/mxml"
      layout="absolute"
      backgroundGradientAlphas="[1.0, 1.0]"
      backgroundGradientColors="[#FFFFFF, #FFFFFF]">

      <mx:HTTPService      id="motionService"
                           url="xml/myMotion.xml"
                           resultFormat="e4x"/>

      <mx:Script>
      <![CDATA[
          import fl.motion.Animator;

          public var myMotion:Animator = null;

        private function playMotion():void {
          if (myMotion) myMotion.rewind();
          myMotion = new Animator(XML(motionService.lastResult),motionButton);
            myMotion.play();
          }


        ]]>
```

Listing 12.4-5   **Continued**

```
        </mx:Script>

        <mx:Button
            id="motionButton"
            label="Click Me."
            click="playMotion(); motionService.send();"/>

</mx:Application>
```

Summary

As you can see, you can achieve some really dynamic animation in Flex using Motion XML exported from Flash CS3. Of course, this was a simple example, but with a little more time and an established purpose, you can create even more rich motion sequences to use in your Flex application. However, be considerate of application layout and the capability to "overdo it," as with anything in your application.

For more information regarding Motion XML, visit http://www.motionxml.com for access to libraries of Motion XML files and more in-depth examples.

V

References

A

Skinning and Styling Diagrams

The following series of diagrams describe the "visual anatomy" for nearly every Flex 3 component. Properties for each component are divided between CSS styles and "skinnable" parts. The names for these properties are pulled directly from the Flex framework and can be specified inline in MXML, in an `<mx:Style>` block or via an external CSS file.

To learn more about using these properties to customize the look of your components, refer to Chapter 4," Styling," Chapter 5, "Graphical Skinning," or Chapter 6, "Programmatic Skinning."

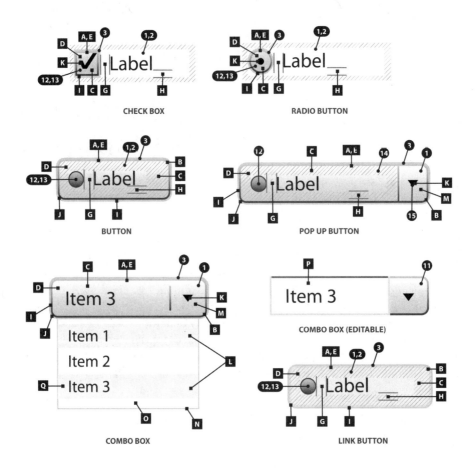

CHECK BOX

RADIO BUTTON

BUTTON

POP UP BUTTON

COMBO BOX (EDITABLE)

COMBO BOX

LINK BUTTON

Styles

A   borderColor
B   cornerRadius
C   fillColors, fillAlphas
D   highlightAlphas
E   themeColor
G   horizontalGap
H   verticalGap
I   focusAlpha, focusBlendMode, focusThickness
J   focusRoundedCorners
K   iconColor, disabledIconColor
L   alternatingItemColors
M   arrowButtonWidth
N   dropdownBorderColor
O   dropdownStyleName (See List styles/skins)

P   textInputStyleName (See TextInput)
Q   rollOverColor, selectionColor

Skins

1   skin, upSkin, overSkin, downSkin, disabledSkin
2   selectedUpSkin, selectedOverSkin, selectedDownSkin, selectedDisabledSkin
3   focusSkin
11   editableUpSkin, editableOverSkin, editableDownSkin, editableDisabledSkin
12   icon, upIcon, overIcon, downIcon, disabledIcon
13   selectedUpIcon, selectedOverIcon, selectedDownIcon, selectedDisabledIcon
14   popUpOverSkin, popUpDownSkin
15   popUpIcon

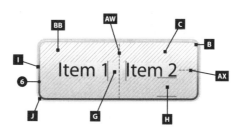

APPLICATION CONTROL BAR

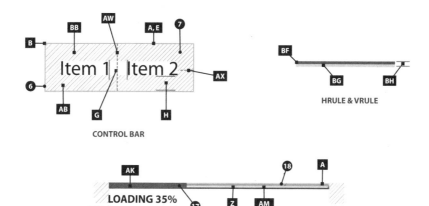

CONTROL BAR

HRULE & VRULE

PROGRESS BAR

Styles

A   borderColor
B   cornerRadius
C   fillColors, fillAlphas
E   themeColor
G   horizontalGap
H   verticalGap
I   focusAlpha, focusBlendMode, focusThickness
J   focusRoundedCorners
Z   trackColors
AB   backgroundAlpha, backgroundColor, backgroundDisabledColor
AK   barColor
AL   labelWidth
AM   trackHeight
AW   horizontalAlign
AX   verticalAlign
BB   disabledOverlayAlpha
BF   strokeColor
BG   shadowColor
BH   strokeWidth

Skins

6   borderSkin
7   backgroundImage, backgroundSize
17   barSkin, indeterminateSkin
18   maskSkin

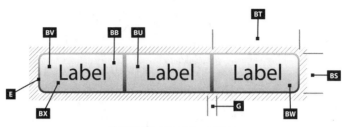

BUTTON BAR & TOGGLE BUTTON BAR

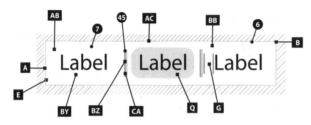

LINK BAR

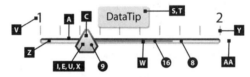

HORIZONTAL & VERTICAL SLIDER

Styles

A   borderColor
B   cornerRadius
C   fillColors, fillAlphas
E   themeColor
G   horizontalGap
I   focusAlpha, focusBlendMode, focusThickness
Q   rollOverColor, selectionColor
S   dataTipStyleName (See ToolTip)
T   dataTipOffset, dataTipPlacement, dataTipPrecision
U   invertThumbDirection
V   labelStyleName, labelOffset
W   showTrackHighlight
X   thumbOffset
Y   tickColor, tickLength, tickOffset, tickThickness
Z   trackColors
AA trackMargin
AB backgroundAlpha, backgroundColor, backgroundDisabledColor

AC borderSides, borderThickness, borderStyle
BB disabledOverlayAlpha
BS buttonHeight
BT buttonWidth
BU buttonStyleName (See Button)
BV firstStyleName (See Button)
BW lastStyleName (See Button)
BX selectedButtonTextStyleName
BY linkButtonStyleName
BZ separatorColor
CA separatorWidth

Skins

6   borderSkin
7   backgroundImage, backgroundSize
8   trackSkin, trackDisabledSkin
9   thumbSkin, thumbUpSkin, thumbOverSkin, thumbDownSkin, thumbDisabledSkin
16 trackHighlightSkin
45 separatorSkin

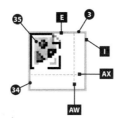

IMAGE & SWF LOADER

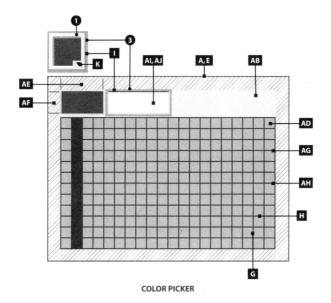

COLOR PICKER

Styles

A   borderColor
E   themeColor
G   horizontalGap
H   verticalGap
I   focusAlpha, focusBlendMode,
     focusThickness
K   iconColor, disabledIconColor
AB   backgroundAlpha, backgroundColor,
     backgroundDisabledColor
AD   columnCount
AE   previewWidth
AF   previewHeight
AG   swatchBorderColor, swatchBorderSize,
     swatchHeight, swatchHighlightColor,
     swatchHighlightSize, swatchWidth

AH   swatchGridBackgroundColor,
     swatchGridBorderSize
AI   textFieldWidth
AJ   textFieldStyleName
AW   horizontalAlign
AX   verticalAlign

Skins

1   skin, upSkin, overSkin, downSkin,
     disabledSkin
3   focusSkin
34   brokenImageBorderSkin
35   brokenImageSkin

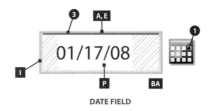

DATE FIELD

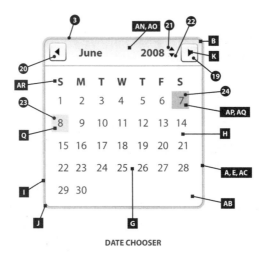

DATE CHOOSER

Styles

A   borderColor
B   cornerRadius
E   themeColor
G   horizontalGap
H   verticalGap
I   focusAlpha, focusBlendMode,
      focusThickness
J   focusRoundedCorners
K   iconColor, disabledIconColor
P   textInputStyleName (See TextInput)
Q   rollOverColor, selectionColor
AB   backgroundAlpha, backgroundColor,
      backgroundDisabledColor
AC   borderSides, borderThickness,
      borderStyle
AN   headerColors
AO   headerStyleName
AP   todayColor
AQ   todayStyleName

AR   weekDayStyleName
BA   dateChooserStyleName (See DateChooser)

Skins

1   skin, upSkin, overSkin, downSkin,
      disabledSkin
3   focusSkin
19   nextMonthSkin, nextMonthUpSkin,
      nextMonthOverSkin, nextMonthDownSkin,
      nextMonthDisabledSkin
20   prevMonthSkin, prevMonthUpSkin,
      prevMonthOverSkin, prevMonthDownSkin,
      prevMonthDisabledSkin
21   nextYearSkin, nextYearUpSkin,
      nextYearOverSkin, nextYearDownSkin,
      nextYearDisabledSkin
22   prevYearSkin, prevYearUpSkin,
      prevYearOverSkin, prevYearDownSkin,
      prevYearDisabledSkin
23   rollOverIndicatorSkin,
      selectionIndicatorSkin
24   todayIndicatorSkin

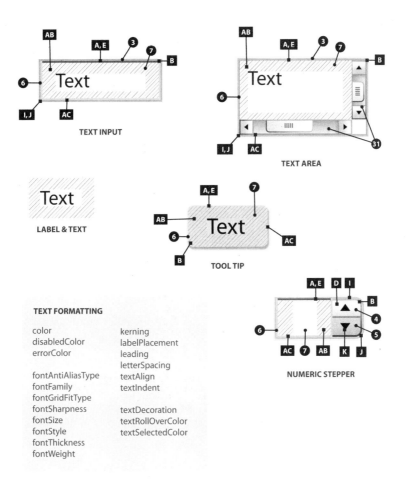

TEXT INPUT

TEXT AREA

LABEL & TEXT

TOOL TIP

NUMERIC STEPPER

TEXT FORMATTING

color	kerning
disabledColor	labelPlacement
errorColor	leading
	letterSpacing
fontAntiAliasType	textAlign
fontFamily	textIndent
fontGridFitType	
fontSharpness	textDecoration
fontSize	textRollOverColor
fontStyle	textSelectedColor
fontThickness	
fontWeight	

Styles

A   borderColor
B   cornerRadius
D   highlightAlphas
E   themeColor
I   focusAlpha, focusBlendMode,
    focusThickness
J   focusRoundedCorners
K   iconColor, disabledIconColor
AB backgroundAlpha, backgroundColor,
    backgroundDisabledColor
AC borderSides, borderThickness,
    borderStyle

Skins

3   focusSkin
4   upArrowSkin, upArrowUpSkin,
    upArrowOverSkin, upArrowDownSkin,
    upArrowDisabledSkin
5   downArrowSkin, downArrowUpSkin,
    downArrowOverSkin,
    downArrowDownSkin,
    downArrowDisabledSkin
6   borderSkin
7   backgroundImage, backgroundSize
31 horizontalScrollBarStyleName (See
    HScrollBar), verticalScrollBarStyleName
    (See VScrollBar)

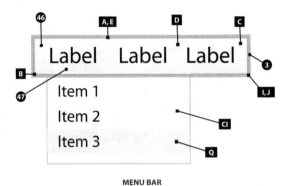

MENU BAR

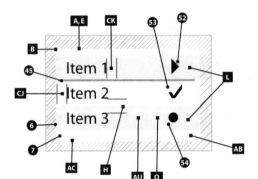

MENU

Styles

A	borderColor
B	cornerRadius
C	fillColors, fillAlphas
D	highlightAlphas
E	themeColor
H	verticalGap
I	focusAlpha, focusBlendMode, focusThickness
J	focusRoundedCorners
L	alternatingItemColors
Q	rollOverColor, selectionColor
AB	backgroundAlpha, backgroundColor, backgroundDisabledColor
AC	borderSides, borderThickness, borderStyle

AU	selectionDisabledColor
CI	menuStyleName (See Menu)
CJ	leftIconGap
CK	rightIconGap

Skins

3	focusSkin
6	borderSkin
7	backgroundImage, backgroundSize
45	separatorSkin
46	backgroundSkin
47	itemSkin, itemUpSkin, itemOverSkin, itemDownSkin
52	branchIcon, branchDisabledIcon
53	checkIcon, checkDisabledIcon
54	radioIcon, radioDisabledIcon

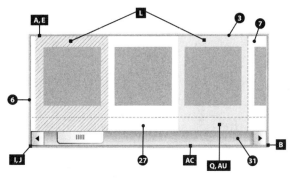

HORIZONTAL LIST

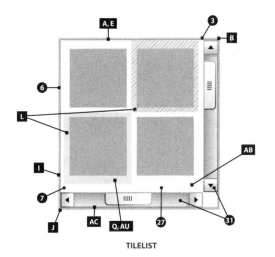

TILELIST

Styles

A   borderColor
B   cornerRadius
E   themeColor
I   focusAlpha, focusBlendMode,
    focusThickness
J   focusRoundedCorners
L   alternatingItemColors
Q   rollOverColor, selectionColor
AB backgroundAlpha, backgroundColor,
    backgroundDisabledColor
AC borderSides, borderThickness,
    borderStyle
AU selectionDisabledColor

Skins

3   focusSkin
6   borderSkin
7   backgroundImage, backgroundSize
27 dropIndicatorSkin
31 horizontalScrollBarStyleName (See
    HScrollBar), verticalScrollBarStyleName
    (See VScrollBar)

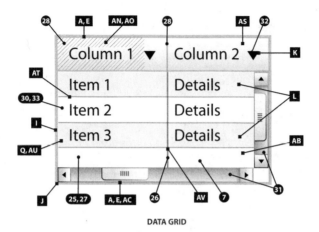

DATA GRID

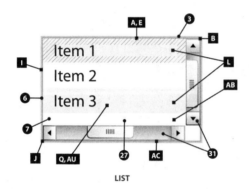

LIST

Styles

A   borderColor
B   cornerRadius
E   themeColor
I   focusAlpha, focusBlendMode,
     focusThickness
J   focusRoundedCorners
K   iconColor, disabledIconColor
L   alternatingItemColors
Q   rollOverColor, selectionColor
AB   backgroundAlpha, backgroundColor,
     backgroundDisabledColor
AC   borderSides, borderThickness,
     borderStyle
AN   headerColors
AO   headerStyleName
AS   headerDragProxyStyleName
AT   horizontalGridLineColor,
     horizontalGridLines

AU   selectionDisabledColor
AV   verticalGridLineColor, verticalGridLines

Skins

3   focusSkin
6   borderSkin
7   backgroundImage, backgroundSize
25   columnDropIndicatorSkin
26   columnResizeSkin
27   dropIndicatorSkin
28   headerBackgroundSkin
30   horizontalLockedSeparatorSkin,
     horizontalSeparatorSkin
31   horizontalScrollBarStyleName (See
     HScrollBar), verticalScrollBarStyleName
     (See VScrollBar)
32   sortArrowSkin
33   verticalLockedSeparatorSkin,
     horizontalSeparatorSkin

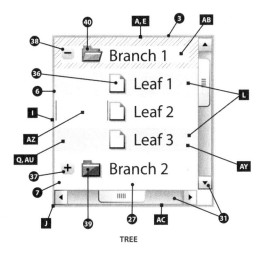

TREE

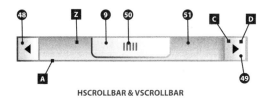

HSCROLLBAR & VSCROLLBAR

Styles

A   borderColor
C   fillColors, fillAlphas
D   highlightAlphas
E   themeColor
I   focusAlpha, focusBlendMode, focusThickness
J   focusRoundedCorners
L   alternatingItemColors
Q   rollOverColor, selectionColor
Z   trackColors
AB backgroundAlpha, backgroundColor, backgroundDisabledColor
AC borderSides, borderThickness, borderStyle
AU selectionDisabledColor
AY depthColors
AZ Indentation

Skins

3   focusSkin
6   borderSkin
7   backgroundImage, backgroundSize

9   thumbSkin, thumbUpSkin, thumbOverSkin, thumbDownSkin, thumbDisabledSkin
27 dropIndicatorSkin
31 horizontalScrollBarStyleName (See HScrollBar), verticalScrollBarStyleName (See VScrollBar)
36 defaultLeafIcon
37 disclosureClosedIcon
38 disclosureOpenIcon
39 folderClosedIcon
40 folderOpenIcon
48 downArrowSkin, downArrowUpSkin, downArrowOverSkin, downArrowDownSkin, downArrowDisabledSkin
49 upArrowSkin, upArrowUpSkin, upArrowOverSkin, upArrowDownSkin, upArrowDisabledSkin
50 thumbIcon
51 trackSkin, trackUpSkin, trackOverSkin, trackDownSkin, trackDisabledSkin

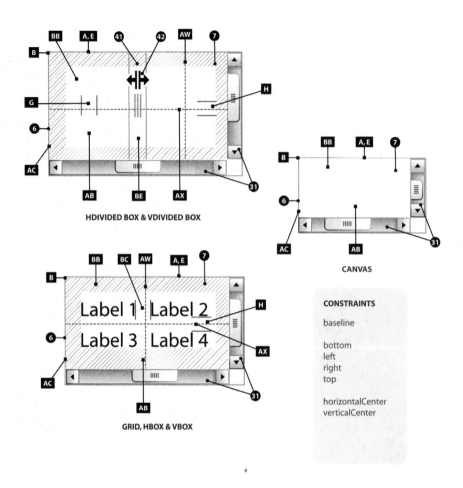

HDIVIDED BOX & VDIVIDED BOX

CANVAS

GRID, HBOX & VBOX

CONSTRAINTS

baseline

bottom
left
right
top

horizontalCenter
verticalCenter

Styles

A   borderColor
B   cornerRadius
E   themeColor
G   horizontalGap
H   verticalGap
AB   backgroundAlpha, backgroundColor,
     backgroundDisabledColor
AC   borderSides, borderThickness,
     borderStyle
AW   horizontalAlign
AX   verticalAlign
BB   disabledOverlayAlpha
BC   indicatorGap
BE   dividerAffordance, dividerAlpha,
     dividerColor, dividerThickness

Skins

6   borderSkin
7   backgroundImage, backgroundSize
31   horizontalScrollBarStyleName (See
     HScrollBar), verticalScrollBarStyleName
     (See VScrollBar)
41   dividerSkin
42   horizontalDividerCursor,
     verticalDividerCursor

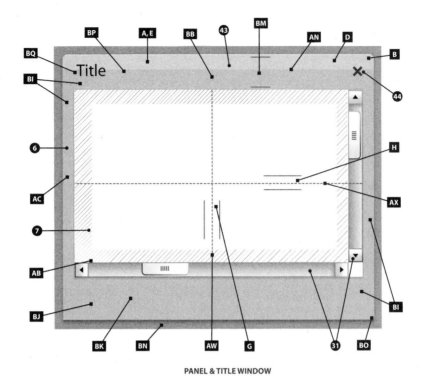

PANEL & TITLE WINDOW

Styles

A   borderColor
B   cornerRadius
D   highlightAlphas
E   themeColor
G   horizontalGap
H   verticalGap
AB   backgroundAlpha, backgroundColor,
     backgroundDisabledColor
AC   borderSides, borderThickness,
     borderStyle
AN   headerColors
AW   horizontalAlign
AX   verticalAlign
BB   disabledOverlayAlpha
BI   borderThicknessBottom,
     borderThicknessLeft,
     borderThicknessRight,
     borderThicknessTop
BJ   controlBarStyleName
BK   footerColors

BM   headerHeight
BN   modalTransparency,
     modalTransparencyBlur,
     modalTransparencyColor,
     modalTransparencyDuration
BO   roundedBottomCorners
BP   statusStyleName
BQ   titleStyleName

Skins

6   borderSkin
7   backgroundImage, backgroundSize
31   horizontalScrollBarStyleName (See
     HScrollBar), verticalScrollBarStyleName
     (See VScrollBar)
43   titleBackgroundSkin
44   closeButtonSkin, closeButtonUpSkin,
     closeButtonOverSkin,
     closeButtonDownSkin,
     closeButtonDisabledSkin (For TitleWindow

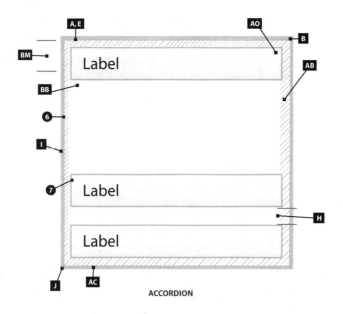

ACCORDION

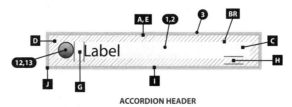

ACCORDION HEADER

Styles

A   borderColor
B   cornerRadius
C   fillColors, fillAlphas
D   highlightAlphas
E   themeColor
G   horizontalGap
H   verticalGap
I   focusAlpha, focusBlendMode,
     focusThickness
J   focusRoundedCorners
AB   backgroundAlpha, backgroundColor,
     backgroundDisabledColor
AC   borderSides, borderThickness,
     borderStyle
AO   headerStyleName
BB   disabledOverlayAlpha

BM   headerHeight
BR   selectedFillColors

Skins

1   skin, upSkin, overSkin, downSkin,
     disabledSkin
2   selectedUpSkin, selectedOverSkin,
     selectedDownSkin, selectedDisabledSkin
3   focusSkin
6   borderSkin
7   backgroundImage, backgroundSize
12   icon, upIcon, overIcon, downIcon,
     disabledIcon
13   selectedUpIcon, selectedOverIcon,
     selectedDownIcon, selectedDisabledIcon

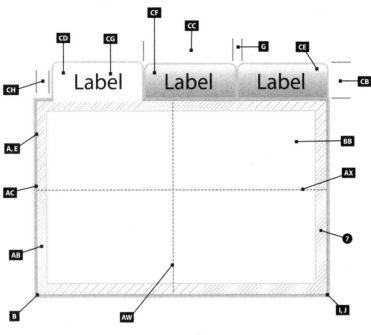

TAB NAVIGATOR

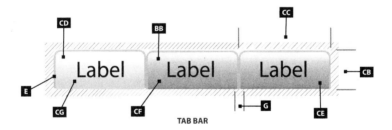

TAB BAR

Styles

A	borderColor
B	cornerRadius
E	themeColor
G	horizontalGap
I	focusAlpha, focusBlendMode, focusThickness
J	focusRoundedCorners
AB	backgroundAlpha, backgroundColor, backgroundDisabledColor
AC	borderSides, borderThickness, borderStyle
AW	horizontalAlign

AX	verticalAlign
BB	disabledOverlayAlpha
CB	tabHeight
CC	tabWidth
CD	firstTabStyleName (See Button)
CE	lastTabStyleName (See Button)
CF	tabStyleName (See Button)
CG	selectedTabTextStyleName
CH	tabOffset

Skins

7	backgroundImage, backgroundSize

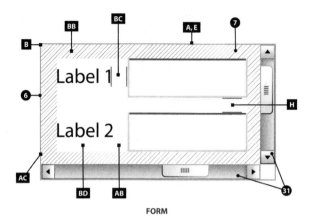

FORM

ALERT
(SEE PANEL)

Styles

A   borderColor
B   cornerRadius
E   themeColor
H   verticalGap
AB backgroundAlpha, backgroundColor,
     backgroundDisabledColor
AC borderSides, borderThickness,
     borderStyle
BB disabledOverlayAlpha
BC indicatorGap
BD labelWidth
BU buttonStyleName (See Button)

Skins

6   borderSkin
7   backgroundImage, backgroundSize
31 horizontalScrollBarStyleName (See
     HScrollBar), verticalScrollBarStyleName
     (See VScrollBar)

Styles

A   borderColor
B   cornerRadius
C   fillColors, fillAlphas
D   highlightAlphas
E   themeColor
F   paddingTop, paddingLeft, paddingRight, paddingBottom
G   horizontalGap
H   verticalGap
I   focusAlpha, focusBlendMode, focusThickness
J   focusRoundedCorners
K   iconColor, disabledIconColor
L   alternatingItemColors
M   arrowButtonWidth
N   dropdownBorderColor
O   dropdownStyleName (See List styles/skins)
P   textInputStyleName (See TextInput)
Q   rollOverColor, selectionColor
R   popUpStyleName
S   dataTipStyleName (See ToolTip)
T   dataTipOffset, dataTipPlacement, dataTipPrecision
U   invertThumbDirection
V   labelStyleName, labelOffset
W   showTrackHighlight
X   thumbOffset
Y   tickColor, tickLength, tickOffset, tickThickness
Z   trackColors
AA   trackMargin
AB   backgroundAlpha, backgroundColor, backgroundDisabledColor
AC   borderSides, borderThickness, borderStyle
AD   columnCount
AE   previewWidth
AF   previewHeight
AG   swatchBorderColor, swatchBorderSize, swatchHeight, swatchHighlightColor, swatchHighlightSize, swatchWidth
AH   swatchGridBackgroundColor, swatchGridBorderSize
AI   textFieldWidth
AJ   textFieldStyleName
AK   barColor
AL   labelWidth
AM   trackHeight
AN   headerColors

AO   headerStyleName
AP   todayColor
AQ   todayStyleName
AR   weekDayStyleName
AS   headerDragProxyStyleName
AT   horizontalGridLineColor, horizontalGridLines
AU   selectionDisabledColor
AV   verticalGridLineColor, verticalGridLines
AW   horizontalAlign
AX   verticalAlign
AY   depthColors
AZ   indentation
BA   dateChooserStyleName (See DateChooser)
BB   disabledOverlayAlpha
BC   indicatorGap
BD   labelWidth
BE   dividerAffordance, dividerAlpha, dividerColor, dividerThickness
BF   strokeColor
BG   shadowColor
BH   strokeWidth
BI   borderThicknessBottom, borderThicknessLeft, borderThicknessRight, borderThicknessTop
BJ   controlBarStyleName
BK   footerColors
BL   headerColors
BM   headerHeight
BN   modalTransparency, modalTransparencyBlur, modalTransparencyColor, modalTransparencyDuration
BO   roundedBottomCorners
BP   statusStyleName
BQ   titleStyleName
BR   selectedFillColors
BS   buttonHeight
BT   buttonWidth
BU   buttonStyleName (See Button)
BV   firstStyleName (See Button)
BW   lastStyleName (See Button)
BX   selectedButtonTextStyleName
BY   linkButtonStyleName
BZ   separatorColor
CA   separatorWidth
CB   tabHeight
CC   tabWidth
CD   firstTabStyleName (See Button)

CE lastTabStyleName (See Button)
CF tabStyleName (See Button)
CG selectedTabTextStyleName
CH tabOffset
CI menuStyleName (See Menu)
CJ leftIconGap
CK rightIconGap

Skins

1   skin, upSkin, overSkin, downSkin,
    disabledSkin
2   selectedUpSkin, selectedOverSkin,
    selectedDownSkin, selectedDisabledSkin
3   focusSkin
4   upArrowSkin, upArrowUpSkin,
    upArrowOverSkin, upArrowDownSkin,
    upArrowDisabledSkin
5   downArrowSkin, downArrowUpSkin,
    downArrowOverSkin,
    downArrowDownSkin,
    downArrowDisabledSkin
6   borderSkin
7   backgroundImage, backgroundSize
8   trackSkin, trackDisabledSkin
9   thumbSkin, thumbUpSkin,
    thumbOverSkin, thumbDownSkin,
    thumbDisabledSkin
10 thumbIcon
11 editableUpSkin, editableOverSkin,
    editableDownSkin, editableDisabledSkin
12 icon, upIcon, overIcon, downIcon,
    disabledIcon
13 selectedUpIcon, selectedOverIcon,
    selectedDownIcon, selectedDisabledIcon
14 popUpOverSkin, popUpDownSkin
15 pupUpIcon
16 trackHighlightSkin
17 barSkin, indeterminateSkin
18 maskSkin
19 nextMonthSkin, nextMonthUpSkin,
    nextMonthOverSkin, nextMonthDownSkin,
    nextMonthDisabledSkin
20 prevMonthSkin, prevMonthUpSkin,
    prevMonthOverSkin, prevMonthDownSkin,
    prevMonthDisabledSkin
21 nextYearSkin, nextYearUpSkin,
    nextYearOverSkin, nextYearDownSkin,
    nextYearDisabledSkin
22 prevYearSkin, prevYearUpSkin,
    prevYearOverSkin, prevYearDownSkin,
    prevYearDisabledSkin

23 rollOverIndicatorSkin,
    selectionIndicatorSkin
24 todayIndicatorSkin
25 columnDropIndicatorSkin
26 columnResizeSkin
27 dropIndicatorSkin
28 headerBackgroundSkin
29 headerSeparatorSkin
30 horizontalLockedSeparatorSkin,
    horizontalSeparatorSkin
31 horizontalScrollBarStyleName (See
    HScrollBar), verticalScrollBarStyleName
    (See VScrollBar)
32 sortArrowSkin
33 verticalLockedSeparatorSkin,
    horizontalSeparatorSkin
34 brokenImageBorderSkin
35 brokenImageSkin
36 defaultLeafIcon
37 disclosureClosedIcon
38 disclosureOpenIcon
39 folderClosedIcon
40 folderOpenIcon
41 dividerSkin
42 horizontalDividerCursor,
    verticalDividerCursor
43 titleBackgroundSkin
44 closeButtonSkin, closeButtonUpSkin,
    closeButtonOverSkin,
    closeButtonDownSkin,
    closeButtonDisabledSkin (For
    TitleWindow)
45 separatorSkin
46 backgroundSkin
47 itemSkin, itemUpSkin, itemOverSkin,
    itemDownSkin
48 downArrowSkin, downArrowUpSkin,
    downArrowOverSkin,
    downArrowDownSkin,
    downArrowDisabledSkin
49 upArrowSkin, upArrowUpSkin,
    upArrowOverSkin, upArrowDownSkin,
    upArrowDisabledSkin
50 thumbIcon
51 trackSkin, trackUpSkin, trackOverSkin,
    trackDownSkin, trackDisabledSkin
52 branchIcon, branchDisabledIcon
53 checkIcon, checkDisabledIcon
54 radioIcon, radioDisabledIcon

Filters Cheat Sheet

The following tables are your cheat sheet for filters. Enjoy!

Property	Description
Bevel filter	
angle	Angle of bevel.
blurX	Amount of blur on the horizontal axis.
blurY	Amount of blur on the vertical axis.
distance	Inset or outset distance of the bevel.
highlightAlpha	Alpha of the highlight.
highlightColor	Color of the highlight.
knockout	Sets the target object to transparent.
quality	Severity of the blur softness.
shadowAlpha	Alpha of the shadow.
shadowColor	Color of the shadow.
strength	Harshness of the highlight and shadow.
type	Options are inner, outer, and full. Specifying full uses both inner and outer.
Blur filter	
blurX	Amount to blur the target on the horizontal axis.
blurY	Amount to blur the target on the vertical axis.
quality	Severity of the blur softness.
Color Matrix filter	
matrix	Matrix for the color filter.
Convolution filter	
alpha	Defines the alpha of the substitute color.
bias	Defines harshness of the influence on the "brightness" of the image.

Property	Description
Convolution filter	
clamp	Whether or not the image uses the nearest shifted pixel to fill in empty spaces created by the filter.
color	The color to replace the pixels that are based off the edges of the image.
divisor	A value that acts as the divisor for the transformation.
matrix	A defined array that defines the transformation.
matrixX	Defines the number of columns in the matrix.
matrixY	Defines the number of rows in the matrix.
preserveAlpha	Whether or not the convolution filter should affect the alpha of the color channels.
Displacement Map filter	
alpha	Alpha of the color used to fill in empty spaces created by shifted pixels.
color	Color to use to fill in any empty spaces created by shifted pixels.
componentX	The color channel that affects the x position of the pixels.
componentY	The color channel that affects the y position of the pixels.
mapBitmap	Defines the area of the bitmap to be affected.
mapPoint	The position of the area that will be affected by the filter using values to specify the x and y coordinates of the top-left point of the displacement map.
mode	Specifies what should be done with empty spaces as pixels are shifted away from the affected area. Options include IGNORE, WRAP, CLAMP, and COLOR.
scaleX	Defines the strength of the x axis displacement.
scaleY	Defines the strength of the y axis displacement.
Drop Shadow filter	
alpha	Alpha of the shadow.
angle	Angle of the shadow in degrees.
blurX	Amount of blur on the horizontal axis.
blurY	Amount of blur on the vertical axis.
color	Color of the shadow.
distance	Offset of the shadow in the direction of the angle specified.
hideObject	Hides the target.
inner	Set drop shadow to the inner area of the target.
knockout	Subtract target from the shadow.
quality	Severity of the blur softness.
strength	Harshness of the shadow.

Property	Description
Glow filter	
alpha	Alpha of the glow.
blurX	Amount of blur on the horizontal axis.
blurY	Amount of blur on the vertical axis.
color	Color of the glow.
inner	Set glow to the inner area of the target.
knockout	Subtract target from the glow.
quality	Severity of the blur softness.
strength	Harshness of the bevel edges.
Gradient Bevel filter	
alphas	Gradient alphas of the bevel.
angle	Angle of the bevel in degrees.
blurX	Amount of blur on the horizontal axis.
blurY	Amount of blur on the vertical axis.
colors	Gradient colors of the bevel.
distance	Inset or offset of the bevel in the direction of the angle specified.
knockout	Subtract target from the bevel.
quality	Severity of the blur softness.
ratios	Gradient ratios of the bevel.
strength	Harshness of the bevel edges.
type	Options are inner, outer, and full. Specifying full uses both inner and outer.
Gradient Glow filter	
alphas	Gradient alphas of the glow.
angle	Angle of the angle in degrees.
blurX	Amount of blur on the horizontal axis.
blurY	Amount of blur on the vertical axis.
colors	Gradient colors of the glow.
distance	Inset or offset of the glow in the direction of the angle specified.
knockout	Subtract target from the glow.
quality	Severity of the blur softness.
ratios	Gradient ratios of the glow.
strength	Harshness of the bevel edges.
type	Options are inner, outer, and full. Specifying full uses both inner and outer.

C

Resources and Cool Stuff

User Experience Design

Flex Interface Guide
http://www.adobe.com/devnet/flex/fig

Designing for Flex Series
http://www.adobe.com/devnet/flex/articles/fig_pt1.html

Adobe XD
http://xd.adobe.com

User Interface Resource Center
http://www.uiresourcecenter.com/

Boxes and Arrows
http://www.boxesandarrows.com/

Logic+Emotion
http://darmano.typepad.com/

User Interface Engineering
http://www.uie.com/

Flex Skins and Themes

ScaleNine
http://www.scalenine.com

FillColors
http://www.fillcolors.com/

Fleksray
http://www.fleksray.org/Flex_skin.html

Designing Flex Skins
http://www.adobe.com/devnet/flex/articles/flex_skins.html

Flex Component Kit

Flex Component Kit Step-By-Step
http://lordbron.wordpress.com/2007/05/01/flex-component-kit-step-by-step/

Example of Flex Component Kit for Flash CS3
http://weblogs.macromedia.com/pent/archives/2007/04/example_of_the.html

Using the Flex Component Kit for Flash CS3 to Create Flex Containers
http://blogs.adobe.com/flexdoc/2007/08/using_the_flex_component_kit_f_1.html

Flex Explorers

Charts Explorer
http://demo.quietlyscheming.com/ChartSampler/app.html

Component Explorer
http://examples.adobe.com/flex3/componentexplorer/explorer.html

Filter Explorer
http://www.merhl.com/flex2_samples/filterExplorer/

Style Explorer
http://examples.adobe.com/flex2/consulting/styleexplorer/Flex2StyleExplorer.html

Style Explorer with Kuler Integration
http://www.maclema.com/content/sek/

Style Explorer with CSS Export
http://www.flexonrails.net/stylescreator/public/

Custom Easing Explorer
http://www.madeinflex.com/img/entries/2007/05/customeasingexplorer.html

Kuler
http://kuler.adobe.com/

Easing Equations Demo
http://www.robertpenner.com/easing/easing_demo.html

Community Flex Components

FlexLib
http://code.google.com/p/flexlib/

FlexBox
http://flexbox.mrinalwadhwa.com/

ASTRA
http://developer.yahoo.com/flash/

Flex Libraries and Frameworks

Degrafa: Declarative Graphics Framework
http://www.degrafa.com

Papervision3D
http://www.papervision3d.org/

Away3D
http://away3d.com/

Alternativa: 3D
http://blog.alternativaplatform.com/en/

Tweener: Animation
http://code.google.com/p/tweener/

KitchenSync: Animation
http://code.google.com/p/kitchensynclib/

TweenLite: Animation
http://blog.greensock.com/tweenliteas3/

FOAM: Physics Engine
http://code.google.com/p/foam-as3/

APE: Physics Engine
http://www.cove.org/ape/

Motor2: Physics Engine
http://code.google.com/p/motor2/

Maté: Application Framework
http://mate.asfusion.com/

Cairngorm
http://labs.adobe.com/wiki/index.php/Cairngorm

PureMVC
http://puremvc.org/

Reference

Flex 3 LiveDocs
http://livedocs.adobe.com/flex/3/html/

Flex 3 Language Reference
http://livedocs.adobe.com/flex/3/langref/index.html

Flex 3 Documentation Resources
http://www.adobe.com/support/documentation/en/flex/

Adobe Open Source
http://opensource.adobe.com/wiki/display/site/Home

Adobe Labs
http://labs.adobe.com/

Flex 3 CSS Properties List
http://www.loscavio.com/downloads/blog/flex3_css_list/flex3_css_list.htm

Downloads

Adobe Software Trials
http://www.adobe.com/downloads/

Flex Skin Design Extensions & Flex Component Kit
https://www.adobe.com/cfusion/entitlement/index.cfm?e=flex_skins

Adobe Exchange
http://www.adobe.com/cfusion/exchange/index.cfm?event=productHome&exc=15

Community

Flex.org
http://flex.org/

FlexCoders Mailing List
http://tech.groups.yahoo.com/group/flexcoders/

Adobe Feeds
http://feeds.adobe.com

CFlex: Community Flex
http://www.cflex.net/

SearchCoders Dashboard
http://www.searchcoders.com/

The Flex Show
http://www.theflexshow.com/

360|Flex Conference
http://www.360conferences.com/360flex/

WebManiacs
http://www.webmaniacsconference.com/

InsideRIA
http://www.insideria.com/

Adobe Blogs

Rob Adams
http://usereccentric.com/

Lee Brimelow
http://theflashblog.com/

Mike Chambers
http://www.mikechambers.com/blog/

Matt Chotin
http://weblogs.macromedia.com/mchotin/

Christopher Coenraetes
http://coenraets.org/

Mike Downey
http://madowney.com/blog/

Daniel Dura
http://www.danieldura.com/about

Ethan Eismann
http://eismann-sf.com/news/

Renaun Erickson
http://renaun.com/blog/

Kevin Hoyt
http://blog.kevinhoyt.org/

Alex Harui
http://blogs.adobe.com/aharui/

Ely Greenfield
http://www.quietlyscheming.com/blog/

Narciso "NJ" Jaramillo
http://www.rictus.com/muchado/

Ted Patrick
http://www.onflex.org/

Brett Rampata
http://www.graviti.tv/blog/

Ryan Stewart
http://blog.digitalbackcountry.com/

Deepa Subramaniam
http://iamdeepa.com/blog/

James Ward
http://www.jamesward.com/wordpress/

David Zuckerman
http://www.davidzuckerman.com/adobe/

Other Blogs

Laura and Nahuel Arguello
http://www.asfusion.com/

Sean Christmann
http://www.craftymind.com/

Adam Flater
http://adamflater.blogspot.com/

Patrick Hansen
http://www.patrickhansen.com/blog/

Peter Hall
http://www.peterjoel.com/blog/

David Hassoun
http://david.realeyes.com/

Jun Heider
http://www.iheartair.com/

Doug McCune
http://www.dougmccune.com/blog/

RJ Owen
http://www.rjria.blogspot.com/

Darron Schall
http://www.darronschall.com/weblog/

Grant Skinner
http://www.gskinner.com/blog/

Ben Stucki
http://blog.benstucki.net/

Brad Umbaugh
http://bradumbaugh.blogspot.com/

Jesse Warden
http://jessewarden.com/

Flex and AIR Showcase

Flex.org Showcase
http://flex.org/showcase/

RIApedia
http://riapedia.com/

Adobe Developer Flex/AIR Samples
http://www.adobe.com/devnet/air/flex/samples.html

Adobe AIR Samples
http://labs.adobe.com/technologies/air/samples/ and
http://www.adobe.com/products/air/showcase/

AIR Applications Wiki
http://airapps.pbwiki.com/

O2 Apps: AIR Applications
http://www.o2apps.com/

Icons

20+ Fresh and Free Icon Sets
http://www.smashingmagazine.com/2007/08/25/20-free-and-fresh-icon-sets/

Icon Factory
http://iconfactory.com/

FamFamFam
http://www.famfamfam.com/

Stock Icons
http://stockicons.com/

Glyph Lab
http://www.glyphlab.com/

Icon Buffet
http://www.iconbuffet.com/

Interface Lift
http://interfacelift.com/

Fast Icon
http://www.fasticon.com/

Icon Shock
http://www.iconshock.com/

Icon Base
http://www.iconbase.com/

Icon Fish
http://www.iconfish.com/

Itookia
http://www.itookia.com/

Fonts

sIFR Flash Fonts Library
http://www.isarie.com/?p=17

Adobe Fonts
http://www.adobe.com/type/index.html

Fonts For Flash
http://www.fontsforflash.com/

Font Freak
http://www.fontfreak.com/index3.htm

Orgdot
http://www.orgdot.com/aliasfonts/

Veer Fonts
http://www.veer.com/products/type/

DaFont
http://www.dafont.com/

Free Fonts
http://www.free-fonts.com/

Graphics

Vecteezy
http://www.vecteezy.com/

COLOURlovers: Color and Patterns
http://www.colourlovers.com/

Index

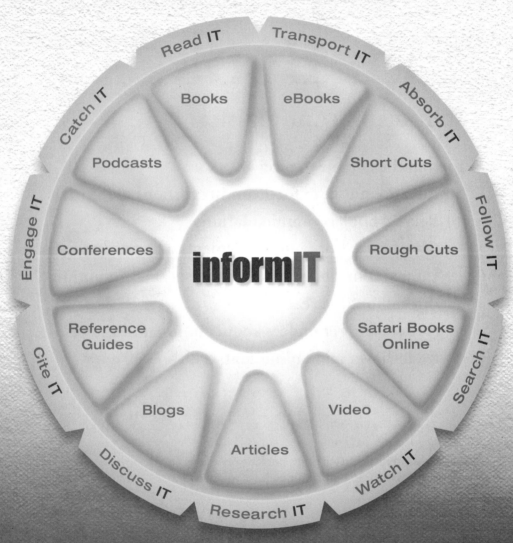